P9-CQC-670

COMPLETE TOURIST GUIDE

THE PELOPONNESE

SIGHTSEEING

GUIDED TOUR OF THE ARCHAEOLOGICAL SITES

COMPLETE LIST OF HOTELS

GENERAL INFORMATION

South of mainland Greece, like "the leaf of a plane tree floating on the sea", stretches the peninsula of the Peloponnese. Joined to the rest of the country by a narrow strip of land, it was detached from the continental body when the Corinth Canal was opened, at the turn of the century. It was overrun by any number of invaders; Romans, barbarians, Franks, Venetians, Turks, all in turn passed this way, but the Peloponnese shook off every foreign element.

In medieval times it was known as the Morea, from the many mulberry trees (*moreai*) growing here. In Byzantine times, these mulberry trees fed the sillk-worms that produced the fine silk which found its way to Western Europe through the intermediary of Venetian and Genoese merchants.

It is a land strewn with the remains of remote and Classical antiquity, with Byzantine monuments and medieval castles. It is a land richly endowed by nature.

As we travel along its highways and byways, we shall encounter majestic mountains, fertile plains, verdant valleys, sparkling streams, placid ponds, fairy-tale caves, beautiful beaches, picturesque villages and attractive towns. Let's set out to make their acquaintance.

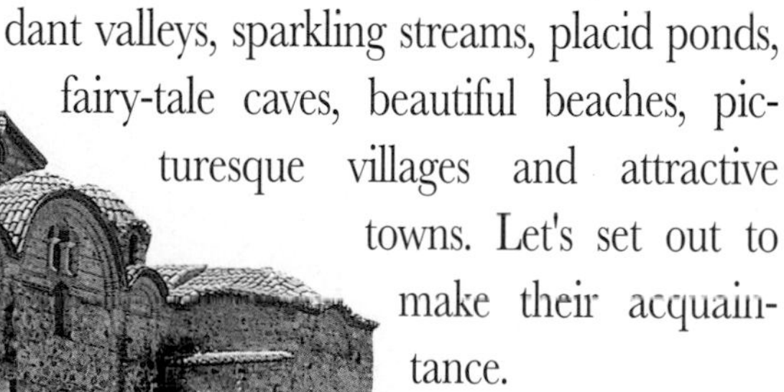

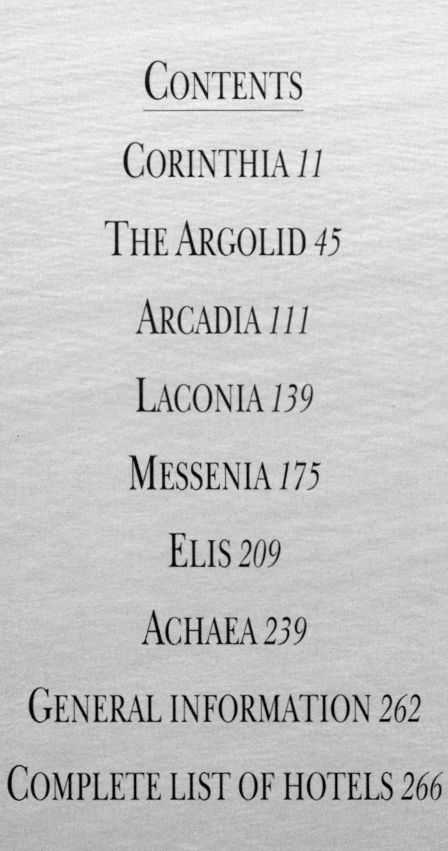

Contents

CORINTHIA

MYTHS AND TRADITIONS

HISTORY

GUIDED TOUR OF THE ARCHAEOLOGICAL SITE OF ANCIENT CORINTH

ACROCORINTH

GETTING TO KNOW THE PROVINCE

ITINERARY 1:
LOUTRAKI-ISTHMIA-KENCHREAE

ITINERARY 2:
LECHAION-SIKYON-KASTANIA-XYLOCASTRO-TRIKALA

ITINERARY 3:
NEMEA

Corinthia, the gateway to the Peloponnese, is the first stop on our journey.

In antiquity, the inhabitants of Corinthia claimed that the sun-god Helios and Poseidon, the god of the sea, ruled their land. Acrocorinth belonged to Helios, while Poseidon was master of the Isthmus. The people believed that, in a cave in the mountains by Nemea, lived the lion killed by Heracles during one of his Labours. They also believed that the lake of Stymphalia further west was the site of another important Labour successfully accomplished by the mythical hero. It was there he killed the terrible Stymphalian birds that were causing such devastation in the area and sowing terror in the hearts of the inhabitants.

Geographically, the boundaries of Corinthia are much the same boundaries as those of antiquity.

Its northern shores are washed by the waters of the Corinthian Gulf, while the mountains of the Geraneia (alt.1032 m) form a natural barrier between Corinthia and Attica. To the east is the Saronic Gulf, to the south the Argolid and Arcadia, while to the west lies Achaea.

The larger part of the prefecture is mountainous. Strabo calls it "rough and rugged".

Along the Gulf of Corinth extends a particularly fertile strip of land, with beautiful pebbly beaches. This is where most of the towns and villages of the prefecture have developed: Corinth, the capital, beautiful Xylokastro, picturesque Kiato and many fishing villages bustling with life during the summer months.

Just opposite Corinth, across the bay on the northern shore of the Corinthian Gulf which washes the coasts of mainland Greece, rise the modern hotel complexes of the spa of Loutraki.

The western part of the province is the most mountainous.

Here towers the imposing bulk of Mt. Zereia (also known as Kyllene), the highest peak of which reaches 2376 m, making it the second highest mountain of the Peloponnese after Mt. Taygetus. Moun-

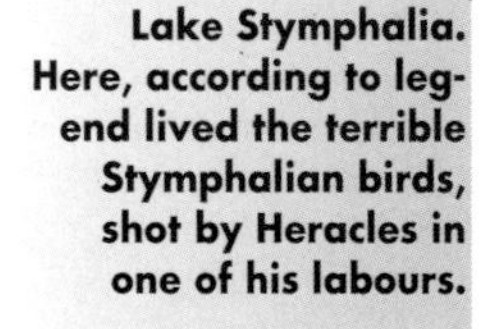

Lake Stymphalia. Here, according to legend lived the terrible Stymphalian birds, shot by Heracles in one of his labours.

tain torrents and small streams flow down its flanks, which are covered with fir trees. To the south of Mt. Zereia, nestling among the mountains at an altitude of 626 m, lies lake Stymphalia, famous for its connection with the legendary hero, Heracles. It is the home of many aquatic plants, while around its shores the vegetation is particularly lush.

Marking the border between Corinthia and the Argolid are the peaks of Megalovouni and Trikorfo, with the historical town of Dervenakia between them, and the villages of Harvati and Trapezona further to the east.

Corinthia's main products are its famous sweet seedless raisins (fresh or dried), juicy lemons, perfumed apricots, delicious oranges, its olive oil, and of course, its excellent wines. The Nemea region, the ancient Phliasian plain, has been famous since antiquity for the quality of its wine.

Terracotta figurine of Aphrodite with Eros, from Corinth. Athens, National Archaeological Museum.

History

The history of the province follows in essence that of the fortunes of Corinth, its most important city, which knew periods of great prosperity and fame.

Traces of its first inhabitants (Neolithic shards, stone implements and figurines) date back to 5000 BC and were found on the site where, during historic times, ancient Corinth had stood.

Indications of human activities, however, have also survived from the Bronze Age. The small settlement of the time appears to have declined during the middle Helladic and the late Helladic period. This was a period of prosperity for other settlements, ranging in geographical location from the Isthmus to Kenchreae and up to Corinth. The most important of these, during Mycenean times, was the settlement of Korakou, between Corinth and Lechaeon. At this time, the small towns which had developed in the area of the prefecture of today formed a province of the Mycenean state.

Before 1000 BC Corinthia was inhabited by Phoenicians from the East and by Aeolians, who came down from Thessaly. The first Dorians arrived from the Argolid

Myths and Traditions

The imagination of the ancient inhabitants of this land created mythical figures such as Sisyphus, Bellerophon and Glaucus. The best-known of these was Sisyphus, the son of the god of the winds, Aeolus. Sisyphus was famous for his intelligence and cunning. It was said that he had even managed to deceive the gods of the Underworld. When he died, Zeus condemned him to eternally push a huge rock up a high mountain. However, every time he came close to the top, the rock would roll back down again to the bottom, obliging Sisyphus to begin his laborious effort all over again. Glaucus was the son of Sisyphus. At the Isthmus, where he was worshipped under the name of Taraxippus, "terrifier of horses", he was known as a breeder of horses. To make them wilder, he would feed them on human flesh. One day, however, the horses turned on their master and tore him to pieces. The inhabitants of the Isthmus believed that Glaucus frightened the horses running in the Isthmian races, which is why they always offered propitiatory sacrifices to Glaucus at the start of the games. Bellerophon, king of Corinth at the time when the city was under the domination of Argos, was the city's greatest hero. According to myth he had two fathers, one of whom was a god — Poseidon— and the other a mortal—Glaucus. He was thus the grandson of Sisyphus. Poseidon gave him the winged horse Pegasus as a gift, and it was Pegasus who helped him kill the terrible Chimaera, a monster with the head of a lion, a tail ending in the head of a snake, and the body of a goat. Pegasus also helped Bellerophon overcome the wild Solymnans and the Amazons.

in 900 BC. After the Dorian invasion of the Peloponnese, Corinth came under the domination of Argos, under which it remained until the 8th century BC.

The 8th century is of particular significance for the city, because it was at this time that its development and its economic prosperity began.

THE DIOLKOS

During the time of the tyrants, the *diolkos*, a paved road linking the Corinthian to the Saronic Gulf, was constructed. Ships needing to cross from one gulf to the other were hauled along this road on rollers.

In 734 BC Corinth founded two colonies, that of Corcyra (present-day Corfu) and that of Syracuse, in Sicily. The founding of these cities favoured the development of seafaring and trade, and Corinth developed into an important maritime power, boasting two harbours, Lechaeon in the north and Kenchreae in the east. It was Corinthian shipbuilders that perfected the trireme, a kind of warship with three banks of oars.

Besides being excellent mariners, the Corinthians were also noted for their artistic skill.

The city's pottery workshops were renowned throughout the Greek world.

From the middle of the 7th century BC, the development of Corinth progressed at a fast pace, with the city reaching the peak of its prosperity under the rule of Periander, son of the tyrant Cypselus. Intellectual and artistic life also flourished at this time. One of the members of Periander's court was the poet and musician Arion, who originated the classical dithyramb, while another poet, Eumelos, distinguished himself in the writing of epic poetry. Corinthian pottery, ceramic work, painting, bronze-work and sculpture in bronze were famous. Superb examples of the work produced by Corinthian workshops are the Proto Corinthian or Corinthian vases, the clay plaques with represen-

Kenchreae. A section of the south mole of the ancient harbour.

tations of gods and the marvellous painting representing a sacrifice, executed by an artist of the Archaic period. The latest architectural style of ancient Greece, created by the Corinthians, became known as the Corinthian order.

The 7th and the 6th centuries BC, were also a period of prosperity for Sikyon, the second most important city of the region. Here, too, there were important workshops whose skilled artisans turned out fine paintings and fashioned splendid works in stone or in bronze. One of the most renowned of the city's artists was Lysippus, who lived during the second half of the 4th century BC and who produced some superb bronze sculptures.

In the 5th century BC Corinth was one of the three most important cities of the Greek world and a major maritime power. The city took part in the struggle against the Persians. After the Persian wars there was a breach in relations between Corinth and Athens, and during the Peloponnesian Wars the latter took the side of the Spartans.

The end of the war did not bring to Corinth the result she had hoped for, that is supremacy at sea. Indeed, it was Sparta that became the preeminent Greek city.

The next step taken by Corinth was to forge an alliance with the Athenians and turn against the Spartans. The Corinthian war which followed (395/4-387 BC) greatly weakened the city.

In 338 BC, after the victory of Philip of Macedon at Chaeroneia, a Macedonian guard was established on the citadel of Acrocorinth. In 333 BC Sikyon in turn fell to the Macedonians.

At the time of the Macedonian domination, Corinth became a commercial and manufacturing centre for the region.

In 251 BC, having restored democracy to his city, general Aratus of Sikyon joined the Achaean League. In 243 BC the Acrocorinth was taken by Aratus and restored to the Corinthians, who became members of the League. In 200 BC Corinth became the capital of the Achaean League. In 146 BC the Roman Lucius Mummius was victorious over the army of the Confederacy, taking Sikyon and Corinth, which he sacked, killing her menfolk, selling the women and children as slaves, pulling down her walls and transporting her treasures to Rome. Some parts of the city were declared public areas and others were ceded to neighbouring Sikyon, which thus benefited

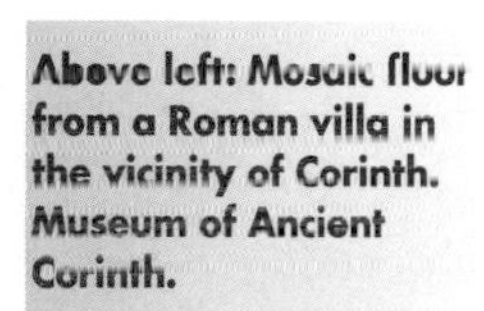

Above left: Mosaic floor from a Roman villa in the vicinity of Corinth. Museum of Ancient Corinth.

Above right: Geometric oinochoe on a tripodal base. 8th century BC. Museum of Ancient Corinth.

Below: Painted wooden panel from Pisa, Corinth. 6th century BC. Athens, National Archaeological Museum

from the destruction of Corinth.The second period of prosperity for Corinth occurred in 44 BC, when Julius Caesar decided to build and repeople it. This was also the end of Sikyon's ascendancy.

During this second period we find Corinth mentioned on coins as Colonia Laus Julia Corinthiensis. In the years that followed, together with its harbours -- Lechaeon on the Corinthian Gulf and Kenchreae on the Saronic Gulf -- it became the most important city in Greece and the capital of the province of Achaea, which included the region extending south of the river Spercheios.

The city was enriched with public works and adorned with public buildings.

In the first century AD (67 AD), during the time of the emperor Nero, the first attempt was made to cut a canal through the Isthmus. In the second century AD, during the reign of the emperor Hadrian, an aqueduct was built to bring water to the city, while the puplic benefactor Herodes Atticus (2nd century AD), embellished the agora and repaired the Peirene fountain . The city attracted merchants, seamen and tradesmen, many of whom came from Egypt; a significant number of these were Jews.

Initially the official language was Latin, but gradually, as the Greek population increased, it ceded its place to Greek.

In 52 AD St. Paul visited Corinth and established the Christian church of Corinth, which, together with the churches of Patras and Sparta, became the most important centres for the propagation of Christianity in the Peloponnese.

From the middle of the 3rd century AD onwards, as a result of the invasion of Corinth by barbarian tribes, the whole region began to decline. The Erulians invaded Corinth in 267 AD, followed in 395 AD by Alaric's Visigoths, who set fire to the city.

In the 6th century AD Corinth experienced a new period of prosperity. To ensure the security of the region, the emperor Justinian built a wall, using ancient building materials from Isthmia. This wall, with its 153 towers, which started from the sanctuary of Poseidon at the Isthmus and ended up at the Corinthian Gulf, was known as the

Hexamilion or "six-mile wall", because its total length was 7300 m or approximately six Roman miles.
After 521 AD Corinth once again fell into decline.
From the 7th century AD to the middle of the 11th the town became the capital of the Greek *theme* (province), which, after the second half of the 11th century, also included the eastern regions of central Greece.
In medieval times, Corinth suffered the same fate as the other towns of the Peloponnese.
One occupier after the other asserted his dominion over the city. It was plundered by the Normans in 1147, fell into the hands of the Franks in 1210 and, in 1358 the Florentine prince, Nicholas Acciajuoli, became lord of the region. In 1395 it became a Byzantine possession and in 1400 it was sold by Theodore Palaeologus to the Knights of St. John of Rhodes. However, submitting to the demands of the people, Palaeologus was forced to reconquer Corinth in 1408. In 1458 the city fell into Turkish hands, in 1618 it was taken by the Knights of Malta, who were followed by the Venetians in 1687. In 1715 it was once again taken by the Turks, and it finally threw off the Turkish yoke in 1822.
However, the vicissitudes of Corinth did not end there. In 1858 the small settlement which stood on the site of the ancient city was destroyed by an earthquake. A new town began to be laid out a short distance away and closer to the Isthmus, but was once again devastated by earthquakes in 1928 and in 1930. Thereafter, building began again rapidly, and today Corinth is an attractive town and the commercial centre of the Peloponnese as well as an important road and railway junction.

A GUIDED TOUR OF THE ARCHAEOLOGICAL SITE OF ANCIENT CORINTH

The archaeological site of ancient Corinth is only a twenty-minute drive away from the modern town.
The ruins that have been brought to light mostly belong to Roman times, to the second period of the city's economic prosperity, which, as we have seen, began in 44 BC, after the older city was totally destroyed by the Romans in 146 BC.
The main entrance to the area of the Corinthian agora was through the propylaea where ended the Lechaeon road which linked the city to one of its two harbours at Lechaeon.
In Roman times this road was paved with stone slabs and was flanked by paved pedestrian paths and lined with shops behind colonnades. Gutters channelled off the rainwater.
At the time of Pausanias' visit to Corinth, in the 2nd century AD, two gilded chariots surmounted the roof of the propylaea. On one of them rode Phaethon, the son of the sun god Helios, and on the other the sun-god himself.
East of the propylaea, on a lower level, we can still see the ruins of the fountain of Peirene. Peirene was a nymph, the daughter of the river-god Asopos. According to myth, she was turned into a spring because of her ceaseless weaping over the death of her son, Cenchrias. In Classical and Hellenistic times, in front of the fountain there was a court-

Above left: Amphora with stopper. It is decorated with two cocks on either side of a double anthemion. c 600 BC. Museum of Ancient Corinth.

Below: View of the fortifications of the Acrocorinth.

Below right: Ancient Corinth. The paved Lechaeon road led to the propylaea of the ancient agora.

yard to which there was access from the Lechaeon road. The water of the spring which brought water to the Peirene fountain was collected in four cisterns and from there was fed into three basins. Six long and narrow openings led to a corresponding number of chambers which were connected to the basins in which the water collected.

The Peirene fountain was given the form in which it survives today by the wealthy puplic benefactor Herodes Atticus. At that time the water flowed into an open-air fountain. On the south side of the structure housing the Peirene fountain rose a two-storey wall in which there were six arched openings leading to the basins. On the other three sides of the edifice there where three arches with statues in the niches.

North of the Peirene fountain lies an area known as the *Peribolos* of Apollo. This is a paved courtyard with Ionian colonnades on all four sides. The area was used for public open-air gatherings.

Before 44 BC, about halfway along the western side of this precinct there stood a small temple of Apollo, dating from the fourth century BC.

North of this precinct excavations have brought to light ruins of a building, identified as the baths of Eurycles.

West of the Lechaeon road rose a large two-storey Roman basilica. On its façade,

Left: Ancient Corinth. The Archaic temple of Apollo.

Below: Aerial view of Ancient Corinth.

which faced the agora, besides the columns, four colossal statues of barbarian chiefs supported the entablature of the second storey.
North of the basilica stood the old square agora, over which was later built a semicircular edifice.West of this edifice the new (northern) agora was later laid out, the southern part of which, as well as a section of the western wing have been excavated. This agora was also square, bordered with shops, and its interior open-air area was surrounded by a peristyle. This agora formed the northern boundary of the precinct of the Archaic temple of Apollo.
The temple, a Doric peripteral building with six columns on the short sides and fifteen on the long sides, was built in the centre of a levelled area, which was the sanctuary of the god and which stood on the northern side of the central section of the agora.
The temple consisted of a cella, divided into two rooms, and a *pronaos* and *opisthodomos*. It was built in the middle of the 6th century BC. An older temple, perhaps built in the 7th century BC, must have stood on the same site but further to the north. The 6th-century temple was probably restored in Roman times.
South of the temple of Apollo extends the northern part of the agora, consisting of

Right: Ancient Corinth. View of the interior of the Peirene fountain.

Below: Ancient Corinth. Dominating the northern part of the central area of the ancient agora, the Temple of Apollo.

sixteen small shops, built in imperial times, which survive today in fairly good condition. Almost in the middle of this row of shops has been preserved a vaulted edifice, which was used in the early Christian years as a church.
On the western side of the agora stood six small temples and a small circular peripteral edifice, known as the monument of Babbius.
The small temples, which opened up towards the east, and which were built on tall rectangular platforms, must have been built after 160 AD. It is not certain to which gods they were dedicated. According to Pausanias, the first temple starting from the south, identified by the letter F, must have been dedicated to the goddess Tyche (Fortune). Further north, temple G has been identified as a Pantheon, that is as a shrine dedicated to all the gods. Temple H may have been dedicated to Heracles and temple J to Poseidon, while temple D was probably dedicated to Hermes.
In front of the temple, which was the only one whose entrance was on the south side, stood a small peripteral building, which, judging from a Latin inscription found on its epistyle, appears to have been built by the magistrate of the eparchy of Corinth Gn. Babbius Philinus. This edifice stood on a tall square platform. It consisted of a wing of eight Corinthian columns supporting an Ionian entablature and a conical roof.
West of the temples extended a row of shops, the so-called western shops.
To the south, another row of shops bounded the central area of the agora. In the middle, between the so-called central shops, stood a *bema* (rostrum) used by the Roman proconsul when he wished to address the people.
It was from this rostrum that St. Paul defended himself, in 52 AD, before the Roman governor of Achaea, Lucius Julius Gallio, against the charge made by the Jews of Corinth that by his teachings, "this man persuadeth the people to worship God against the law".
South of the main shops and of the rostrum extended a long and narrow stoa (portico), measuring 160 m in length, with an interior colonnade of Ionic columns and a row of 33 rooms. This southern stoa was originally built in the 4th century BC and was rebuilt after 44 BC.
Southeast of the stoa stood a Roman basilica, while another, similarly-designed basilica, the so-called Julian Basilica, closed the central area of the agora to the east.
The Julian Basilica appears to have been built by the family of the emperor Augustus and was used as a venue for trials and public gatherings. It owes its name to the

TEMPLE OF OCTAVIA

Southwest of the present-day museum have been preserved the ruins of yet another temple, built in Roman times. It was a peripteral temple in the Ionic style, and surrounded by a built enclosure. This temple, which is also mentioned by the ancient travel-writer Pausanias, has been identified as a temple of Octavia, the sister of Augustus. Inside it stood a statue of a seated Roman matron.

Ancient Corinth: The Peirene fountain.

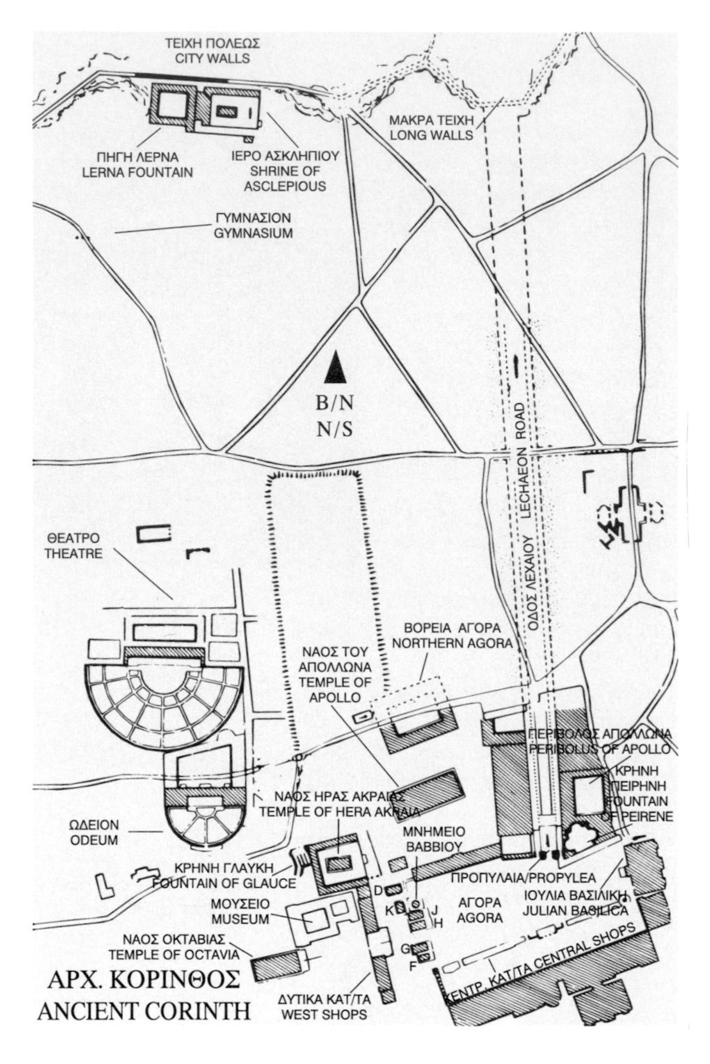

sculpted portraits of members of the family of Julius Caesar and of Augustus, which stood inside it.

Before the Roman period, at the point where the entrance stairs to the basilica once stood, was set a stone marking the starting point for the races held in an area in the middle of the agora, which also doubled as a stadium. In this central space were found the remains of a large sacrificial altar dating from the Roman period and, beside it, the foundations of a pedestal on which was set a large bronze statue of Athena, dating from the same period.

North of the museum and west of the precinct of the Archaic temple of Apollo, stood another temple dating from the early imperial period, with a built enclosure and an interior peristyle, most probably dedicated to Hera Acraea.

West of the temple of Hera have been preserved the ruins of the rock-cut Glauce fountain, similar in construction to the fountain of Peirene. It drew its water from the spring which flowed under the Acrocorinth.

Glauce, as Pausanias tells the story, was the daughter of the king of Corinth, Creon. Jason, deserting Medea, had decided to marry Glauce. Among the wedding gifts sent by Medea through the intermediary of her children to Jason's future wife, was a beautiful robe. As soon as Glauce put on

Ancient Corinth. Ruins of shops in the northwestern part of the ancient agora.

this robe, she was enveloped by devouring flames. To save herself, she leapt into the waters of the fountain, which from then on took her name.

To the west of the Archaic temple and outside the area of the agora can be seen to this day the ruins of the seating area and of the foundations of the stage of an Odeon, built at the end of the first century AD and restored during the time of Herodes Atticus.

In the early 3rd century AD, after it was destroyed by fire, the Odeon was turned into an arena for gladiatorial combats and other such contests. North of the Odeon, at a distance of only 150 m and at a lower level, has been excavated the seating area of the city's large ancient theatre. The remains of an earlier theatre, which had a wooden stage, date from the 5th century BC. Of the 3rd-century BC theatre, which must have had a stone stage and could seat 18,000 spectators, only traces have survived. The shape of the theatre was altered in the early part of the first century AD, acquiring a more impressive stage adorned with columns. After that it was altered again several times, in response to the needs of the times. In the early 3rd century AD the orchestra was turned into an arena for animal fights, while a later intervention transformed the arena into a reservoir for water.

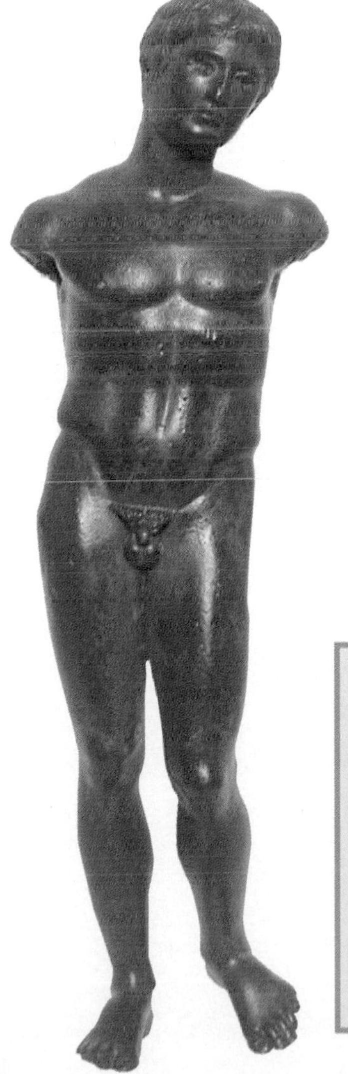

Above right: cup from Kenchreae, with green glaze and relief decoration. Museum of Ancient Corinth.

Below left: bronze statuette of an athlete, from Sikyon. Dated to the second half of the 5th century BC. Athens, National Archaeological Museum.

Below right: Mycenean kylix with tall foot. 13th century BC. Museum of Ancient Corinth.

ARCHAEOLOGICAL MUSEUM OF ANCIENT CORINTH

In this interesting museum are mainly exhibited finds from the area of the agora of ancient Corinth, but objects discovered at other sites are also included. (tel.: 0741/31.207)

To the east of the theatre and of the Odeon must have stood the shrine of Athena Chalinitis, mentioned by Pausanias. This epithet was given to the goddess because, according to Pindar, Athena gave Bellerophon, while he was sleeping, a golden bridle (chalinos), with which to tame the wild horse Pegasus.
North of the theatre and at a distance of approximately 300 m, the stylobate of a colonnade and parts of columns indicate the position of a gymnasium. A little to the north stood the shrine of Asclepius The temple, which was dedicated to the god, consisted of a cella and a pronaos and had four Doric columns in front. It was built in the 4th century BC and restored in the early imperial period. The enclosure of the shrine was linked on the west side with another enclosure, which is believed to have belonged to the Lerna fountain. It is conjectured that, west of the Asclepieion, there may have been a temple dedicated to Zeus.

ACROCORINTH

From the plain encircling the present-day town of Corinth rises the sheer rocky mass of Acrocorinth, girded by its strong walls with their towers and battlements. The view from the top of the hill is impressive, as our gaze reaches beyond the plain to the sea and to the mountains of central Greece across the water.
A tarred road leads up to the entrance of the fortress, which was the citadel of ancient and medieval times. The hill is about 575 metres high, and all its sides, apart from the western flank, are abrupt and dif-

ficult to scale. A gorge on the western side was converted into a deep moat. On the same western side, where the walls are particularly strong, stands the entrance to the citadel with its three consecutive gates.. A bridge and a steep paved road led to the first gate, and from there on to the other two. The two first gates still preserve their arched medieval form, while the third gate was much later topped by a horizontal lintel. The foundations of the medieval enceinte of the fortress rest on the ruins of the ancient fortifications.

The summit of the hill is relatively level and since ancient times was provided with its own walls. The relatively large area of the summit and the existence of a spring known as the Upper Peirene on the south-eastern edge of the hill, made possible the habitation of Acrocorinth without a break

up to the end of the period of Turkish occupation. In antiquity, on the highest point of the hill there stood a small temple of Aphrodite dating from the 5th or the 4th century BC. The sun-god Helios, particularly revered by the Corinthians, was also worshipped at Acrocorinth.

In early Christian times, on the site of the temple was built a small basilica, which later was turned into a tower and, at the end of the 17th century, was converted into a paved platform by the Venetians. During the Macedonian and medieval periods a military guard was established on the summit of the hill, in barracks whose ruins are still visible today. In 1210, the Lord of Nauplion, Leon Sgouros, plunged on horseback to his death from the walls of Acrocorinth, to avoid surrendering to the Franks.

Left: Strong walls with towers and battlements encircle the rocky hill of Acrocorinth.

Above: Part of the paved road and the three consecutive gates leading to the interior of the citadel.

Acrocorinth. Coloured lithograph. Théodore de Moncel. *Excursion par terre d'Athènes à Nauplie.* Paris (1845). Gennadius Library.→

A TOUR OF THE PREFECTURE

Corinthia is a region rich in interesting tourist and archaeological sites. Here the visitor will find busy seaside resorts, tranquil mountain villages, the ruins of ancient cities, picturesque fishing villages, lovely beaches, and a wide choice of accommodation.
We shall discover the outstanding monuments and sights of the prefecture by following three main itineraries. On our first trip we shall see the part of Corinthia that lies within the geographical area of mainland Greece, and also its eastern shores. On our second journey we shall get to know the northern coast and part of the inland area, while on our third, we shall be introduced to the archaeological sites south and south-west of Corinth.

ITINERARY 1

Our journey begins as we leave the prefecture of Attica. Just before we reach the Isthmus, to the right, there is a branch in the road which takes us, 6 km. further along, to our first stop, the town of Loutraki.
Built at the foot of the Geraneia mountains, on the site of an ancient settlement, the town is known for its mineral springs, its casino, and its many modern hotels. Its fine pebbly beaches and clear sea attract many visitors, both Greeks and foreigners, during the hot summer months.
We leave Loutraki and continue northwards. Ten kilometres further along, we find ourselves in the village of Perahora.
In its archaeological museum are housed finds from the excavations at the Heraeon - the sanctuary of the goddess Hera - and from the prehistoric settlement of lake Vouliagmeni at Perahora.
Approximately 10 kms west of Perahora we come to the picturesque lagoon of Vouliagmeni, in whose waters are mirrored the Geraneia mountains. Vouliagmeni communicates with the sea through a small opening in the land. In antiquity it was known as Eschatiotis, and although at that time the lake did not connect with the sea, its waters were salty. The narrow strip of land that separated the land from the sea was cut at the end of the last century.
West of the lake extends the peninsula on which the important city of Heraeon developed in ancient times.
In the 8th century Corinthians settled on this peninsula. Before their arrival the area had been inhabited by Megarians.
Leaving the Heraeon, Perahora and Loutraki behind us, we make our way to-

HERAEON.

At the southeastern rocky edge of the headland stands the lighthouse of Perahora. Below the rocks there is a small cove which used to serve as the harbour of the city of Heraeon. Deep inside this small bay, by the sea, have been excavated the ruins of a sanctuary, which, as we can see from inscriptions, must have been dedicated to Hera Acraea. The sanctuary was established in the early 8th century BC. It included a vaulted Geometric temple, while west of the first temple a later one was built during the Archaic period. About two hundred metres further east, inland, the ruins of another sanctuary have come to light, which, as is indicated by an inscription on a vase, was dedicated to Hera Limenia. This sanctuary did not include a temple.
The building which stood here must have been used for religious rituals and to house votive objects. Between the two shrines an L-shaped stoa has been uncovered. It was built around 400 BC and belonged to both sanctuaries.

wards Corinth. Soon we pass over the bridge which spans the canal. Below us, if we are lucky, we may see a ship going through the narrow passage. The cutting of the canal had already been planned during the time of the tyrants of Corinth, particularly in the time of Periander, so that ships might avoid having to sail around the Peloponnese. However, the cost of the project proved to be too great, as were also the difficulties in implementing it. Thus, instead of a canal, the *diolkos* was designed, traces of which may still be seen. This was a paved road linking ancient Schoinous (present-day Kalamaki) to the Corinthian gulf. It was thus made possible for ships to be hauled overland between the Saronic

Left: Aerial view of Loutraki and its lovely beach.

Below: The Vouliagmeni lagoon near Perahora.

Above: Ancient Isthmia

Below: The mosaic floor of the Roman baths in the sânctuary of Ancient Isthmia. It represents Tritons and Nereids.

and the Corinthian gulfs. However, because of the great costs involved, only warships or small vessels without cargo were transported in this way. The ship would be strapped to a cart with rollers, the "olkos neon" (dragger of ships), as it was called, and hauled across to the harbour on the other side.

After Periander, the cutting of the canal was also planned in turn by Demetrios Poliorcetes, Julius Caesar, Gaius and Hadrian. However, the first real attempt was made during the reign of Nero in 67 AD, but was interrupted by the emperor's death.

Construction work on the present-day canal finally began in 1881 and was completed in 1893. The canal was cut along the same line as that which had been planned in Nero's time. Its total length is about 6 kms and its width about 25 m.

As we leave the canal we will make a short halt for a cup of coffee and a rest, before we continue our journey into Corinthia.

We start off again following the left branch of the road, which leads to Isthmia.

In the village of Kyra Vryssi have come to light the ruins of a sanctuary dedicated to Poseidon.

In ancient times, the temples of Poseidon in ancient Isthmia and of Zeus in ancient Olympia were the two largest temples in the Peloponnese.

It is believed that the first temple to Poseidon was built in the middle of the 7th century BC. It was destroyed by fire in the early 5th century BC. A Doric

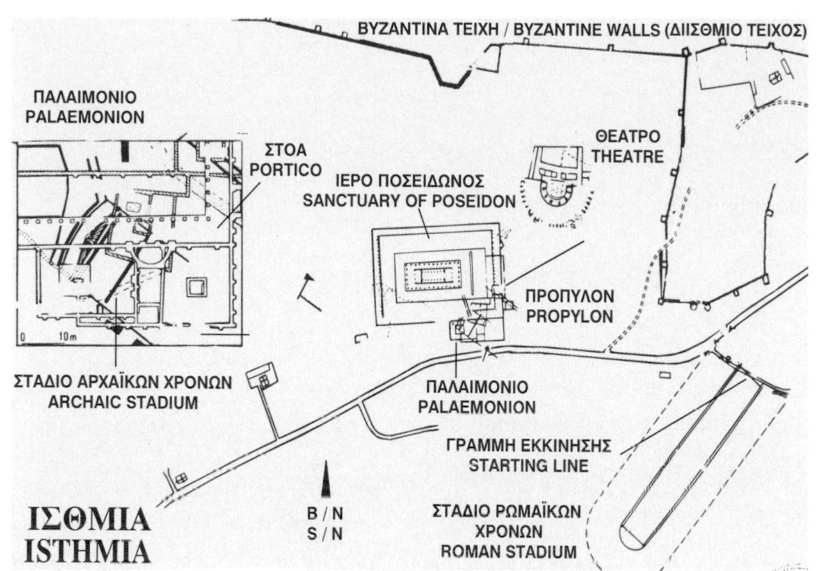

peripteral temple was later built, at about the same time as the temple of Zeus in Olympia. However, the second temple was also destroyed by fire in 390 BC during the Corinthian war. It was repaired in the 4th century BC and was restored again after 44 BC. The temple was demolished during the reign of the emperor Justinian so that its building materials might be used for the construction of the wall along the Isthmus.

In front of the temple, on the eastern side, stood a long and narrow altar. The temple was surrounded by an enclosure which, in the 2nd century AD, was replaced by porticoes which opened up towards the temple. Outside the south-eastern corner of the temple of Poseidon stood the stadium of Archaic and early Classical times, of which we can still see a part of the triangular starting point of the races, which was paved with poros stone.

The stadium of Roman times was moved further south to a natural depression in the ground, which permitted the construction of an ample seating area.

Near the south-eastern corner, outside the sanctuary of Poseidon, on the site of the old stadium, was founded in Roman times a temple and precinct dedicated to Palaemon, the son of King Adamas and

Attic red-figure kylix, by the Codrus painter. Dated to 440/430 BC, it represents the feats of Theseus, who according to Athenian tradition, had instituted the Isthmian games. London, British Museum.

ISTHMIA

The Corinthians were in charge of the organisation of the games, which originally were local in character but at the time of the tyrants became pan-Hellenic in scope.

However, according to Pausanias, during the period of the decline of Corinth, between 146 BC and 44 BC, the organisation of the games was taken over by the Sicyonians.

Excavations on the site have shown that the sanctuary of Isthmia was plundered by Mummius.

During the period of the hundred or so years in which Corinth lay desolate, the sanctuary also was abandoned and the games neglected, but when the town was repopulated the sanctuary was rebuilt and the games began to take place, as before.

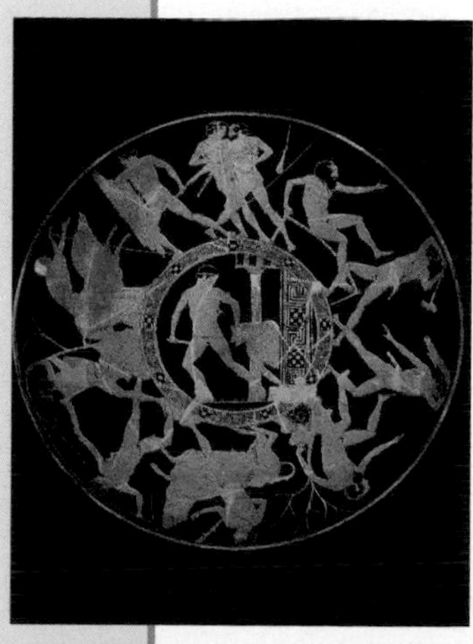

Above: Submerged remains of the harbour of Kenchreae may be made out at the bottom of the sea.

Below: The beach at Loutra Oreas Elenis ("Baths of Helen the Fair").

Queen Ino, whose body, according to legend, was carried to the Isthmian coast on a dolphin's back. The temple dedicated to Palaemon was a circular peripteral temple surrounded by its own enclosure, which communicated with that of the shrine of Poseidon.

The round edifice, which appears on Corinthian coins of the middle of the 2nd century AD, and within which can be seen a young man lying on a dolphin's back, has been identified as the temple of Palaemon, at Isthmia.

Northeast of the temple of Poseidon stood the theatre of Isthmia. The building materials of this edifice, also, were used in the construction of the Justinian wall, and this is why only scant traces survive today. The earliest theatre must have been built just after 400 BC.

Every two years, panhellenic games — the Isthmian games — were held at Isthmia. They included a number of contests: the pentathlon, the pancration, field and track events, horse and chariot races, as well as musical contests. The victors were crowned with pine-branch leaves.

The museum of Isthmia, situated in the village of Kyra Vryssi, houses finds from the excavations at Isthmia and wreaths.

We leave Isthmia behind us and continue along a winding coastal road lined with pine trees, which passes through a succession of fishing villages.

Five kilometres south of Isthmia we come to Kenchreae, the eastern harbour of ancient Corinth. It lay on the northern

side of a natural bay, where, during Roman times, two moles—the northern and southern moles—were built opposite each other. The horseshoe-shaped coast between the two moles was lined with arcades and harbour installations. The southern mole was the wider of the two. Here, besides the harbour installations, stood a shrine dedicated to Isis. Later, possibly during the 4th century AD, a Christian basilica was built a little further inland. On the northern mole a shrine dedicated to Aphrodite is believed to have once stood.
Today the two moles have been covered by the sea. Of the ancient edifices, a small part is on land and has come to light, while other parts are still visible today beneath the surface of the water. Among the ruins of the southern mole can be made out the foundations of the basilica while, on the northern arm, survive the ruins of a square tower of the late Roman period as well as ruins of edifices dating from the late Roman and Early Christian periods.
A few kilometres further south, at the southern end of the bay of Kenchreae, we encounter the coastal settlement known as "Loutra tis Elenis" (Helen's baths). Here, from the foot of a rock just above the surface of the sea, springs salt water, warmer than the sea water and endowed with therapeutic qualities. In the 5th century BC this spring was known as Reiton, but in Pausanias' time, that is in the 2nd century AD, it was already called by its present name.
We continue to follow a southerly direction and after two kilometres we find ourselves at Kato Almyri, a coastal village with a beautiful sandy beach. South of Kato Almyri, outside the village of Sofiko, stand the churches of the Virgin and of the Taxiarches (the Holy Archangels), dating from the 12th/13th century.
From Kato Almyri our road, winding

Korfos: The green of the shore blends with the blue of the sea on this lovely beach with the picturesque tavernas.

Aerial view of the modern city of Corinth. →

Above left: Assos.

Below left: Lechaeon. Here was the second harbour of Ancient Corinth.

Above right: One of the two fountains in the gymnasium of Ancient Sicyon.

Below right: the theatre of Ancient Sicyon.

through pine-clad mountains, leads to the Argolid. Thirty-nine kilometres south of Corinth, just before we cross the border into the Argolid, we shall see below us the picturesque village of Korfos, built in the crook of a deep green bay.

ITINERARY 2

The capital of the prefecture of Corinthia is the modern town of Corinth, which has been built 5 kms west of the Isthmus, on the shores of the Corinthian Gulf. Corinth, which is an important commercial centre of the Peloponnese, has an attractive waterfront, wide streets, modern buildings and a cathedral which is dedicated to the patron saint of the city, the Apostle Paul. St. Paul lived in the ancient town for quite a long period of time and founded there one of the most important Christian churches in Greece.

West of the town lies the most densely-inhabited part of Corinthia—during the summer months, anyway. Village succeeds village along the coastal road. They face the cool, deep blue Corinthian Gulf, while behind them lies the fertile verdant plain of Corinthia.

Approximately 5 kms west of the town, we come to the northern harbour of ancient Corinth, Lechaeon. The harbour of Lechaeon, which was an artificial one, also served as a naval base. It was linked to ancient Corinth by long walls, built in the 5th century BC. The foundations of the walls have come to light between Lechaeon and Corinth. On the beach have been uncovered the foundations of a large Christian basilica which was probably built around 500 AD. According to Pausanias, there was a sanctuary dedicated to Poseidon at Lechaeon, while Plutarch

mentions the existence of a sanctuary of Aphrodite. As we continue westwards our road passes through a series of villages— Periyiali, Kato Assos, Vrahati, Kokkoni, Nerantza—nestling among gardens and orange groves. In the spring, the air is redolent with the fragrance of lemon and orange blossoms.

We arrive in Kiato, a modern town, important in the production of currants and citrus fruit.

From here, a branch in the road leads southwards, and six kilometres further on, brings us to the ruins of Hellenistic Sicyon.

Ancient Sicyon flourished more or less at the same time as Corinth. At that time the city stood by the sea, on the site of present-day Kiato. When, in 303 BC, Demetrius Poliorcetes became master of the region, it was moved further south, to a height near the village of Vas-

siliko, where the ruins of public buildings have now been uncovered. The hill which rose above the city became its citadel.
Demetrius built a wall around Sicyon and laid out its agora. The city of Archaic and Classical times became the seaport of the new town and many inhabitants of Sicyon remained there.
In 251 BC, the general of the Achaean League Aratus, himself from Sicyon, freed the city from the Macedonians and made it a member of the League.
In 87 BC the city was sacked by the Roman dictator Sulla.
Of Hellenistic and Roman Sicyon visible today is the theatre at the foot of the acropolis. Of this theatre can be seen the semicircular orchestra, the foundations of the stage, the lower tiers of seats and the two vaulted passages leading directly from the acropolis to the upper section.
Further east lie the ruins of the gymnasium of Cleinias, built on two levels, and the poros stone foundations of an Archaic temple, believed to have been dedicated to Artemis, and to have been rebuilt at the time of the foundation of Hellenistic Sicyon.
North of the temple is preserved in good condition the bath-house of Hellenistic times, which has been converted into a museum (tel. No.0742/28900), in which are housed finds from the ancient city of Stymphalos and from Sicyon, architectural elements from the Christian basilica of Sicyon etc.
In the southern part of the site, excavations have brought to light the foundations of the *bouleuterion* (assenbly house), which stood in the middle of the city's agora. It is a square edifice, in the centre of which stood the speaker's rostrum. East of the bouleuterion extended a long stoa.
Northwest of the theatre can be seen the stadium, of which a part of the retaining wall has survived.
After Sicyon, if we take the road towards Gonousa, we will come to the ruins of ancient Titane. The acropolis of the city

Above: Perched on the slopes of Mt. Zereia, verdant Kastania offers a cool refuge in the hot summer months.

Below: Zereia is one of the most beautiful mountains of Greece. Tall firs cover its slopes and peaks.

Xylocastro on the coast of the Gulf of Corinth is a favourite summer resort. Among its attractions are the deep blue sea which caresses its shores and the green pine forest that surrounds it.

stood on a low hill, where the cemetery of the village is situated today. Parts of its ancient walls and towers have survived. Pausanias tells us that on this acropolis stood a temple dedicated to the goddess Athena. In the ancient town there was also an Asclepieion, famous throughout the Peloponnese. Northwest of the hill the heating installations of Roman baths have recently come to light.

As we continue southwards from Kiato, we might wish to drive up to the village of Kastania, after passing by lake Stymphalia, of legendary fame, where the ancient city of Stymphalos once flourished. From the road we are able to see the remains of a Gothic church, on the right of which stands part of the impressive gateway of the medieval monastery. To the left of the ruins can be seen the hill where the acropolis of the ancient town once stood.

The picturesque village of Kastania clings to the slopes of Mount Zereia, at an altitude of 920 m. Higher up, at an altitude of 1300 m, outside the village, is situated the Xenia hotel, set among fir trees and enjoying a marvellous view.

After Kiato, the road continues westwards towards Achaea, after going through picturesque seaside villages such as Melissi and Sykia.

Xylokastro is the second largest town in

Trikala - another beautiful village clinging to the green slopes of Mt. Zereia.

Above right: An Attic black-figure amphora decorated with a representation of the struggle of Heracles with the Lion of Nemea. c520 BC. Brescia, Museo Civico.

Below right: Sarcophagus with a carving in relief showing the expedition of the "Seven against Thebes", and the death of Opheltes. 2nd century AD. Museum of Ancient Corinth.

Corinthia, and is a modern holiday resort with an attaractive waterfront, where one can enjoy a rest while gazing at the sea. Along the pebbly beach, between Sykia and Xylokastro, lies the verdant pine grove known as Pefkias. From Xylokastro the road continues in a southwesterly direction and brings us to the mountain village of Trikala, built on the slopes of Mt. Zereia. Here begins the ascent of skiers towards the ski centre and of mountaineers towards the two mountain refuges.

We leave Xylokastro behind us. The road follows the coastline, passing through the small settlements and fishing villages of Kamari, Kato Pitsa, Lykoporia, Derveni, which welcome us and line our route all the way to the borders between Corinthia and Achaea.

ITINERARY 3

As we start out on our third and last journey into Corinthia, we shall begin by taking a look at the archaeological treasures of the region.

At Chiliomodi, 18 kms south of the town, a branch in the road leads to the village of Klenia, where in antiquity stood the city of Tenea. From there we shall proceed to Agionori, with its medieval fortress, built to ensure the control of the area. From Chiliomodi the main road continues west and takes us to Kontostavlo, the official name of which is Ancient Cleones, although today only traces survive of the Cleones of antiquity - namely, some parts of the fortified enclosure and, outside of that, the better preserved foundations of a temple dedicated to Heracles. This was a prostyle temple and comprised a cella opening up towards the east. Today we can see the wall posts and the floor, paved with massive stone slabs. In front of the temple stood two parallel raised structures which were most probably altars.

We leave the plain of Cleones and drive uphill towards ancient Nemea. As we ascend, we can see below us the fertile valley planted with vineyards, which produce the sweet Nemean wine, or "blood of Heracles", as it is called. This is where

the legendary hero performed one of his twelve labours, when he killed the lion that lived in a cave on Mt. Tretos.
The region of Nemea was first inhabited in prehistoric times. On the hill of Tsoungiza, west of the village of ancient Nemea (originally known as Herakleion), a Neolithic settlement has been excavated, while at Nemea itself the ruins of an important sanctuary dedicated to Zeus have been uncovered.
This was a peripteral temple, built in the 4th century BC of poros stone on the site of an Archaic temple. It had a *pronaos* (front porch), a long and narrow cella and an *adyton* (inner sanctuary) instead of an *opisthodomos* (rear porch). Here was worshipped also, together with the father of the gods, Opheltes, the young son of the King of the region, Lycurgus, who died after having been bitten by a poisonous snake.
Of this temple three columns still stand today, two of which continue to support part of the epistyle and stand between the two pilasters of the pronaos, while the third belonged to the colonnade running along the sides.
Many drums from the columns surrounding the temple can still be seen, as can also the three steps of the platform. At the end of the cella there were five steps, of which three have survived, leading to a rectangular area, about two metres below the floor of the cella. It is here, in this area which has been identified as the adyton, that the rites in honour of the young Opheltes probably took place.
To the east and not far from the temple can still be seen the foundations of a long and narrow altar, and south of the temple have been excavated the foundations of a rectangular edifice which may have been used as a guest house and a meeting and banqueting room. In early Christian times a Christian church of which today some ruins survive, was built on the eastern part of the edifice.
Between the temple and the guest house excavations have brought to light the foundations of a rectangular building, which may have been a portico or an enclosed place of worship. West of the guest house are to be seen the ruins of another rectangular edifice, which may have been a palaestra. On its western side were baths, a part of

which has now been converted into a museum (tel. No.0746/22739) housing the finds of the excavations of the surrounding area.
East of the sanctuary has been uncovered the stone marking the starting line of the racing events in the stadium of Nemea. Here, every other year, were held the Nemean games, which assumed a panhellenic character after 573 BC.
Besides Adrastus and the generals who were his companions in his expedition against Thebes, which started off from Argos, the founder of the games was believed to have been Heracles, after he had slain the lion of Nemea. According to legend, Adrastus established the games in honour of Opheltes.
The legend surrounding the tragic death of Opheltes relates that when Adrastus and the other generals were passing through Nemea, they met the child's nurse, Ypsipyle, and asked her to lead them to a spring. Responding willingly to their request, Ypsipile laid the young Opheltes down on the ground, on a bed of wild celery, as a consequence of which the child was bitten by a snake and died. To honour the dead child, who was given the name Archemorus, which means "beginner of doom", were founded the Nemean games.
Initially it was the inhabitants of Cleones who undertook the organisation of the games, but after 573 BC the Argives took over this task. The prize the victors received was a crown of wild celery.
We now leave Ancient Nemea behind us and drive westwards, where lies the modern village of Nemea among endless vineyards. About 4 kms to the north, excavations have uncovered the ruins of ancient Phlious, built in historic times on the north-eastern slopes of the Phliasian plain, an area famous in antiquity for its wine. The Phliasians entertained friendly relations with the Spartans, but were not on good terms with their neighbours the Argives and the Arcadians.
At Nemea and Phlious our third itinerary through Corinthia comes to an end. We shall now direct our course towards neighbouring Argolis, the birthplace of the splendid Mycenean civilisation.

Left page: The three standing columns of the Temple of Zeus in Nemea.

Above: Heracles, the hero honoured at Nemea. From the west pediment of the temple of Athena Alea at Tegea. A work of the famous sculptor Scopas. Tegea, Archaeological Museum

Left: Bronze statuette of an infant, dating from the Hellenistic period. It was found at Nemea and represents Opheltes. Nemea, Archaeological Museum.

THE ARGOLID

Head of a statue of Hera, from the Heraion of Argos. It is dated to c.420 BC and was probably the work of an Argive sculptor. Athens, National Archaeological Museum

The Argolid is a land of myths and legends - the home of Agamemnon and of Clytaemestra, of Electra and Orestes, the domain of Hera. Homer calls it a "very thirsty" land. Here, the rivers were worshipped as deities and the springs were dedicated to the nymphs. Here lie Mycenae "rich in gold", "wall-girt" Tiryns and Argos "the horse-pasturer". It was from Mycenae that the Achaeans under the leadership of Agamemnon, together with the other Greeks, set off in their ships across the Aegean to take Troy, the city of legendary fame.

It was here, too, that Heracles performed the first of his twelve labours; here, in the lake of Lerna, that lived the terrible monster, the Lernaean Hydra; here, finally, that, according to legend, Danaus and his fifty daughters, the Danaids, set foot after their expulsion from Egypt, bringing water to Argos, which had suffered from drought ever since Poseidon caused its rivers to run dry.

The highest peak of the Argolid, the Arachnaeon (1100 m), rises grey and austere, bringing to mind the ancient citadels of the mighty kings of old, girded on all sides by strong walls, the "Cyclopean walls", which men believed had been built by the Cyclops, the master-masons from Lycia, in Asia Minor.

There are other mountains, too, in the Argolid – some bare, some covered with dense green forests of pine – but they are not as high. Between them lies the fertile plain of the Argolid with its rich soil, bearing orange trees that perfume the air with the scent of their blossoms, and olive groves rippling with silver as the wind plays among their leaves. In the background, the sea laps on bays and capes, its cool, salty tang mixing with the sweet smell of the earth.

HISTORY

The Argolid is a fertile land, well-situated geographically, and this attracted settlers from a very early date.

In the Francthi cave, near the village of Koilada in the Hermionid, traces of human habitation have come to light, which go as far back as the Mesolithic era. Here, too, was found a complete human skeleton dating to 7592 BC. The caves at the springs of the Erasinos river at Kefalari were also inhabited during the same period, in which man was still exclusively a hunter. Permanent settlements were established in the Middle Neolithic period, with the development of farming and animal-breeding. Around 2500 BC, one of these settlements, Lerna, by the lake of the same name, became an important centre in the region. In the Bronze Age (3000/2800-1100 BC) the Argolid was densely populated. Mycenae, Argos, Tiryns, Asine and

Prosymna were some of its settlements. The inhabitants were no longer only farmers and shepherds but were now also involved in trade with the advanced civilisations of the Cyclades, of Crete and of the East, which thus influenced their own development. During the second Bronze Age period, known as the Middle Helladic (2000-1600 BC), new Greek tribes settled in the already established centres and mixed with the indigenous populations. The influence exerted on them by the flourishing Minoan civilisation with which they were in contact created the necessary preconditions for their own cultural development, which occurred in the region during the next period, the Late Helladic (1600-1200 BC).

The important Achaean centre of Mycenae flourished greatly from 1600 to 1120 BC, and the Minoan civilisation was supplanted in the Greek world by the Mycenean. Mycenae was at the apogee of its power around 1350 BC, however the cities of Tiryns, Argos, Prosymna, Asine, Nauplion and Midea also flourished at this time.

The Mycenean state extended beyond the borders of the Argolid, and the Myceneans spread throughout the Peloponnese, through Thessaly, the eastern mainland of Greece and Euboea.

Mycenean palaces were built at Iolkos,

Wall painting of the 13th century BC from the acropolis of Mycenae, showing the head and upper part of the body of a female figure. Athens, National Archaeological Museum.

MYTHS AND LEGENDS

Inachus, Phoroneus, Perseus and Thyestes are some of the main figures in the myths of the Argolid. Pausanias makes particular mention of the river bearing the name of Inachus, the river-god who, together with Asterion and Cephissus was called upon as judge in the dispute between Hera and Poseidon over the mastery of the Argolid. Their decision was in Hera's favour, which provoked the anger of Poseidon, who then caused the waters of his judges' streams to dry up, turning the region into a barren land. Inachus was believed to have been the ancestor of the Argives and the founder of one of the three dynasties ruling the Argolid before the descent of the Dorian Heracleids. After he had dried up the stagnant waters of the plain of the Argolid and laid out the bed of the river that took his name, Inachus, gathered around him the inhabitants of the area, who until then had been living in the mountains,. Phoroneus was the son of Inachus, and, according to another legend, was the first inhabitant of the Argolid. He gathered together into a single community the people who until then had been living scattered in family tribes. The place in which they settled was named "Phoronikon asty". It later took the name of Phoroneus' grandson, Argos, who became the lord of the land and the eponymous leader of the city. Another famous hero is Perseus, the son of Zeus and of Danae. It is said that he exchanged his kingdom, Argos, for Tiryns, which belonged to Megapenthes, and that he founded Mycenae. Perseus' descendants were known as the Perseids, the last king of whom was Eurystheus, who imposed the Twelve Labours on Heracles. Finally, we might conclude our references to the demigods and heroes of the region by mentioning Atreus and his brother Thyestes, sons of Pelops, who came to the Argolid from Elis and succeeded Eurystheus to the Mycenean throne. The dynasty of the Atreids was the last Achaean dynasty to rule Mycenae before the descent of the Dorians, who, according to legend, were the descendants of Heracles returning to their ancestral land.

Thebes, Athens, Pylos, Tiryns and elsewhere. Transcending the borders of the land of the Achaeans, the Myceneans reached as far as Crete and the Dodecanese, founded colonies In Asia Minor and trading posts in Cyprus, established cultural and commercial relations with the peoples of the coasts of Asia Minor, from Troy to Halicarnassus, as well as with those of the Syrian and Palestinian coasts, Egypt, Sicily and southern Italy.

The products of Mycenean art, which adorned the Mycenean palaces or were sold on foreign markets, now supplanted those produced by the Minoans. From 1450 BC on, Mycenean art was no longer subject to the influence of Minoan art, and began to develop independently.

Acroterion from the temple of Asclepius at Epidaurus, showing a woman riding a horse. Athens, National Archaeological Museum.

The combative spirit of the Achaeans and the value they attached to symmetry left its mark on their creations, whereas the Minoans had shown an interest primarily in depicting the natural world.

Thus, despite superficial similarities, there are major differences between the two types of art. The palaces of Knossos were embellished with frescoes depicting animals and flowers, goddesses and athletic contestants, while those adorning Mycenean palaces portrayed hunters and warriors.

In the late 13th-early 12th century the Mycenean citadels were destroyed, while in the late12th - early11th century began the decline of the Mycenean state, which became final in the middle of the 11th century BC.

In the meantime, in the last quarter of the 12th century, the first Dorian invaders swept down from mainland Greece into the Peloponnese.

There were three groups of Dorians, the first of which, under the leadership of Timenos, one of the descendants of Heracles, seized the cities of Mycenae and Argos (in 1120 or 1104 BC, according to Thucydides).

Later, in the second half of the 11th century BC, the Dorians of Argos spread out across the rest of the Argolid. Nevertheless, many of the old centres continued to be inhabited, although their populations dwindled. The fact, however, that the economy of the region no longer was based on commerce but instead on the agricultural exploitation of the plain, favoured the city of Argos which, after the fall of Mycenae, became the major power in the Argolid.

In 710 BC, the sphere of influence of Argos expanded. It now controlled not only other centres in the Argolid but also the Heraeon at Prosymna, the most important of the sanctuaries of the goddess Hera on the Greek mainland. During the period from 700 to 480 BC Argos was at the height of its power.

Under the Timenid king

Pheidon, who appears to have ruled during the second quarter of the 7th century BC, the city came to extend its domination over the remaining cities of the Argolid – Epidaurus, Troezen, Hermione, Phlious (which at that time was part of the Argolid) and Aegina (where he minted a special coin) – and even beyond the boundaries of the province, throughout the eastern Peloponnese all the way to Cape Maleas.

Pheidon introduced a uniform system of weights and measures. He won back the city-states which had been colonised by Argives, and obtained the permission of the Pisans to occupy Pisa (the region to which Olympia belonged) and thus to preside over the Olympic games. Pheidon's successor, Damocratides, seized Nauplion and drove out its former inhabitants.

The expansionist tendencies of her rulers brought Argos into conflict with Sparta, with whom Argos became involved in a series of conflicts. In 494 BC, at the battle of Sepeia (near Tiryns), the Spartan army, under the leadership of king Cleomenes, annihilated the army of the Argives.

Ten years later, however, the Argives seized Tiryns and Mycenae, which had taken the side of the Spartans.

At the time of the Persian Wars the Argives turned to Athens for support against the Spartans, and established a democratic regime in Argos.

In 245 BC Epidaurus and Troezen became part of the Achaean League and in 230/299 BC Argos, Hermione and Phlious followed suit.

In 146 BC the Argolid shared the fate of the rest of Greece and came under the domination of the Romans. During Roman times the city of Argos was the second most important city in the Peloponnese.

In 267 BC the Argolid was invaded by hordes of Erulians, and in 395/396 BC by the Visigoths led by Alaric, who destroyed Argos and Epidaurus.

From the 5th century on, the Peloponnese was under Byzantine administration and, during the reign of the emperor Heraclius (610 AD), the Argolid became part of the *theme* of the Peloponnese, which, after the 11th century, was renamed the *theme* of Greece. Argos continued to be an important city.

In 1210, after the fall of Constantinople in 1204 to the Crusaders, the Franks became masters of Argos and of Nauplion, after a long siege by Geoffrey de Villehardouin. Together with the rest of the Peloponnese, it made up the principality of Achaea, which was divided into *timaria* (fiefs).

One of these, the fief of the Argolid, was

Roman copy of a classical statue of Asclepius from the sanctuary of the god at Epidaurus. Athens, National Archaeological Museum.

granted to the Duke of Athens, Otto de la Roche.

After 1460, one by one the various regions of the Argolid fell into the hands of the Turks.

In 1686 Nauplion and Argos came under Venetian rule, until 1715, when they were recaptured by the Turks. Argos attracted the Greek farmers, craftsmen and tradesmen of the region, while Nauplion became the headquarters of the Turkish pasha.

The inhabitants of the Argolid took an active part in the revolution of 1821 against the Turks, and in December of 1821 the town of Nea Epidavros was chosen as the venue for the first National Assembly of the insurgent Greeks. In 1822 Argos became the seat of the revolutionary government, to be succeeded, a year later, in 1823, by Nauplion, which, in 1828, became the capital of the newly-established Greek state, a position it retained until 1834, when the capital was transferred to Athens.

LERNA

In Proto-Helladic times Lerna was the most important centre in the Argolid. It was built at the foot of Pontinos hill, near the present-day town of Myloi (approximately 10 kms south of Argos) in a region with abundant springs. Many of the waters of these springs flowed out into the sea, while others formed a small but deep lake surrounded by dense vegetation. This was Alcyonia lake, the depth of which, according to Pausanias, was "fathomless". Here, in one of the springs of the lake, called Amymone, lived, according to legend, the Lernaean Hydra, the terrible many-headed monster.

Lerna was inhabited continuously from the 5th and 4th millennia BC until the second century AD, at which time it was visited by Pausanias, who informs us that the city he saw extended further north than the prehistoric settlement. From the finds (stone implements, clay female figurines, vases) brought to light by excavations, it

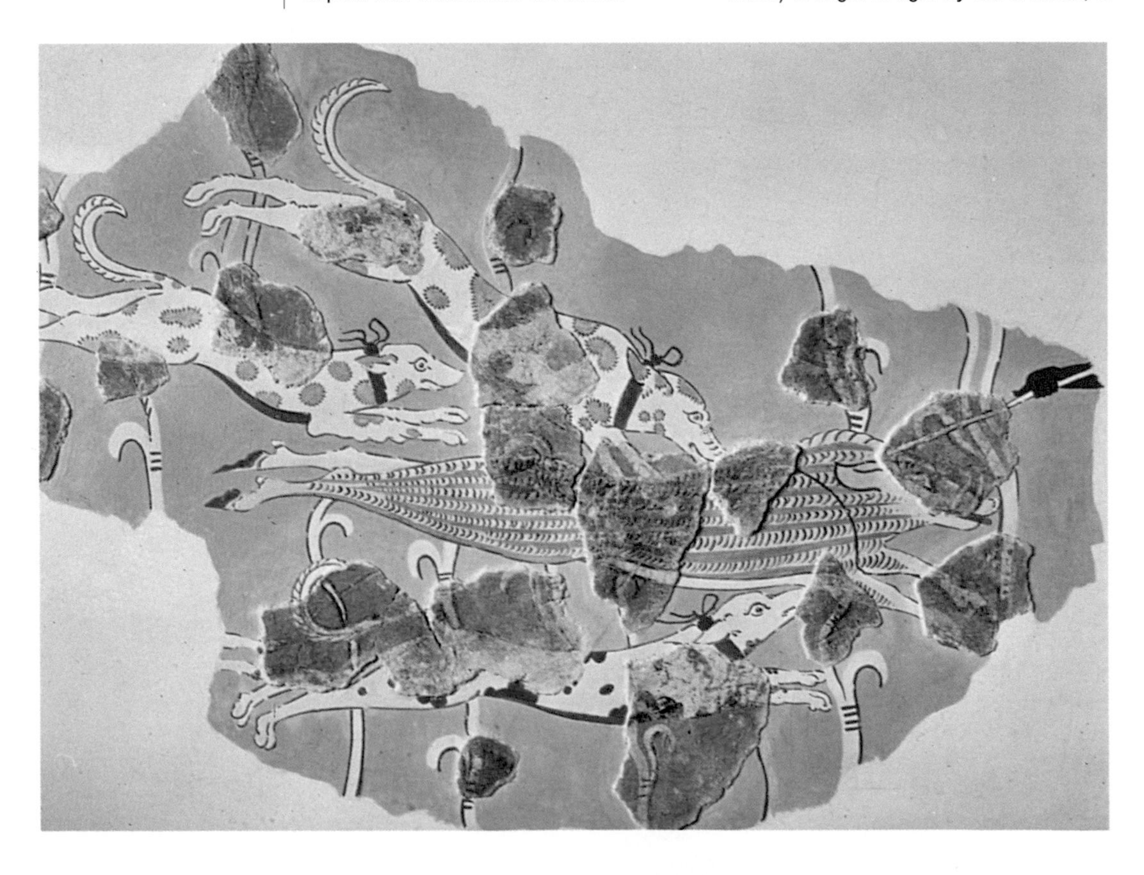

appears that the inhabitants of Lerna had very early on established contacts with the islands of the Aegean.

The settlement began to develop from the beginning of the 3rd millennium, reaching its peak around 2500 BC. At this time, the houses built were large and stood on stone foundations. To the late years of the Proto-Helladic period belongs the "House of the Tiles", which took its name from the many clay tiles of its roof which were found here. The building, which appears to have been the palace of a prince, was two-storied. On the ground floor were four consecutive rectangular rooms, two of which (the first and third) were spacious, while the other two were narrow. The rooms communicated with each other through doors set in the northern walls. On the south and north sides of the building there were narrow corridor-like rooms that must have been stairwells leading to the first floor, or storerooms. We can still see some steps, which led to the upper storey. At the entrance of the building there was a narrow vestibule.

The settlement was fortified during the same period as that in which the "House of the Tiles" was erected. Part of the fortifications have been preserved.

The Proto-Helladic settlement of Lerna was destroyed by fire before 2000 BC, but continued to be inhabited during the Meso-Helladic period. In the Late Helladic period, Lerna was eclipsed by Mycenae and Tiryns, but continued to be inhabited, as we have said, after the Mycenean period.

MYCENAE THE GOLDEN

As Lerna retreated into the background, another city moved into the limelight - Mycenae the Golden, whose king, Agamemnon, was the general commander of the Greek forces and "king of kings" during the Trojan war.

Left: Wall painting from Tiryns (13th c. BC), showing a boar hunt. Athens, National Archaeological Museum.

Above: The "House of the Tiles" at Lerna.

At the time when the city was at the peak of its prosperity, its houses and palaces, built on the top of a high hill, were girded by gigantic walls. Here lived the legendary and tragic figures of Agamemnon, Clytaemestra and Aegisthus, whose violent and overwhelming human passions inspired the tragic poets of antiquity to recount, in vivid verse, their turbulent lives and violent deaths. According to legend, the founder and first king of the city was the hero Perseus, said to have reigned during the first half of the 14th century, that is around 1400 to 1350 BC.

However, according to historical sources, the hill of Mycenae began to be inhabited around 2500 BC and Mycenae was already flourishing at the end of the 17th century BC.

It was given the name of Mycenae because the point *(myces)* of Perseus' sword was said to have fallen on the site where the city was built, something which was considered to be a good omen. According to another version, it took its name from the mushrooms *(mycetes)* that grew on the site. Feeling thirsty, Perseus sought their cool taste, and when he pulled some up, a spring of fresh water, later named the Perseian spring, gushed out from beneath their roots.

Funerary stele in poros stone from grave V of Grave Circle A. It bears a spiral decoration, while the lower part represents a horse race. Athens, National Archaeological Museum.

Many identify Mycenae with the capital of the strong empire which was known to the Hittites by the name of Ahhiyawà. From the middle of the 15th century BC on, the commercial activities of the Myceneans extended to the eastern and western shores of the Mediterranean, where their trading posts gradually displaced those of the Minoans. After the Minoan palaces were destroyed by a powerful earthquake around 1550/1500 BC the Minoan state began to decline and, in 1450 BC, the Myceneans seized the opportunity to take Knossos and become masters of Crete.

The 14th and 13th centuries were a time of prosperity and expansion for the Myceneans, who fortified their city with strong walls, the so-called "Cyclopean walls". Wide roads were built both inside and outside the citadel. The inside road led to the imposing palace built on the summit of the hill.

The roads outside the walls, complemented with bridges, linked the citadel to the small settlements or to other Mycenean centres such as Tiryns and Argos.

The Myceneans were able soldiers. They are said to have fought as mercenaries for the Pharaoh of Egypt, and to have helped him drive out the Hyksos, a service for which they were rewarded with large quantities of gold.

They were also merchants and seamen; they transported their wine, oil, honey and artefacts to various Mediterranean ports, where they exchanged them for the raw materials – gold, copper and ivory – they needed.

They were farmers and herdsmen, too. Their lands were planted with olive, ap-

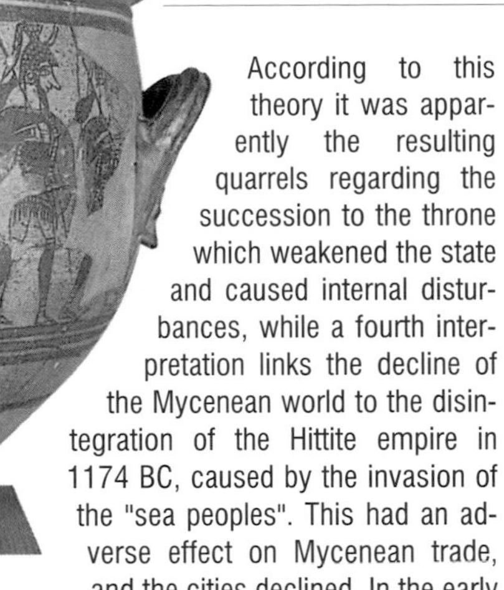

ple, pear, fig and almond trees. They cultivated the vine, grew cereals and kept bees. Fishing was an activity they had little interest in, as they seem to have only cared for shellfish. They raised pigs, sheep and goats, bred horses and were good hunters. The supreme ruler of the Mycenean state was the "anax", the king, who was surrounded by his officials. Among the greatest of the Mycenean kings were Atreus and Agamemnon. The former appears to have reigned around 1250 BC and the latter between 1220 and 1184 BC. In the second half of the 13th century (around 1200 BC) the citadel of Mycenae was destroyed by fire. A variety of interpretations on the causes of this fire are given by scholars. Some say neighbouring invaders or others, from further away, set fire to Mycenae, while others believe they were the result of internal conflicts, due to the lengthy absence of the city's leaders on the Trojan expedition, which is believed to have taken place during this period (1200-1184 BC). Still others connect these events with the death of Agamemnon right after his return from Troy and with the murder, eight years later, of Aegisthus and Clytaemestra by Agamemnon's son, Orestes.

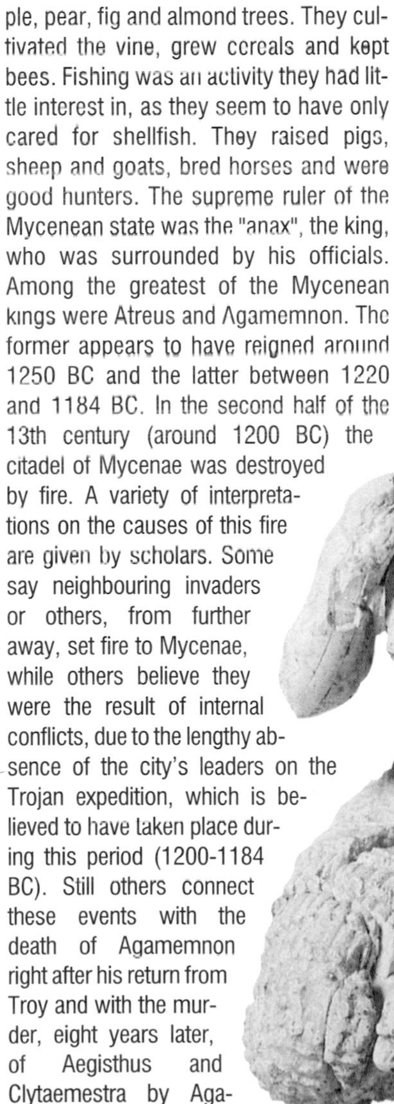

According to this theory it was apparently the resulting quarrels regarding the succession to the throne which weakened the state and caused internal disturbances, while a fourth interpretation links the decline of the Mycenean world to the disintegration of the Hittite empire in 1174 BC, caused by the invasion of the "sea peoples". This had an adverse effect on Mycenean trade, and the cities declined. In the early 12th century an effort was made to reconstitute the Mycenean state, without great success, however, owing to the invasion of the Dorians. This century was a period of gradual decline of the power of the Myceneans. In the years of the reign of Orestes' son, Tissamenes, the Dorians were able to take Mycenae (1120 BC). Although the city itself was

Above: Krater decorated with a scene of marching warriors. Found in a house outside Grave Circle A. Athens, National Archaeological Museum.

Below: Ivory figurine of two female figures and a child in the middle, with their arms around one another. 15th century BC, Athens, National Archaeological Museum.

Above: Blade of a dagger with an inlaid decoration of gold and silver. It represents a hunting scene and was found in grave IV of Grave Circle A. Athens, National Archaeological Museum.

Below: Silver cup with inlaid gold heads. Athens, National Archaeological Museum.

destroyed, some of the inhabitants continued to live in the citadel. However, the once powerful city was reduced to the status of a small village. In spite of this, the Myceneans took part in the common struggle of the Greeks against the Persians by sending a contingent of soldiers to Thermopylae in 480 BC and, a year later, in 479 BC, to Plataeae. In 468 BC the citadel was destroyed by the Argives, who repaired it again in the 3rd century BC.

Pausanias, visiting Mycenae in the 2nd century AD, reports that, of the ancient citadel, parts of the walls, as well as the lion gate, the Perseian fountain, the underground treasure chambers of Atreus and his sons and the tombs of Atreus, Agamemnon, Clytaemestra, Aegisthus and others could still be seen. In the Byzantine period and the Middle Ages the small town continued to live on, forgotten by all. It is once again mentioned in the 18th and beginning of the 19th century in the accounts of foreign travellers. During the last years of the Turkish occupation, European travellers visiting the area attempted to plunder its treasures.

In 1836, after the liberation of Greece, Mycenae was placed under the jurisdiction of the Greek Archaeological Society, which carried out extensive excavations. In 1876 Heinrich Schliemann began to dig in the area of the citadel, uncovering the famous palace and the "treasures of Atreus".

A GUIDED TOUR OF THE ARCHAEOLOGICAL SITE

THE ACROPOLIS

The acropolis (citadel) of Mycenae, the hub of the Mycenean world, the extent of which is approximately 30,000 sq. m. stands on the summit of a high hill. Its shape is almost triangular and it is surrounded by strong walls 5.50 m thick. Their height, which is about 8 metres today, must have originally been about 12 metres The rough, irregular blocks of stone used for the building of the wall are so huge that it seemed that only gigantic beings such as the legendary Cyclops could possibly have lifted them, which is how the walls came to be known as "Cyclopean" walls. The gaps between these stones were filled by smaller stones and clay.

The Myceneans do not appear to have used hoisting mechanisms such as pulleys and winches, but to have applied the same methods as those used by the Egyptians in building the pyramids. That is, they built sloping earthen ramps for rolling the stone blocks up to the level of the wall,

which were demolished after the work was completed.
The fortifications of the Mycenean acropolis were constructed in three phases. The older cyclopean walls were built in 1360/1340 BC and encircled a smaller area. In 1250 BC these walls were extended to surround the first circle of graves, while at the end of the 13th century BC the acropolis assumed its final form by the addition of a small area on the north-eastern side which enclosed an underwater cistern.
Before the central entrance, the Lion Gate, there is a small courtyard. On the eastern side of this long and narrow courtyard rises the wall and on the western side a strong tower. This disposition of the external area limited the strength of potential invaders, since only a few soldiers at a time would be able to approach the gate. On the inside of the entrance area there is a square courtyard of 4 x 4 metres, which was initially covered. From here the guards could easily climb up onto the walls.
On the right of the entrance have been preserved the ruins of a two-storey edi-

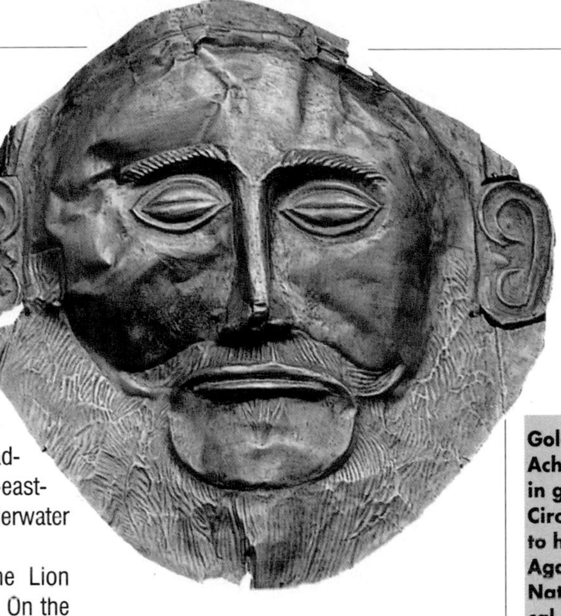

Gold mask of an Achaean king, found in grave V of Grave Circle A, and thought to have been that of Agamemnon. Athens, National Archaeological Museum.

THE LION GATE

The sides of the hill on which Perseus built Mycenae are steep, and the only approach to the citadel is from the north-west, where the main gate was built. This entrance is known as the Lion Gate from the relief representing two lions carved over its lintel and which has been preserved to this day in good condition. Besides the central gate there is also a smaller one on the northern side of the enceinte.
The Lion Gate was built in 1250 BC. It measures 3.10 metres in height, and 2.95 metres in width at the bottom, while the top is slightly narrower (2.85 m). It is built of four gigantic dressed stone blocks. It has two jambs of about 3 metres in height and 1.70 metres in width, which support the lintel on which rests the relieving triangle bearing the relief representation of two animals on its outside face. The heads of the animals - probably lionesses - have not survived, possibly owing to the fact that they were made of a softer stone, perhaps steatite, and were then attached to the stone slab with the help of bronze pins The gate was closed by a double wooden door sheathed in bronze. Each of the two leaves swung on a wooden pivot, thus allowing the door which was secured by a wooden bar on the inside, to open and shut.

Right: The acropolis of Mycenae. We can make out Grave Circle A.

Below: Gold ring with a representation of a ritual scene. Athens, National Archaeological Museum.

fice whose west wall rests on the encircling wall of the acropolis. The English archaeologist and scholar A.J.B. Wace called this building a granary, because of the storage jars containing charred grains of wheat found in its basement.

In front of the "granary" lies the cemetery of the Myceneans, known as Grave Circle A, which was excavated by Schliemann in 1876. Grave Circle A is part of a larger cemetery, which also extended to the west, outside the enceinte. One part remained outside the acropolis when, in the middle of the 13th century BC, the western cyclopean wall was built. Grave Circle A is a circular area of about 28 metres in diameter, encircled by an enclosure formed by a double row of upright stone slabs with a third slab placed vertically over the other two. At this point the wall curves to include this part of the cemetery.

In Grave Circle A were found six royal shaft graves. Above each one had been

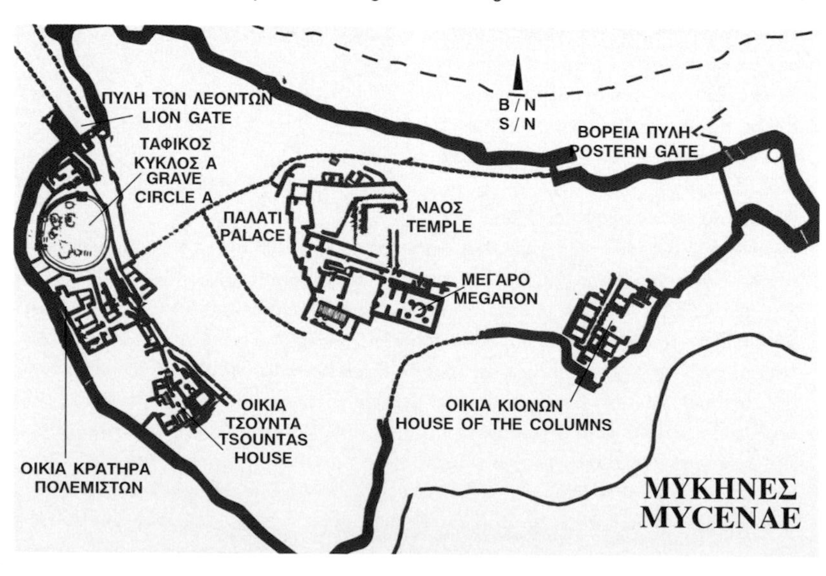

Right, above: Mycenean dagger with a richly decorated hilt, from grave IV of Grave Circle A. Athens, National Archaeological Museum.

Right, below: The acropolis of Mycenae. We can see the inner side of the Lion Gate, the "granary", and the ascending road leading to the palace.

placed a poros stone stele, many of which bear relief representations of men riding on chariots, while others are adorned with geometric designs. Inside the graves were found nineteen skeletons and many grave offerings which are now exhibited in the National Archaeological Museum in Athens.
Among the grave offerings, particular mention must be made of the bronze swords and daggers, the gold and silver cups and the five gold masks (one of which was initially erroneously believed to be that of Agamemnon), gold plaques, gold jewellery, and gold and silver rhytons. The total weight of the gold objects amounted to about 14 kilograms.
The graves of Grave Circle A were believed by Schliemann - who followed Pausanias' account - to have been those of Agamemnon and his retinue, who were murdered by Clytaemestra. However, later scholars proved that the graves are older and date from the 16th century BC (that is approximately 1600-1510 BC). Professor G. Mylonas, in charge of the excavations since 1963, has argued that these graves must have belonged to the royal family reigning at Mycenae at the time.
To the south of the graves have come to light the foundations of houses of the Mycenean period, which have been given various names, such as the House of the Warrior Vase, because of the krater found inside it bearing a representation of warriors on a march, the House of the Ramp, the West House, the Wace House, the Tsoundas House.
East of the Tsoundas House Professor G. Mylonas excavated a temple with a sacrificial altar, while south-east of these buildings was uncovered the religious centre of the Myceneans, including the houses of the priests and, among them, an edifice which was perhaps the residence of the high priest.
To the latter building, the walls of which were adorned with frescoes, belong the frescoes of the "Mycenean woman" and of the "figure-of-eight-shaped shields".
An uphill road, known as the Great Ramp, part of which has survived, leads from the Lion Gate to the summit of the hill where stood the palace.
The right side of this ramp is supported by a Cyclopean retaining wall. The steps leading up are a later construction to fa-

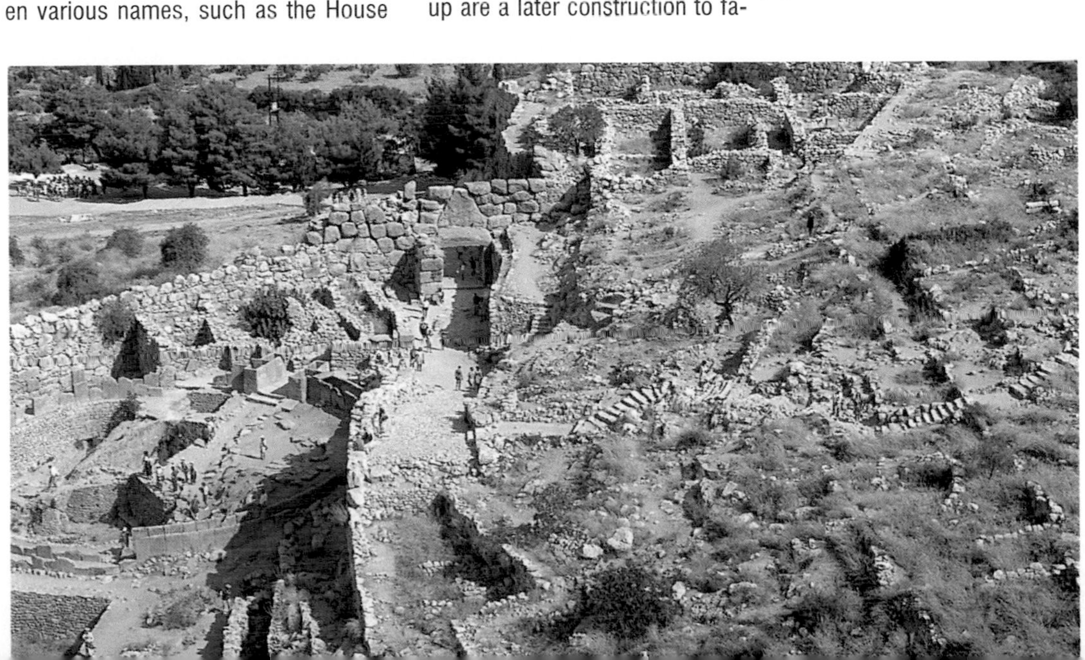

cilitate the access of visitors to the palace. The path is interrupted, at one point, by a building of Hellenistic times, believed to have been an olive press.

On the summit of the acropolis stood the impressive residence of the king and of the members of his family. One entered through a propylon on the northwestern corner of the hill. Two porches, one on the inside and one on the outside, adjoined the propylon, the roof of each resting on a column.

From the propylon a long corridor led to the western entrance, which was the main entrance of the palace. Today only the threshold, consisting of a massive block of conglomerate, survives.

To the north of the entrance have been excavated the foundations of a room which must have served as a sentry room.

We come to the south corridor, parallel to which runs another smaller one leading to the great courtyard of the palace, which was paved with cement and adorned with a polychrome decoration. The southern corridor led to a succession of rooms, which occupied the highest level of the hill. Of these has been excavated a long and narrow room, the *prothalamos* (antechamber). The walls were lined with low benches and there was a quadrilateral hearth. Professor Mylonas gave this room the name of "antechamber of the curtains" after the frescoes that were found here.

Of the apartments which lay north of the southern corridor only vestiges remain. Here, on the summit, was built in the 7th century BC a temple dedicated to the goddess Athena, of which only part of the foundations are still visible today. Later, in Hellenistic times, and on the same site, a second larger temple was built, of which the platform has survived.

On the eastern side of the great courtyard stood the *Megaron,* which measured 23 metres in length and an average of 11.50 metres in width. Its western side was open towards the courtyard and formed a porch, which Homer calls "aithousa".

A door in the eastern wall of the hall led to the vestibule of the Megaron. From here, a wide doorway, which closed only with a curtain, and the sill of which, made of conglomerate stone, is still vis-

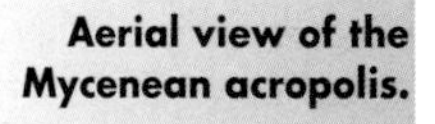

Aerial view of the Mycenean acropolis.

ible today, led to the *domos*, that is to the main room of the Megaron.
The dimensions of the domos are 12.95 by 11.50 metres approximately. The centre was occupied by a circular hearth, of which only a part survives. It was surrounded by four wooden pillars, the bases of two of which, as well as the foundations of a third, can still be seen. These pillars supported the roof, in which there was an opening to allow the smoke to escape. The walls of the domos were covered with frescoes, and on the south side stood the king's throne.
South of the small corridor have been preserved the foundations of a roughly square room with a small courtyard on its south side, which must have been a guest chamber. South of the guest chamber, in the southwestern corner of the palace, we can still see a part of a grand staircase.
East of the Megaron are the Artists' and Craftsmen's Workshops, and the House of the Columns, which made up the main part of the eastern wing of the palace and which owes its name to the colonnade running around the central courtyard. East of the House of the Columns has been excavated a building known as Building Δ, and to its north another edifice known as building Γ. Both of these must have served as storerooms for provisions.
The north-eastern extension of the acropolis, which was built during the last phase of construction of the fortified wall, includes another two buildings, A and B. In building B must have lived the guard entrusted with the security of the underground cistern north of the building. This cistern, which was built at the end of the 13th century BC to provide the Myceneans with water in case of siege, and which was of vital importance to the citadel, still impresses the visitor today.
A vaulted passage and a flight of 93 steps interrupted by two landings, lead down to the reservoir. The path passes under the wall and continues beyond it. At the lowest point of the descent is the

Another view of the acropolis. On the top of the hill can be seen the palace.

cistern, shaped like a well, into which the waters of springs outside the acropolis, brought to the cistern by means of subterranean conduits, were gathered and stored.
Two sally ports, one in the north wall and one in the south wall of the extension of the enclosure served as escape routes in the case of surprise attacks.
The circular cistern which has survived on the north-eastern side of the north tunnel dates from the Hellenistic period.
On the north side of the enclosure, west of the north sally port, is the second gate of the acropolis, the North Gate, which is smaller than the Lion Gate, but which was built in the same period using identical techniques.
West of the North Gate, within the width of the wall, have been uncovered the foundations of storehouses for food and weapons, which were built at the end of the 12th century BC.
To the south-west of these have come to light the ruins of a building of Mycenean times, known as building M, which is believed to have been the dwelling of the officer responsible for the security of the wall. West of this building and to the north-east have been excavated the foundations of an edifice of the early 12th century BC, which was perhaps used by the guards of the Mycenean acropolis.

STRUCTURES OUTSIDE THE CITADEL

The citadel of Mycenae was the residence of the royal family and of the state officials. The Mycenean citizenry lived outside the citadel, in "villages" that were not very far apart, each "village" having its own cemetery nearby.

After 1900 BC the ordinary inhabitants buried their dead in square pits, hewn out of the rocks and covered with stone slabs.

In the 17th and 16th centuries BC the members of the royal families were buried in shaft graves, such as those in Grave Circles A and B.

From 1550 BC up until the end of the year 1120 BC it is chamber and tholos tombs that are the most prevalent - chamber tombs being used for the burial of ordinary citizens and tholos tombs for the kings and the members of the royal families.

The chamber tombs are cut out of the rock and have a *dromos* (path) leading to the entrance, which is small and closed by a dry stone wall. Many of these tombs have come to light around Mycenae.

The tholos tombs also consist of a chamber cut out of the rock and a *dromos* leading to the entrance. Here, however, the chamber is covered by a domed roof made of circular layers of stones placed so that each circle has a smaller diameter than the previous one. At the top, the structure is closed by a single slab over the hole.

Wace divided the tholos tombs into three groups, according to the period in which they were built, which also determined their particular features.

In the oldest tombs (1510-1460 BC) the dromos leading to the chamber was bordered by unfaced walls. A dry stone wall closed off the entrance. The blocks of stone used as lintels were not smoothed on the inside so that they followed the curve of the dome, as in the more recent tombs. The dome was built of rough-hewn stones, and there was no relieving triangle over the lintel. In tombs of a somewhat later period (1460-1400 BC) the façade was adorned, but the decoration was not as carefully executed as that in the still later tombs, and the walls of the dromos leading to the chamber were more simply faced.

Below, left: The entrance to the tholos tomb of Clytaemestra.

Above, right: The façade of the "Treasure of Atreus".

Below, right: The inside of the vaulted roof of the "Treasure of Atreus".

The most recent tombs of all (dating from after 1400 BC) had a dromos bordered by walls of well-shaped stones set in straight courses, while the carefully finished façades were adorned with half-columns, and relieving triangles bearing a relief decoration. They also had wooden doors, probably sheathed in bronze.

As the visitor leaves the Mycenean acropolis behind him, he will find, north of it, the tholos tomb of the Lions which derives its name from its location beside the Lion Gate. It was built around 1350 BC. Three shaft graves cut out of the floor of the tomb were found, at the time of their discovery, to have already been plundered.

South of the road are to be found the tholos tombs of Aegisthus and Clytaemestra - these names, of course, being simply conventional. Aegisthus' tomb dates from around 1500 BC, while that of Clytaemestra appears to have been built around 1220 BC. On the way leading to the chamber of the grave was built in the Hellenistic period,a theatre, part of tho seating area of which is still visible today. The dromos measures 37 metres in length and its sides are faced with blocks of conglomerate.

The section above the lintel of the door was covered by sculptured marble plaques.

Near the tomb of Clytaemestra has been discovered Grave Circle B, the second royal cemetery of Mycenae. Some of the 24 graves found here are older than those of Grave Circle A (that is, they belong to the end of the 17th and the first half of the 16th centuries BC) while others are contemporaneous with them. Fourteen of these 24 graves, which have been given the letters of the alphabet by archaeologists, are royal shaft graves and the remaining ten are small quadrilaterial ones hewn out of the rock. These belonged to ordinary people who must have had some connection with the palace.

In Grave Circle B have been found sixteen skeletons and many grave offerings made of silver, gold, bronze and rock crystal, as well as clay vases. Some of the grave offerings are now exhibited in the National Archaeological Museum in Athens and others in the Museum of Nauplion.

On the graves of Grave Circle B, as in those of Grave Circle A, have been found stelae, many of them in their original position. In Grave Circle Γ was found a skeleton showing the signs of a surgical operation. Grave P was remodelled in the second half of the 15th century BC and was given the shape of a quadrilaterial chamber with a narrow corridor, a form of grave unknown in Greece and only found in Cyprus and in Syria.

South of Grave Circle B have been excavated the foundations of four houses of the 13th century BC: the West House, the House of the Shields - so named because of the shields found there - the House of the Oil Merchant and the House of the Sphinxes - in which was found a plaque decorated with sphinxes.

In the House of the Oil Merchant were found fragments of large jars (pithoi) used for storing olive oil or for the preparation of perfumed oils.

To the south of the four houses has come to light the "Treasury of Atreus", built around 1250 BC and the most impressive of the tombs found. It may indeed have belonged to king Atreus, who had reigned at that time. The dromos leading to its entrance measures 36 metres in length, 6 metres in width, and is cut out of the rock. Its sides are faced with blocks of conglomerate.

The decorated façade of the grave measures 10.50 metres in height, while the opening measures 2.70 metres at the threshold and 2.45 metres at the level of the lintel. It was also decorated on the inside of the dome.

Parts of the decoration of the façade are to be seen in the National Archaeological Museum in Athens and in the British Museum in London. A double wooden door closed the entrance, and on the façade, on either side of the door, stood a half-column. Finally, stone slabs adorned with a carved relief decoration, covered the relieving triangle.

None of the grave offerings, which must have been particularly sumptuous, has been found, because the tomb had already been plundered in antiquity.

Aerial photograph of the acropolis of Tiryns.

TIRYNS

A second important centre in the region during the period of Mycenae's greatest prosperity was Tiryns. This is confirmed not only by Homer, who refers to the city as "wall-girt" because of its impressive fortifications, but also by the ruins of its acropolis, which covered an area of 20,000 sq.m.

When Pausanias visited the city, in the 2nd century AD, he only found ruins. According to him, the city was named after Tiryns, a son of Argos and grandson of Zeus.

According to other myths, the founder and king of the city was Proetus, a descendant of Danaus and twin brother of Acrisius. The two brothers shared out the Argive territory between them and Argos fell to Acrisius while Proetus kept Midea, the Heraeon and Tiryns, which he girded with walls built by the Cyclops. Tiryns was first inhabited in Neolithic times and became a flourishing settlement during the Proto-Helladic period.

Legends relate that it was fortified two generations before Mycenae. Excavations prove that the first walls were built shortly after 1400 BC and were completed in three stages, the last walls being built just before 1200 BC (1230 BC).

Around 2500 BC on the site of the Megaron stood a circular edifice of about 28 m in diameter, which may have been the residence of the ruler, or a fort. Traces of this edifice have been excavated under the foundations of the Megaron, those of the exterior courtyard and of the two smaller buildings to the east.

In the Middle Helladic period (2000-1600 BC), after the settlement in the area of the first Hellenic tribes, the appearance of the place changed and just after 1400 BC the first Mycenean acropolis took shape. The first palace was built and the highest part of the rock was encircled by a girdle of defensive walls, interrupted by a single gate. The entrance was narrow, and was flanked by towers on either side. In the early 13th century (1300 BC approximately) another palace was built on the site of the first, which had been destroyed by fire. The fortifications of the acropolis were extended towards the north and the lowest northern part of the rock was surrounded by a makeshift wall of brick laid over a stone base.

In the second half of the 13th century BC (1230 BC) the acropolis was destroyed by fire or by an earthquake, and then rebuilt in the form in which we see it today. The northern, lower part of the rock, the "lower acropolis", was encircled by "Cyclopean walls" and in this area were set up workshops and storerooms. The Megaron was rebuilt.

A section of the western side of the cyclopean walls of Tiryns. We can see the sickle-shaped bastion.

On the southern and southeastern sides, the old wall was reinforced and within it were created galleries for the storing of provisions. Two subterranean tunnels were dug out in the north and northwest part of the wall in order to ensure the citadel's water supply.

Around 1200 BC the acropolis of Tiryns was once again destroyed by fire or by a powerful earthquake. This time the city was rebuilt, both within the acropolis and outside its walls.

Tiryns continued to be inhabited even after the end of the Mycenean period, and the Dorians who invaded the region continued to use its acropolis.

In the early Geometric period, an edifice of about 21 metres in length and seven in

width, believed to have been a temple dedicated to the goddess Hera, was erected on the site of the Megaron.
Tiryns laid claim to being the oldest place of worship of the goddess. That Hera was worshipped here is also confirmed by legend, according to which Peirasus, the builder of the first statue of Hera, was a son of Argus, the hundred-eyed giant who guarded Io at Mycenae. The statue, made of the wood of the wild pear tree, stood in the highest temple dedicated to the goddess. When the Argives destroyed Tiryns in the 5th century BC, they carried off the statue and set it up in the Heraeon in Argos.As Argos reached the height of its prosperity, Tiryns began to fade into insignificance; however, its inhabitants, following the example of the Myceneans, contributed to the victories of Thermopylae and Plataeae by joining the Athenians and Spartans who were standing up against the Persians.

Gallery within the wall of the acropolis of Tiryns, which served as a storeroom and magazine.

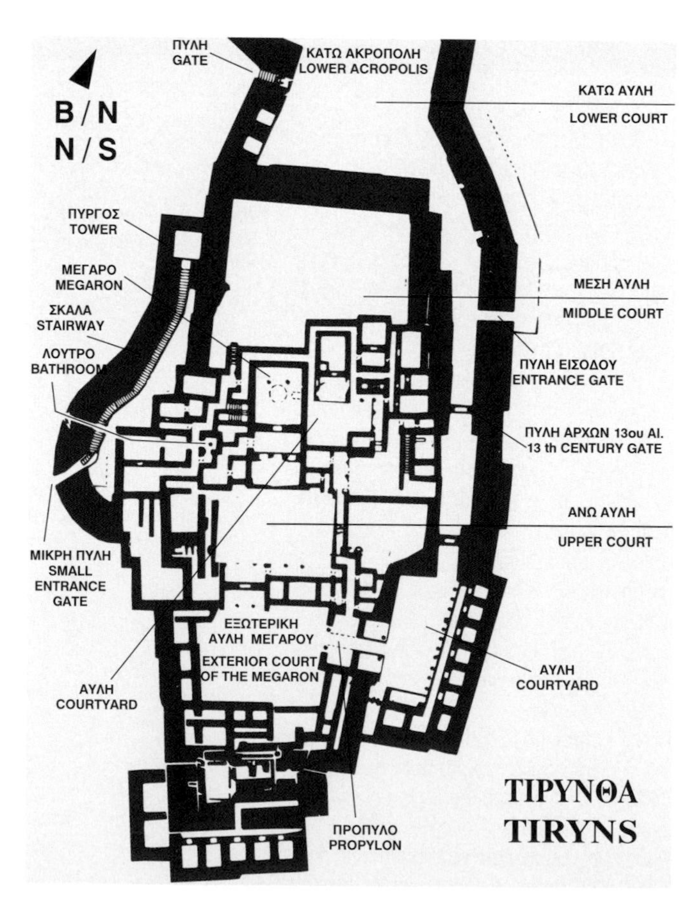

Ten or fifteen years later, according to Strabo, Tiryns was destroyed by the Argives, after which a good number of its inhabitants settled in Argos, while others established themselves in Epidaurus or in the city of Alieis (present-day Porto Heli).

A GUIDED TOUR OF THE ARCHAEOLOGICAL SITE

The low hill, rising above the fertile Argolic plain, very near the sea, was an ideal site for the establishment of the Mycenean centre of Tiryns. The acropolis of late Mycenean times was reached by following an uphill road approximately 4.50 metres in width, on the east side of the hill.
The entrance gate, with its two jambs and double wooden door, resembled the Lion Gate in Mycenae.
At a certain point north of the entrance there is a curve in the wall. This was a device intended to impede the approach of enemy forces which, as they neared the gate, would thus be vulnerable to attack from three sides (front, behind and right) at once.
A person wishing to reach the Megaron from the gate had to turn left and pass through another two gates. The first was probably the entrance gate to the acropolis at the beginning of the 13th century BC. From the other gate, a small forecourt led

to a larger court with a porch on its eastern side. Below the porch ran the eastern gallery, reached through the steps which must have existed south of the porch. These galleries, the roof of which was made of huge stones forming a pointed vault, had been accommodated within the wide wall, and served as storerooms. From the courtyard, a great propylon with an interior and exterior porch, each of which had two supporting columns, led to the outside courtyard of the Megaron. South of the courtyard, below the wall, which here, too, is very thick, we find the south gallery and the steps leading to it. North of the exterior courtyard a smaller propylon, similar to the first, led out into an interior courtyard. Here there are traces of a circular altar dedicated to Zeus Erkeios ("protector of the house"). North of the courtyard stood the Megaron, which, as in Mycenae, consisted of a porch, a vestibule and the main room. Its stuccoed floors and its walls were lavishly decorated. Parts of the frescoes which had adorned them have survived and are

Left: Part of the fortifications of the acropolis of Asine.

Below: View of the hill of Asine.

ASINE

Asine was yet another flourishing settlement of Mycenean times. Prehistoric Asine is mentioned by Homer in the *Iliad* while, in our day, the city lent its name to a poem by the Greek poet and Nobel prize winner, George Seferis. It was first inhabited in the Bronze Age and was an important centre, not only in Mycenean times, but also in the Proto-Geometric and Geometric periods. Asine lies 11 kilometres to the south-east of Nauplion, very near Tolo. It was built on an idyllic site, on the summit of a steep rock, 85 metres high, the western side of which drops sharply down to the sea.

Its inhabitants were Dryopes, whose religious centre was near the sanctuary of the Pythian Apollo. After the destruction of the city around 700 BC by the Argives, many of its inhabitants settled in the province of Messenia.

Asine once again became an important town in the area during the Hellenistic period. It was then that was built the wall, parts of which, together with its medieval additions, has survived to this day.

This second period of prosperity lasted until the early Roman period, but when Pausanias visited it he found only ruins. In medieval times the citadel was used by the Franks, who repaired its ancient fortifications.

now exhibited in the National Archaeological Museum in Athens. They represent hunting scenes, processions of women taking part in religious ceremonies, chariots and figure-of-eight shields.
Three doors in the northern wall of the porch opened out onto the vestibule. From the vestibule, the dimensions of which were approximately the same as those of the porch, a door led to the western apartments, while another larger one led to the main room, which measured about 11 metres in length. The throne stood against the eastern wall of the room, while in the centre of the room there was a hearth surrounded by four columns.
In the western apartments there was a small square room which seems to have been used as a bathroom. The floor consists of the smoothed surface of a rock guttered with a channel for the water. The channel ended up at an adjoining T-shaped conduit, which led to a sewer designed to collect the rainwater from the roofs.
To the east of the Megaron lies a smaller courtyard and two smaller Megara, access to which was gained through a narrow corridor starting from the large propylon.
The Megaron and the western wing communicated through a narrow paved corridor with the large back courtyard, the "middle acropolis", which lay to their north.
To the west of this courtyard stood a tower. From here, a narrow stairway led to a postern gate. Where the tower stood, the defensive wall took on the shape of a sickle; the bastion thus formed, together with the gate, afforded the inhabitants some protection in the case of a siege, when they needed to bring in water from the springs outside the walls.
North of the back courtyard extends the "lower acropolis", which the inhabitants of Tiryns approached through the central gate or through two other arched gates, the one on the north and the other on the south side of the rock. At the western end of the "lower acropolis" have come to light the foundations of buildings .
One of these stands at the entrance of two subterranean parallel galleries leading to two underground cisterns.

Bronze helmet and breastplate of the 8th century BC from a late-Geometric tomb of Argos. Argos Archaeological Museum

ARGOS

With the decline of the Mycenean state and the coming of the Dorians, Argos now took over, growing in importance until it became, in the 8th century BC, the most powerful city of the Argolid.
Built on the western side of the verdant plain of the Argolid, it is hemmed in by mountains on the east, the west and the north, its only outlet being the sea to the south.
The poetess Telesilla hailed from Argos, as did Cleobis and his brother Biton, whose figures, carved in relief, adorned ancient Argos. According to Pausanias, it was Telesilla who organised the Argive women and saved the city in 494 BC, when it was besieged by the Spartans under king Cleomenes.

As for Cleobis and Biton, Herodotus tells us that they yoked themselves to their chariot and travelled 45 *stadia* to bring their mother Cydippe, a priestess of Hera, to the Heraeon. In answer to the proud and happy mother's prayer, the gods recompensed the two brothers by granting them what was considered the supreme blessing for a human being, a peaceful death.

According to the local myths, Argos, the "Phoronikon asty", was the most important city not only of the Argolid but also of the entire Peloponnese, and was founded by Phoroneus,the son of the river Inachus.

Excavations have proved that the region has been inhabited without interruption since Neolithic times.

In the Mycenean period, Argos, under Diomedes, its king, was second in importance among the cities of the Argolid only to Mycenae and Tiryns.

At the height of its prosperity (7th century BC), the city's rivalry with Sparta came to a head over the mastery of the region of Cynuria. The two rival cities became involved in a war which ended with Sparta emerging as the greatest land power in the Peloponnese.

In the 6th century BC Argos flourished as an artistic centre. Its artistic skills, pottery, metal and bronze work, were renowned. Among its most famous artists were the great sculptors Ageladas and Polycleitus.

In the 5th century BC the agora was laid out, while in Hellenistic times Argos acquired a drainage and road system. In Hellenistic and Roman times, the town extended beyond the boundaries of present-day Argos, but, in 395 BC, the raids of the Visigoths left the city in ruins.

During Byzantine times little was heard of Argos. Of that period, the only buildings of any importance are the bishop's residence and the cathedral. After 1397, at which time the town first fell into Turkish hands, Argos came under the domination of a succession of masters. In 1463 it was again taken by the Turks, in 1686 it was captured by the Venetians, to be re-conquered by the Turks in 1715.

In 1822 the acropolis of Larissa was finally once again in Greek hands, while in 1829 the ancient theatre of Argos was chosen as the venue for the Fourth National Assembly of the newly-liberated Greek state.

A GUIDED TOUR OF THE ARCHAEOLOGICAL SITE

The excavations aiming to bring to light ancient Argos began in the early years of the 20th century. They were interrupted in 1930, and began once again in 1952. Uncovering the remains of the ancient city has run into many difficulties, because present-day Argos has been built on the site of the ancient one.

In antiquity the city was bounded, to the north-west, by the hill of Larissa and the somewhat lower hill of the Prophet Elijah. Both hills were surrounded by walls and their fortified enclosure constituted a part of the fortifications of the city. Traces of the wall are evident on the saddle between the two hills and on the western side, from the citadel of Larissa down towards the area of the theatre and of the odeon.

To the east, and not far from the theatre, begins the area of the agora, the hub of the ancient city's life. Here stood many important edifices and, as Pausanias informs us, many temples and sanctuaries. Among them, of particular importance was that of the Lykeian Apollo, on the north side of the agora,

Above: Fragment of a krater of the 7th century BC showing the blinding of the Cyclops Polyphemus by Odysseus and his companions. Archaeological Museum of Argos.

Below: Clay figurine of the Neolithic period representing a fertility goddess. From Lerna. Archaeological Museum of Argos.

Above: The ancient theatre of Argos.

Below: Argos. Roman "thermae" (public baths), with the ancient theatre in the distance.

in the precinct of which the Argives set up the resolutions adopted by the city.
The sanctuary, as Pausanias tells us, was established by Danaus, when he became king of Argos after overthrowing Gelanor, the son of Sthenelos, and it is probably to the sanctuary that the agora owes its name of "Lykeios".
The excavations carried out to date have only uncovered a small part of the ancient agora - mostly the foundations of public buildings - mainly in the southern part, opposite the theatre. Parts of the starting line of a stadium of Classical times have come to light, and south of the stadium has been excavated a square area which looks like a structure around a courtyard, and which dates from the 5th century BC. Its front faced north and it had a Doric portico of which the foundations have survived. The functions of this edifice were changed several times: in the first century BC it housed a gymnasium, in Roman times it was turned into a complex of public baths, while later still, it accommodated shops and workshops, most of which were abandoned after the Slavic invasion.
North of the portico were found the ruins of a round edifice (tholos) with eight Corinthian columns, which, in the 3rd century BC, was turned into a *nymphaeon* (fountain). Southeast of the tholos (at the junction of Theatre road and Tripolis road) have been uncovered the poros stone foundations of a building identified as the temple of Demeter Pelasgis which, according to Pausanias, stood on the eastern side of the agora.
In this area, which may have been the western boundary of the agora, has come to light a square building of Classical times, with an entrance on the eastern side. It consisted of a room measuring 32.60 metres in length, with four colonnades of four Ionian columns each.
The famous athletic training centre of Cylarabes probably lay outside the walls of the city, to the southeast of the ancient agora.
West of the agora and in a better state of preservation, have been excavated the city's theatre and the Roman baths next to it, while north of the agora was found a nymphaeon and south of it an odeon and a shrine to Aphrodite.
The theatre lies on the south-eastern slopes of Mt. Larissa and is the best preserved construction of the ancient city. It had 81 tiers of seats, divided by two flights of steps into three sections. The central section and part of the circular orchestra, measuring 26 metres in diameter, were cut out of the rock. The seats in the first row were made of marble and were intended for the officials. Two wings of stone seats complemented those which were cut out of the rock. The theatre was probably built at the end of the 4th century BC and could accommodate 20,000 spectators. It is believed to have taken the form in which we see it today during the Roman period. An inscription informs us that the proscenium was remodelled by the em-

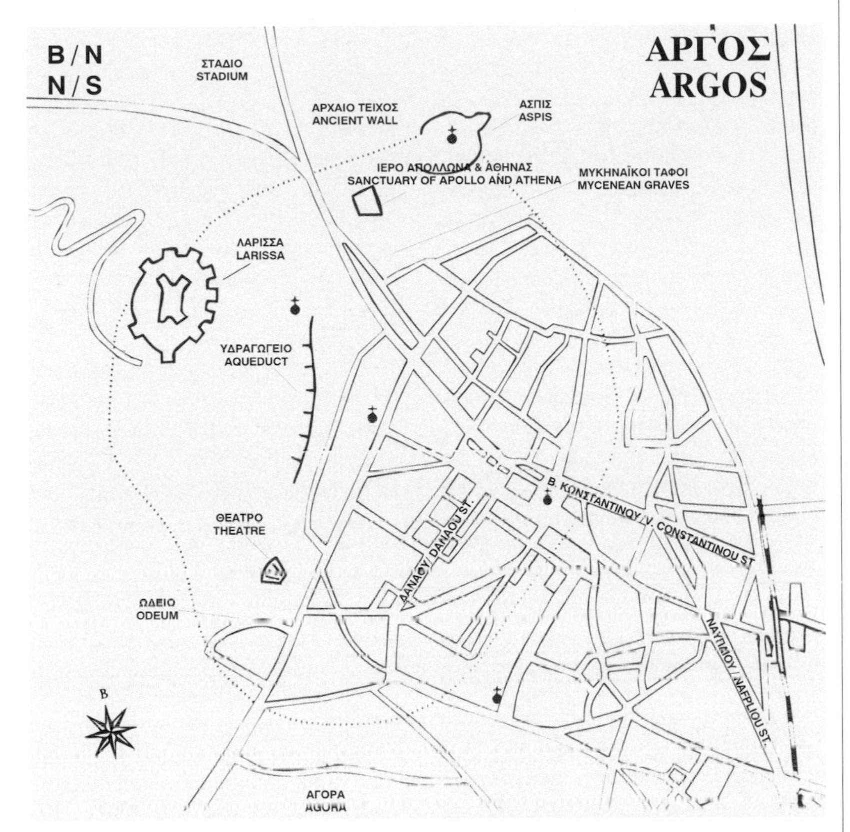

peror Hadrian. To the south of the theatre has been preserved an odeon, which was probably erected in the first century AD. It had a semicircular orchestra and arched side passages with mosaic floors. The seating area, with its 18 tiers of semicircular seats, was divided into two parts. The façade of the brick-built proscenium, on the side of the orchestra, was adorned with niches in which statues would have been set.

On the site of the odeon had once stood a building in the form of a theatre, with 35 straight tiers of seats carved out of the rock. This was probably used by the Argives from the 5th century BC as a place of assembly.

South-west of the stage of the odeon have been uncovered the ruins of the shrine to Aphrodite, which was probably first set up in the late 7th century BC. In the 6th century BC an enclosure was built around the precinct of the shrine, in which there must already have existed an altar and a small temple housing the statue of the goddess. The temple, part of the foundations of which have come to light, was built between 430 and 420 BC. It consisted of a *sekos* (cella) and a *pronaos* (porch) with two columns be-

Argos. To the east of the ancient theatre was erected, towards the middle of the 2nd century AD. this complex of public baths.

tween the jambs, but there was no *opisthodomus* (rear porch). Worship at the shrine ceased after it was destroyed when paganism was proscribed by the emperor Theodosius and his successors. Around the middle of the 2nd century BC, east of the theatre and the odeon were built the public baths. The brick edifice has been preserved to this day to a considerable height (at some points the walls measure up to 10 metres in height). Also well preserved are the *hypocausts,* the furnace and heating installations under the floor, which heated the water for the *caldarium* and the *sudatorium*.

About 100 metres to the north-east of the large theatre lies the place which has been identified by many scholars as the *kriterion* the Areopagus (Supreme Court) of the Argives. Here, according to legend, Danaus brought to trial Hypermestra, one of his fifty daughters, for refusing to follow his orders to kill her husband, Lynceus. This is a levelled area, measuring 35 metres in length and 21 in width, with a polygonal retaining wall of the Classical period and a series of six steps in the centre carved out of the rock. In the area there are traces of the small precinct of a pre-Classical temple.

Behind the kriterion, on a higher level, was built in the 2nd century AD a nymphaeon, (fountain), with two vaulted cisterns carved out of the rock. From the lower cistern, through a system of conduits, the water was channelled into the city.

LARISSA

To the west of the city of Argos rises the hill of Larissa, now known as Kastro. The name "Larissa" is pre-Hellenic and was used for fortified settlements. According to Pausanias, the Argives named their citadel after Larissa, the daughter of Pelasgus.

Larissa was first inhabited in prehistoric times and was fortified in the early historic period. Of the ancient walls, built in the 6th and 5th centuries BC, several sections survive. The ramparts were rebuilt in the 10th century, were repaired in the 13th century by the Franks and later, in the 15th

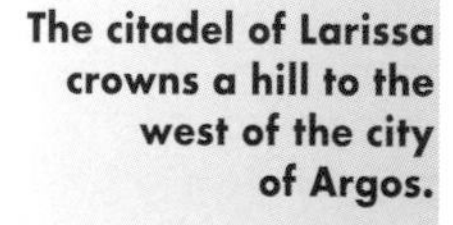

The citadel of Larissa crowns a hill to the west of the city of Argos.

century, by the Venetians. They consisted of an external wall surrounding the levelled summit of the hill and of an inner circuit of ramparts, measuring approximately 70 metres in length, which encircled the central area. The water supply was ensured by cisterns, which collected the rainwater, and with which both enclosures were provided.
Within the area of the acropolis the foundations of two temples have been excavated. Pausanias tells us that one of them was dedicated to Zeus Larissaios and the other to Athena Polias. For the construction of the now ruined Christian church in the southeastern corner of the exterior enclosure, which was restored in 1175 during the time of Manuel I Comnene, a great deal of the ancient building material was used. Again according to Pausanias, on the eastern slopes of Mt. Larissa stood the sanctuary of Hera Acraea. On the site, at the entrance to a cave, was built during the period of Ottoman rule the church of the Panaghia Katakekrimmeni (the Well-Hidden One), or Virgin of the Rock (Panaghia tou Vrachou) which belonged to a monastery.

SANCTUARY OF APOLLO DEIRATIOTES AHD ATHENA OXYDERKES

A little higher up, on the western end of the saddle between the two hills, known as Deiras (mountain-top), ruins of a sanctuary have been uncovered, in which, as Pausanias again informs us, Apollo Deiradiotes and Athena Oxyderkes ("the Sharp-Sighted") were worshipped.
Very few remains of pre-Christian edifices have been preserved in the area of the sanctuary, owing to the construction there of a large Christian basilica. Best-preserved is the altar of Apollo, carved out of the rock, and immediately to the east of the altar ten oblong steps also cut out of the rock. From these steps the faithful could follow the religious rituals and sacrifices which took place at the altar, or they might climb to the upper terrace, where the sanctuary of Apollo is believed to have stood. On its site was built a Christian basilica, the best preserved parts of which are the foundations. The south ends of the steps and the altar are interrupted by the walls of the narthex of the basilica. North of the altar have come to light the foundations of two structures, which appear to have been parts of porticoes. The second portico is believed to have housed the oracle of Apollo mentioned by Pausanias. East of the Christian basilica, on a lower level, has been uncovered a small part of the foundations of a circular building (tholos), which has been identified as the sanctuary of Athena. North of the tholos, on a higher level, excavations have brought to light the foundations of an edifice with a rectangular cistern, which is believed to have belonged to the sanctuary of Apollo or to an Asclepieion which existed in the area.

ARCHAELOGICAL MUSEUM OF ARGOS

The Archaeological Museum of Argos houses exhibits from the excavations at Lerna, vases of various periods, mosaic floors etc.
Archaeological Museum of Argos (Vassilissis Olgas Street, tel.no.: 075/28819)

The sanctuaries of Apollo Deiradiotes and Athena Oxyderkes, near Argos.

It is believed that, north of the site where stood the sanctuaries of Apollo and Athena, in a hollow of the slope of the Deiras, lay the stadium of Argos. Here, in historic times, were held the athletic contests in honour of Hera as well as the winter Nemean festival. South of the sanctuary have come to light Mycenean tholos tombs.The hill of the Prophet Elijah was the site of a settlement of the middle-Helladic and the Mycenean periods. The hill was fortified in Classical times, and parts of the wall survive to this day.

THE HERAEON OF ARGOS

Northeast of the town of Argos lies the Heraeon. Excavations have brought to light the foundations of buildings which

Argos. Coloured lithograph. Théodore de Moncel. *Excursion par terre d'Athènes à Nauplie.* Paris (1845). Gennadius Library. →

were part of the sanctuary of Hera, one of the chief centres of worship of the goddess in the Greek world and the most important sanctuary of Argos in the historical period. It is from this sanctuary that the worship of the goddess started, which later spread to the rest of the Argolid, to Samos and to certain areas of southern

Above: Heraeon, Argos. The platform of the later temple of Hera built in 410/400 BC.

Right: Nauplion.

Greece. The sanctuary was built on the slopes of Mt. Euboea, named - as the legend tells us - after one of the daughters of the river Asterion. On the top of the mountain was built the citadel of the prehistoric city of Prosymna. Of the sanctuary, still surviving on the topmost levelled part are the foundations of the older temple of Hera, built towards the end of the 8th or the beginning of the 7th century BC, and destroyed by fire in 423 BC, as a result of the negligence of the priestess Chryseis. South of the old temple, which after its destruction was still respected by the Argives as a "*sevasma*" ("venerable edifice"), there stood a long stoa or colonnade of the 6th century BC, and to the east of it another smaller one built in the same period. A stairway gave access to the site of the Archaic temple. To the southeast of this second stoa there stood a large rectangular hall with rows of columns in the interior, the *telesterion* (ceremonial room), which bounded the area of the sanctuary on the eastern side.

Northeast of the telesterion rose the impressive new temple of Hera, built by the architect, Eupolemos, in 410/400 BC. It was a peripteral Doric temple consisting of a front porch (the pronaos), a cella and a back porch. In the cella stood the gold and ivory statue of the goddess, the work of the sculptor Polycleitus. The goddess was seated on a throne, holding in one hand a sceptre surmounted by a cuckoo, and in the other a pomegranate. The pomegranate was a symbol of fertility, while the cuckoo symbolised the coming of spring and the awakening of the earth. The cuckoo was connected to the goddess in another way, as well. According to the myth, Zeus had assumed the form of a cuckoo in order to approach Hera.

Next to the statue of Hera stood a gold and ivory statue of Hebe, while in the cella was also preserved the older statue of Hera, made of the wood of a wild-pear tree by Peirasos, the son of the hundred-eyed giant, Argus. In Hellenistic times, in front of the temple was built a long and narrow altar dedicated to the goddess.

South of the temple there was a stoa, of which we see the foundations today. From there a stairway led to the level of the later temple. East of the temple of Hera there was a hostel equipped with beds and tables which served for communal meals. North of the hostel there was another stoa, while on the northwestern side of the sanctuary there was a Roman bathhouse, with mosaic-floored rooms, under which was the hollow space which housed the furnace and the heating system. The festival held in honour of the goddess was called the "Heraea". It was the greatest festival of Argos and was related to fertility. During the celebrations, a big procession was formed, in which took part matrons, maidens and armed men, who accompanied the chariot of the priestess of Hera, drawn by cows, the sacred animals of the goddess. The procession made its way to the Heraeon, where a ritual was performed in which one hundred oxen were sacrificed. This ritual sacrifice gave the festival its earlier name of *Hecatomboia* ("a hundred oxen"). The meat was then distributed to all those who participated in the celebration. In the course of the festivities there were also athletic contests in which the winners were crowned with wreaths of myrtle and received a shield as a prize.

NAUPLION

The capital of the prefecture of the Argolid is the town of Nauplion, built in the crook of the Argolic gulf and at a distance of only 12 kilometres from Argos. Above the picturesque town rises the rocky promontory of Acronauplia and the steep rock of Palamidi, while at the entrance of the bay, well-protected by its small fort, floats the little island of Bourtzi.

Above: Strongly fortified Bourtzi controlled the entrance to the harbour of Nauplion during medieval times.

Below: Part of the fortifications of Palamidi.

The area was first inhabited in Neolithic times, and continued to be so throughout the Mycenean era, as is confirmed by the presence of tholos tombs found on the northeastern slopes of Palamidi, but the settlements were never as brilliant and important as those of the neighbouring Mycenean centres. In the early Archaic period, on the site of present-day Nauplion flourished a city then known as Nauplia, which was one of the founding states of the Amphictyonic league and the league of Calauria.

According to Pausanias, it was Nauplios, the son of Poseidon and of one of Danaus' daughters, Amymone, who was the founder of Nauplia and gave the city its name. A descendant of this Nauplios bearing the same name was one of the Argonauts who took part in the quest of the Golden Fleece. A son of this younger Nauplios was Palamedes, a sage, doctor and astronomer, who is said to have conceived the idea of the lighthouse and to have devised the four letters which, added to the Phoenician alphabet, made up the Greek alphabet. Before the end of the 7th century BC the Argives seized Nauplia and made it their seaport. The inhabitants of Nauplia took refuge in the province of Messenia and established themselves in Methone (Modon).

In Hellenistic times Nauplion once again became an important centre in the region. The western side of Acronauplia was fortified by the construction of a strong polygonal wall and the summit was used as a citadel.

The main god worshipped by the Nauplians was Poseidon.

When Pausanias visited the city in the 2nd century AD he found it deserted; only ruins of the walls remained, and a temple dedicated to Poseidon.

In Byzantine times, Nauplion recovered its importance and the town developed to the west beyond the walls, beneath Acronauplia. Around 879 AD it became a bishopric, and in 1180 the Byzantine emperor Manuel Comnene appointed Theodore Sgouros as its governor.

Acronauplia was fortified by strong walls, built over the ancient ramparts, and Nauplion became the see of a metropolitan bishop. The town flourished. Leon Sgouros, son of Theodore Sgouros, seized the castles of Argos and of Corinth, besieged Athens and extended his dominion all the way to Larissa in central Greece. In 1210, Anapli - as it became known from late Byzantine times on - surrendered after a siege to Geoffrey de Villehardouin, who ceded it in 1212 to the Duke of Athens, Otto de la Roche, as a reward for the help the latter had offered him during his conquest of the Peloponnese.

The Franks added new fortifications to the citadel of Acronauplia. In 1389 Marie d'Enghien ceded the town to the Venetians who kept it until 1540, at which time it fell into Turkish hands. During the period of the first Turkish occupation, Nauplion, which became the capital of the "*Sandjak* of the Morea" and the seat of the pasha, developed into a commercial exporting centre for the entire Peloponnese. After a century and a half of Turkish occupation, in 1686, the Venetians, under Francesco Morosini, recaptured Nauplion, which was made the capital of Venice's eastern possessions under the name of Napoli di Romania. During the first period of Venetian occupation (1389-1540), the Venetians built their own walls and strengthened the fortifications of Acronauplia, in 1470, by building the fortress known as the Castel del Toro, an elongated addition to the eastern heights, which ends in a circular bastion. Acronauplia, at the time, was connected to the mainland by a narrow isthmus.

After 1460 the population of Nauplion increased as a result of an influx of people from the rural areas and of citizens of Chalkis expelled from their city. This created pressing housing needs, and the major public works of this period concerned the building of a "lower town" on land reclaimed from swampy areas by the sea, north of Acronauplia and Palamidi, the construction of houses on piles and, finally, the building of sea walls for the defence of the lower town. A moat dug

Above: Nauplion. Lion carved in the rock, in 1834, by the Bavarians.

Below: View of Nauplion. We can see part of Palamidi, Acronauplia and the town.

outside the eastern wall provided security from the landward side.
Nauplion thus increased fourfold in size and acquired the form it has today. Access to it from the land could only be effected across the narrow strip joining it to the mainland and through the "Land Gate", on the eastern side, where a wooden bridge was flung over the moat. In 1471 the islet of Aghioi Theodoroi (present-day Bourtzi) was also fortified by the addition of walls, a tall square tower and a semicircular bastion. The port (between Acronauplia and Bourtzi), became known as Porto Cadena, from the chain which barred its entrance, linking the mole to the

islet which was called Castello dello Scoglio.
During the second period of Venetian rule (1686-1715) the 216 metre-high hill of Palamidi was fortified according to the plans drawn up by the French engineers Lasalle and Levasseur. A path of 857 steps carved out of the rock and passing through a series of gates providing protection from enemy fire, leads to the fortress, allowing its defenders to communicate with Acronauplia. Above the castle's main gate was set the Venetian symbol of the Lion of St. Mark.
The fortress of Palamidi itself consisted of eight independent bastions, which were linked to each other but could also be totally self-sufficient - since each had its own cisterns, storerooms and its arms and ammunition. Each bastion could defend the others but, if any was to fall into enemy hands, each could also attack the others. At the same time the city was embellished with impressive edifices which lent it its characteristic appearance.
In 1715 Nauplion was captured by the Turks. In 1821, at the time of the Greek War of Independence, the Greeks made successive attempts to recapture the town, and in 1822 they were finally successful. In 1828 Nauplion was proclaimed the capital of the Greek state and the seat of the government of the first governor of the new state, Ioannis Capodistrias, who arrived there in January of the same year. As the capital of the state Nauplion flourished. The city was reconstructed according to the town plans designed by Voulgaris and Vallianos. Three years later, however, outside the church of St. Spyridon, Capodistrias was assassinated. In 1833 Nauplion welcomed the first king of Greece, Otho of Bavaria, who, in 1834, moved the capital to Athens. In memory of the king's Bavarian soldiers, who died between 1833 and 1834 during an epidemic of the plague, a lion, the "Lion of the Bavarians", was carved in the hollow of a rock outside the town.
Today, picturesque Nauplion, a fine example of a 19th-century neo-classical town, attracts many visitors all the year round. Its character has remained largely unchanged and owes much to the three civilisations which have left their mark on its identity. The narrow streets, lined with old double-storied and three-storied neo-classical buildings, with their balconies resting on marble corbels, the small paved squares and the steep alleys, where bougainvillaea and jasmine grow, and which lead up to the castle with its ramparts and embrasures, the harbour and the attractive waterfront lined with pastry shops and restaurants facing the calm sea, the busy shops along the streets, all contribute to the charm of modern Nauplion. At dusk, looking down from the castle, we see the town change, as it is successively bathed in red, orange and mauve by the setting sun, and a unique atmosphere of tranquillity and peace descends upon it.
At the same time, the visitor is reminded at every corner of the town's chequered history, thanks to the many monuments that

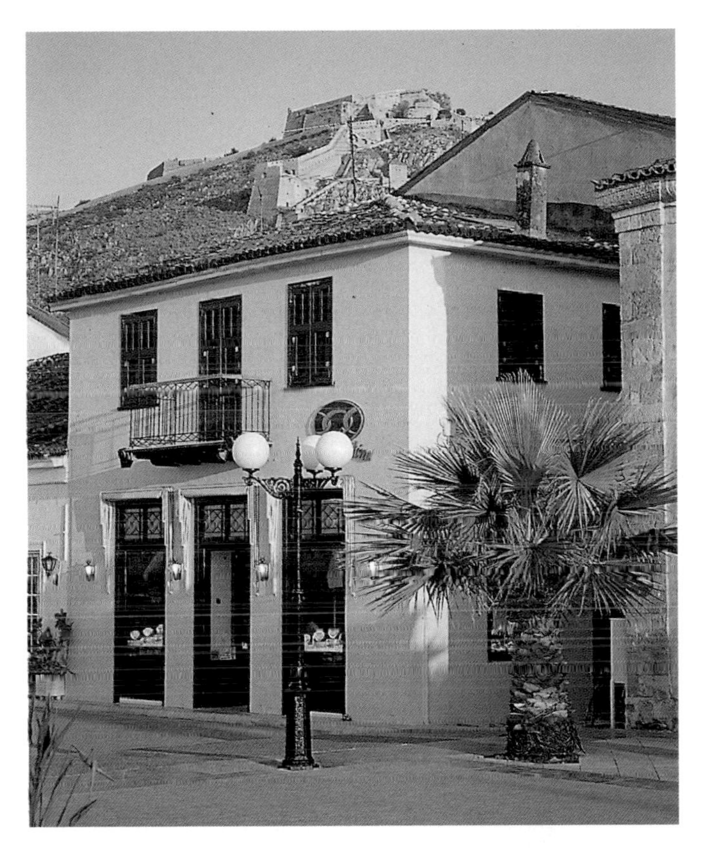

In the protecting shadow of the fortress of Palamidi lies the town of Nauplion, showing off its attractive two- and three-storied neo-classical houses, adorned with colourful bougainvillaea, its pleasant squares and picturesque alleys, its busy waterfront lined with restaurants and pastry-shops.

have survived from various periods in the recent past. Among the buildings dating from the first period of Venetian rule are the Catholic church of Frangoklissia and the church of the Holy Virgin (Theotokos), behind Syntagma square.

In the second period of Venetian rule the Armoury (1713) was built in baroque style by the Venetian *Provveditore,* Sagredo, to the west of Syntagma square. Today it houses the Archaeological Museum of Nauplion. Dating from the same period are the churches of St. Nicholas (1713) and St. Spyridon (1702).

A reminder of the period of Turkish occupation is the *Bouleuterion*, south of the museum, a mosque made of white stone, which was later used for the assemblies of the first Greek Parliament.

On the eastern corner of Syntagma square, opposite the museum, has been preserved one of the first schools of the modern Greek state, the *Allilodidakteirion*, originally a mosque.

To the south-east stands the present-day cathedral of St. George, which was built by the Venetians during the first period of Venetian rule and was adorned with frescoes by Italian painters.

The Seminary behind the Bouleuterion is also known as the Prison of Leonardos. East of this is the Byzantine church of St.

Above: Palamidi, Acronauplia, a section of the city and Bourtzi (aerial photograph).

Right: Palamidi

Above: Another view of Palamidi.

Below, left: Head of a clay male figurine of the 13th century BC from Asine, known as "the gentleman of Asinee". Nauplion, Archaeological Museum.

Below right: Mycenean armour and helmet of boar's teeth (15th century BC). Nauplion, Archaeological Museum.

Nauplion, Coloured lithograph. Théodore de Moncel. *Excursion par terre d'Athènes à Nauplie.* Paris (1845). Gennadius Library. →

Sophia, the oldest of Nauplion's churches to have survived. Among the monuments of the past are also the residence of Otho's viceroy, George Ludwig von Mauer, and the Army Cadet School (which now serves as a War Museum). The fortress of Palamidi, finally, is also very much worth visiting, whether the visitor prefers to take the path with its 857 steps or the tarred road winding up the east side. Another site worth seeing is the castle of Acronauplia, accessible by the road which leads to the beach of Arvanitia. The citadel of Acronauplia is made up of four parts, which represent the four phases of its construction or reconstruction. The oldest part of all is the *Romeiko*, the Byzantine fortifications built over the ancient walls. This part, which is also the largest, is situated at the western end of Acronauplia. Then comes the part known as the *Frangiko,* which was first used by the Franks, and later became the military and administrative centre of the Venetians. After that is the Venetian Castel del Toro, and lastly the low Grimani bastion built in 1706, during the second period of Venetian rule. It stands east of the Castel del Toro, ensuring the access to Palamidi from the west, and linking the walls of the citadel to the defensive system of the lower town. Today, two modern Xenia Hotels stand in the area of Acronauplia.
Of the walls of the lower town only the western part has been preserved, ending in the small bastion of the Five Brothers, opposite Bourtzi, the picturesque fortress-island.

MUSEUMS OF NAUPLION:

ARCHAEOLOGICAL MUSEUM

Archaeological Museum (Syntagma Square, tel. No.: 0752/27502) Here are exhibited finds of prehistoric times (from the Franchthi cave, of Midea, Mycenae and Tiryns) as well as from historic times.

WAR MUSEUM

(Amalias 22) Displayed here are memorabilia of recent Greek history.

MUSEUM OF FOLK ART

(Vas. Alexandrou 1, tel. No.: 0752/28379)
This is housed in a neo-classical building. Among its exhibits are regional costumes, woven and embroidered articles, various utensils and implements, old maps of Nauplion etc.

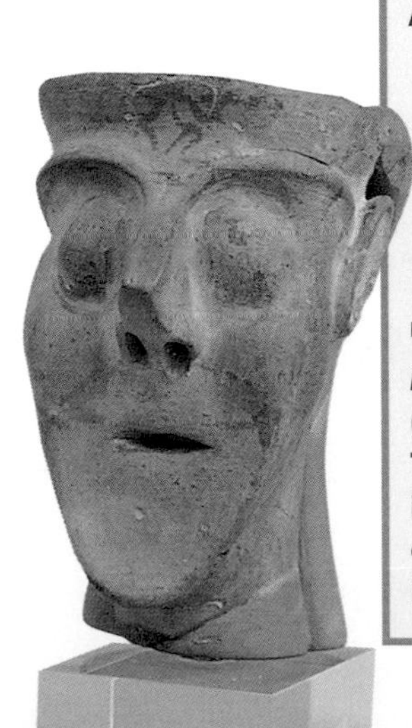

EPIDAURUS

North-east of Nauplion lies the region which in antiquity was known as Epidauria. Its often rugged coastline is washed by the waters of the Saronic Gulf, and forms, here and there, picturesque deep-green inlets. The area is quite hilly, with a few small plains between the pine-clad slopes.

In Classical times, by allying itself with Sparta and Corinth, the region of Epidauria was able to stand up to the powerful Argives. The ancient city of Lessa, which probably stood on the site of present-day Lygourio, and Kazarma - where can be seen the ruins of a 5th-century fortress - formed the borders between Epidauria and the region of Argos. North of Epidauria lay the province of Corinthia, while to the south and south-east it bordered on the regions of Hermionis and Troizene. Its political centre was the city of Epidaurus, built on the shores of the Saronic Gulf, opposite the islands of Aegina and Angistri.

The first traces of life on the site of the ancient city, which stood south-east of the present-day settlement of Ancient Epidaurus, date back to 3000-2000 BC. The verdant peninsula forms two bays, one to the north and one to the south, while in the middle rise two hills. The ancient city extended from the southern limits of the present-day village towards the peninsula. On the neck of land between the two bays stood the houses, the agora and the theatre. On the summit of the lower of the two hills, where today stands the restored church of the Virgin Mary, stood a temple dedicated to the goddess Athena, while to the north of this temple has come to light a small theatre.

On this same summit stood the city's acropolis, which was fortified with an enceinte in Roman times. The two hills were encircled by walls, sections of which, with their medieval extensions, have been preserved to this day.
The city's harbour was of great importance to the region, especially for establishing communication with the port of Piraeus and the islands.
Today the ancient coastline has been submerged, but the foundations of edifices can still be seen, under the water, to the north-west of the ancient agora.
The theatre, although much smaller than the famous theatre of Epidaurus further inland, has been preserved in very good condition. It was built at the time of Alexander the Great and had 18 tiers of seats, thus accommodating 5,000 to 6,000 spectators. The seats, made of poros stone or marble, are inscribed with the names of citizens.
The official sanctuary of the city was the Asclepieion, the oldest on the Greek mainland to be dedicated to Asclepius. It was founded, in Classical times, outside the city, at a distance of 2-3 hours on foot, in a pine-clad area at the foot of Mt. Cynortion. It flourished during the 5th and 4th centuries, and its fame spread throughout all the Greek cities.
According to legend, Asclepius was the son of Apollo and of Coronis, the daughter of the king of Thessaly, Phlegyas. When Coronis was killed by an arrow shot by Artemis, Apollo carried off Asclepius and entrusted him to the care of the centaur, Cheiron, who taught him the art of healing by means of herbs, exorcisms and surgery.
Myths also tell us that Epione, "the gentle one", was Asclepius' wife, and that Hygieia, Iasso, Akeso and Panaceia were their daughters.
Asclepius, after having successfully healed many patients, committed the crime of *hubris* against the gods when he attempted to bring the dead back to life, and for this he was killed by Zeus with a thunderbolt. However, there are many local variations of the story of Asclepius.

At Epidaurus it was believed that Coronis, having given birth to Asclepius, exposed him on Mt. Myrtion. Apollo sent the she goats grazing on the mountain to suckle the infant and the dog which looked after the herd to protect him. This is why Mt. Myrtion was renamed Titthion which means "suckling mountain".
Asclepius, one of the later Olympian

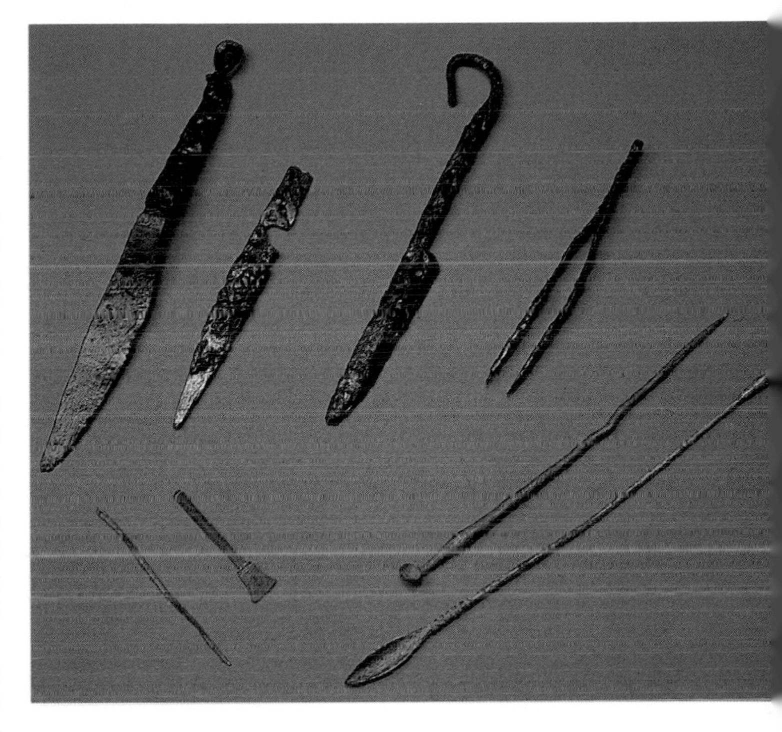

gods, began to be worshipped in the region in the 6th century BC, replacing many local healer-gods. He was a god of the underworld, one of the gods who had power over death. He was worshipped as an "unceasingly gentle" healing god who could postpone death and prolong the life of mortals. His emblem was the snake, who symbolised his connection with the underworld. He was portrayed by sculptors and painters with a snake wound around his staff, and with the faithful dog who had guarded him when he was young, sitting before him.
The inscriptions and dedications found in the sanctuary give us valuable information on diseases and the way in

Left: View of the peninsula where, in antiquity, flourished the city of Epidaurus. Amid the greenery we can make out the small theatre which is situated near the agora of the ancient city.

Above: Bronze surgical instruments. Museum of Ancient Epidaurus.

Ancient Epidaurus. The theatre can be seen on the left. →

which they were treated in antiquity. Patients arriving at the Asclepieion had to follow a certain procedure. After first undergoing ritual cleansing and offering sacrifices, they were lodged in a building of the sanctuary, known as the *enkoimeterion*, or dormitory. During their sleep they were healed by the god or were given advice on the manner in which they would be healed. Often, to ensure a proper cure, some kind of medicine, diet or physical exercise was prescribed. The instruments found in the area of the sanctuary show that surgical operations were also performed here.

To the north-east of the sanctuary of Asclepius established by the citizens of Epidaurus, on a slope of Mt. Cynortion, had once flourished a sanctuary dedicated to Apollo Maleatas. Within the sanctuary had stood, since approximately 2800 BC, a prosperous settlement, which continued to be inhabited after 1600 BC. Between about 1600 and 1100 BC, a sacrificial altar was built here, dedicated to some chthonian nature divinity. After Mycenean times, the cult of Apollo Maleatas was initiated within the enclosure, and later, towards the middle of the 7th century BC an altar to the god was erected.

Around 640 BC the sanctuary on the slope of Mt. Cynortion became the official sanctuary of the Epidaureans. Towards the middle of the 6th century was established the cult of Asclepius, which gradually supplanted that of Apollo Maleatas, who, however, continued to be honoured at the Asclepieion together with Asclepius, the ritual requiring of the worshippers a preliminary sacrifice, the *prothysis*, to Apollo.

Towards the end of the 4th century BC the Asclepieion was adorned with edifices such as the temple of Asclepius, the tholos, the theatre, as well as temples dedicated to Artemis, to Aphrodite and to Themis.

When athletic contests began to be included in the festival of the Asclepieia, the gymnasium, the palaestra, the stadium, colonnades and bath houses were built.

The sanctuary continued to flourish during Hellenistic times. In 86 AD it was desecrated by the Roman general Sulla, but in the 2nd century AD it enjoyed a new period of prosperity. It was then that new bathhouses were built in the area of the sanctuary, and many works carried out by the Roman prefect Antoninus, who came from Asia Minor and was a contemporary of Pausanias.

In 395 AD the sanctuary was once again sacked, this time by the Visigoths under Alaric, but it continued to function until the 4th century AD. In 426 AD it was closed by decree of the emperor Theodosius, as part of his effort to ban the old pagan religion. The sanctuary was completely abandoned after the devastating earthquakes of 522 and 551 AD.

In 1879, Professor P. Kavvadias began excavations, on behalf of the Archaeological Society, and these were continued until 1928. Thereafter, work began again in 1974.

Above: Detail from the carved floral ornamentation of the Tholos. Museum of Ancient Epidaurus.

Below: Corinthian capital from the Tholos. Museum of Ancient Epidaurus.

A GUIDED TOUR OF THE ARCHAEOLOGICAL SITE

The sanctuary of Asclepius extends over a large area. In antiquity the entrance was on the north side. The road which linked the city of Ancient Epidaurus to the sanctuary ended at a grand propylon. From the propylon a "sacred way" approximately 200 metres long, led to the main buildings, that is the temple of Asclepius and the tholos. Approximately one kilometre further along is situated the theatre, to the south-east, at the foot of Mt. Cynortion.

From the Asclepicion an uphill road led to the shrine of Apollo Maleatas, on the northern side of Mt. Cynortion, beyond a small isolated temple, which seems to have been dedicated to Aphrodite.

Today the entrance to the archaeological site of the Asclepieion is situated on the south side. The road taken by the visitor passes by the stadium on the right and ends at the theatre. Northwest of the theatre stands the Museum, where are exhibited the finds from the area of the sanctuary.

The theatre of the Asclepieion, a work attributed to Polycleitus the Younger (4th century BC), must have been built in the late 4th century BC. Its orchestra forms a complete circle of about 20 metres in diameter, with a *thymele* - a round base on which was set an altar - in the centre. The circle of the orchestra has three different centres (instead of one), which aided in the tracing of the curved rows of seats. This technique increases the acoustics of the theatre and allows the spectators in the last rows to have a better view.

The original seating area of the theatre was divided into 12 tiers and consisted of 34 rows of seats accommodating 6,200 spectators. The first row of seats, which had backs and were intended for official guests, were made of red lime-

Remains of buildings in ancient Epidaurus.

stone. The *skene* consisted of the proscenium on a lower level, with its row of Ionic half-columns, between which were placed movable paintings, and the main stage higher up.
Towards the end of the Hellenistic period (2nd century BC), another 22 tiers were added above the promenade on the upper end of the seating area. The addition included 21 rows of seats, thus increasing the capacity of the theatre to 12,300 spectators. The *skene* was also extended and remodelled.
The theatre of Asclepius is one of the most perfect theatres of antiquity and one of the best preserved. It is still used today for performances of ancient drama during the summer festival of Epidaurus.

Northwest of the theatre we find the ruins of a square building, lying at some distance from the other structures of the sanctuary which extend to its northwest. This is the *katagogeion* or guesthouse, built to accommodate the visitors who came to the sanctuary for the festival of the Asclepieia. It was erected in the late 4th or early 3rd century and is 76 metres wide. It was divided into four square areas of equal size, each of which consisted of a courtyard surrounded by a colonnade, with 18 rooms around it. It was probably a two-storey building, disposing of a total of 150 rooms. These rooms had doors opening up on the courtyard but did not intercommunicate. The foundations of the hostel were of stone and the walls of brick.
About one hundred metres to the west of the hostel there is a rectangular edifice dating from the 3rd century BC, which housed baths for the gymnasium and hostel. In its rooms were found bathtubs and basins.
North of the baths we come to the gymnasium, a rectangular edifice measuring 70 x 76 metres, built around 300 BC. It had an interior courtyard surrounded by a colonnade. Along its four sides are large hypostyle rooms and other smaller ones in the corners.

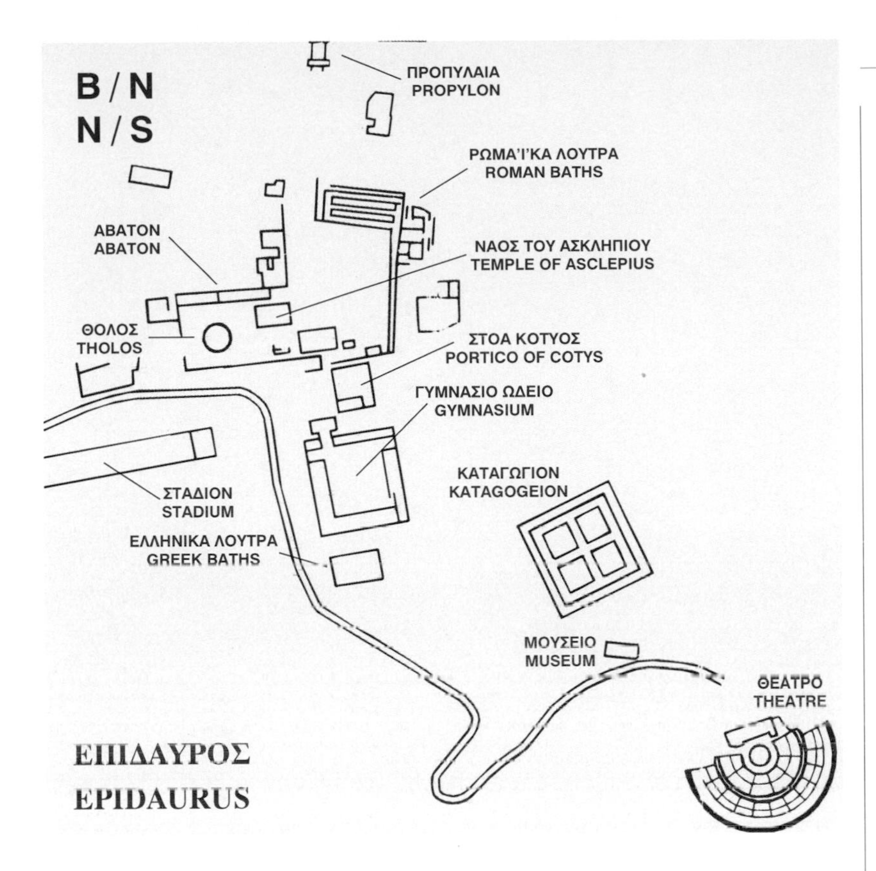

Above left: View of the sanctuary of ancient Epidaurus.

Below left: The "katagogeion", the hostel built to accommodate the visitors to the Asclepieion.

The entrance to the gymnasium, in its north-western corner, had an impressive propylon with six Doric columns on its façade and four each on the eastern and western sides. In Roman times an odeon was erected in the inner court, while the propylon was converted into a small temple to the goddess Hygieia. The odeon had 11 rows of semicircular brick-built seats.

To the west of the gymnasium, and near the temple of Asclepius and the tholos, lies the stadium. It was built in a natural hollow of the land, which was dug out to increase its length and width. In one of the sections of the north and south sides, stone seats in straight rows began to be built during the Hellenistic period, some of which can still be seen. The track, which has a straight, not a curved *sphendone*, was 181 metres long and about 23 metres wide. It is about 11 metres shorter than the track at Olympia and almost 4 metres shorter than that of the Panathenaic stadium in Athens.

A passage beneath the seats of the north side led to the track. It started out from the area to the south-east of the temple of Asclepius, from an edifice consisting of a courtyard surrounded by a colonnade and a long and narrow room with a central row of columns and apartments. This building may have served as the residence of the athletes and as a palaestra.

To the east of the stadium and north of the gymnasium are the remains of a large edifice measuring 34 x 29.5 metres with an entrance on the western side, believed by Professor Kavvadias to have been a palaestra. It had an open space in the centre with rooms on its south, east and west sides. On the north side there is a long and narrow stoa with an interior colonnade. Professor Kavvadias identified this with the Stoa of Kotys referred to by Pausanias; however, the latter edifice has recently been recognised in the colonnade to the south of the complex, which formed the boundary of the sanctuary on the northern side.

In the 2nd century AD one of the edifices of the palaestra was converted in-

Left page above: The ancient theatre of Epidaurus.

Below: One of the two entrances to the theatre

Right page, above left: The goddess Hygieia. Epidaurus, Archaelogical Museum.

Below: The stadium of the Asclepieion.

to a temple dedicated to the healer-gods Apollo and Asclepius, who were given the epithet of "Egyptians", because the ceremonial accompanying their worship followed the Egyptian ritual.
Immediately following the palaestra, to the west, we see the ruins of a small temple, which is thought to have been dedicated to Artemis and built in 330 BC. It had a *pronaos* (porch) and a *sekos* (cella) and six Doric columns on its façade, while Corinthian columns adorned the interior surfaces of the north, south and west walls. On its marble water spouts were carved the heads of dogs and goats, while its *akroteria* were adorned with Nikes. North of the temple of Artemis stands a rectangular building measuring 24.3 x 20.7 metres, known as the *enkoimeterion*, or dormitory, which is of an older date than the one we see north of the temple of Asclepius. It had a stoa on its façade and on three of its sides there were long and narrow rooms to accommodate those visiting the sanctuary.

In the early 5th century, in the northwestern corner of the edifice stood a small temple with a pronaos and a sekos, of which the floor of the building and an altar in the centre have survived. The temple and the altar were dedicated to Apollo. Later, they were incorporated into the building which, after the 4th century, was converted into a residence for the priests. West of the enkoimeterion has been preserved the base of a large altar also dedicated to Apollo.
North of the altar lie the ruins of a temple of Asclepius, designed by the architect Theodotes, which began to be erected in 380 and was completed in 375 BC. This peripteral Doric temple with six columns on the narrow sides and eleven on the long sides measured 13 x 2 x 24.3 metres. It had a pronaos and a sekos and housed the ivory statue of the god, a work by the sculptor Thrasymedes. At the entrance, instead of steps, there was a ramp.

The tympana of the pediments, fragments of which have been preserved, were adorned with sculptures by Timotheos representing scenes from the Fall of Troy and the Battle of the Amazons. The akroteria were decorated with Victories and with Nereids on horseback.
The huge gold and ivory statue of Asclepius showed the god seated, with one hand resting on the head of a serpent and the other holding a staff. A dog crouched at his feet. East of the temple can be seen the base of an altar to Asclepius. Its shape resembled that of a long table, and was similar to that of the temple of Apollo. It stood on a platform and was protected by a roof.
To the south, in front of the façade of the temple, may be seen the bases of votive offerings to the god.
Northeast of the temple there was a square bounded on the south, east and north by a series of impressive votive offerings. Here ended the sacred way, along which the worshippers progressed from the propylaea to the buildings of the sanctuary.
In 395 BC, around the temple of Asclepius, the tholos, the abaton, the altars of Apollo and of Asclepius and the square with the votive offerings, a wall was built to protect the edifices from the incursion of the Visigoths.
South of the temple of Apollo survive the ruins of two edifices of the Classical period. The one on the east, has been identified as a workshop in which the sculptures adorning the pediments of the temple were made, while it is thought that the other comprised ancillary areas of the temple.
West of the altar of Apollo are to be seen the foundations of the Tholos or thymele, as it is referred to in the inscription recording the cost of its erection, which probably began before the end of the 4th century BC. This was a circular building which stood on a three-stepped base. A ramp in front of the entrance led up to the platform.
The tholos consisted of an exterior colonnade (*pteron*) and a circular cella, within which was a second colonnade. The colonnade of the pteron consisted of 26 Doric columns and the internal colonnade of 14 Corinthian columns, whose capitals are considered to be among the most beautiful of their kind. Sculpted fragments of the tholos (capitals, parts of the entablature) are exhibited in the local museum.
According to Pausanias, works by the painter Pausias once adorned the interior of the circular wall of the sekos. A ramp before the entrance led up to the platform. The door and the marble coffers of the ceiling were also richly ornamented with floral designs. The floor inside the tholos was paved with white marble, while in the central area, white and black tiles were placed in such a way as to form lozenges. A white slab in the centre could be lifted to allow access into a crypt below. This was surrounded by three concentric circular corridors, which have been preserved to this day. Here sacrificial offerings were made to Asclepius, at the time when he was honoured as a hero in the sanctuary.
The interior colonnade of the tholos rested on the circular wall of the interior corridor, the wall of the sekos on the middle one, and the pteron on the exterior one. North of the tholos the sanctuary was bounded by two consecutive porticoes measuring 75 metres in total length and 9.5 metres in width. These served as an *enkoimeterion* or *abaton* - a dormitory or hospital ward for the patients. Of the two porticoes, the one on the east was built in the second quarter of the 4th century BC, while the later one, on the west, was built at the end of the 4th or the beginning of the 3rd century BC. Due to the fact that the ground was lower at this point, the later addition is double-storied.
Two Ionic colonnades ran along the southern side of each of the porticoes. In the western portico were set the stelae on which were recorded the "miracles", that is the successful healings performed by the god, while on the eastern end of the enkoimeterion there stood, from the 6th century BC on, a sacred well, which together with the

Above left: The Tholos.

Below left: The Gymnasium and the Odeon built within its courtyard in Roman times.

ARCHAEOLOGICAL MUSEUM OF EPIDAURUS

In its rooms are housed finds from the excavations in the area of Epidaurus. Among them are architectural elements from edifices in the sanctuary, inscribed stelae, bases, surgical instruments etc. (tel. No.: 0753/22009)

Ancient Epidaurus. The Propylaea.

temple and the altar to Apollo were the oldest constructions in the sanctuary.
Behind the enkoimeterion have been preserved the ruins of a 2nd-century BC building complex consisting of a bath-house and a library. The library, besides serving as a reading room for the visitors to the sanctuary, was also the place where the medical books and the sanctuary's archives were kept.
As the visitor progresses northwards, he finds on the west the foundations of a small prostyle Ionic temple, erected in the late 4th century BC, which was probably dedicated to Themis, the goddess of law and justice. A third small temple, similar to the previous one, the ruins of which are to be found east of the sanctuary, on the road leading to the temple of Apollo Maleatas, is thought to be the temple dedicated to Aphrodite to which Pausanias refers.
East of the temple of Themis have survived the ruins of a structure of the 3rd century BC which has been identified by several scholars as the Stoa of Kotys. It consisted of a peristylar courtyard measuring 49 metres in length and containing shops and porticoes.
In Roman times, to the east of the Stoa were built bathhouses, or *aquae.* Their western wall stood against the wall of the Stoa.
South of the baths stood a small edifice, the *Epidoteion*, which may have been dedicated to the "*epidotes*", that is to the gods who bestowed benefits on mortals. This building consisted of an outdoor area and of a room behind it, with a semicircular platform on which were set the statues of the gods.
Southeast of the Epidoteion have been

SANCTUARY OF APOLLO MALEATAS

On a slope of Mt. Cynortion stand the ruins of the sanctuary of Apollo Maleatas. In the area of the sanctuary have survived ruins of the temple of Apollo, which was built in the 4th century BC, a short time before the construction of the temple of Asclepius. North-east of the temple extended a large retaining wall of 45 metres which, at its southern end, had a stoa looking onto the central area of the sanctuary. In the centre of the square, east of the temples, can be seen the ruins of the altar to Apollo, built in the 4th century BC. It was shaped like a large table resting on a platform and was covered by a light roof. East of the altar there was a stairway which in classical times led to the sanctuary. Southeast of the stairway there was a temple and an altar dedicated to the Muses. On the southeastern side, the sanctuary was bounded by structures which, according to inscriptions, were the residence of the priests, a reservoir constructed in the 2nd century AD with funds donated by the emperor Antoninus, and a fountain.

preserved the ruins of the *Anakeion,* or sanctuary of the Dioscuri, erected in the 4th century BC, and further south the ruins of a Roman villa.

On the way to the propylaea of the sanctuary, which are situated at a considerable distance from the Anakeion and the temple of Themis, the visitor finds a well, built in the late 6th century or early 5th century BC.

The grand propylaea of the Asclepieion were built around 300 BC. They had two façades, one on the north and one on the south, each adorned with six Ionic columns. Here, too, a ramp led up to the platform. The square area inside was surrounded by a Corinthian colonnade.

East of the propylaea, outside the sanctuary, can be seen the ruins of a large five-aisled Christian basilica dedicated to St. John. It was built at the end of the 4th or the beginning of the 5th century AD, using ancient building materials.

THE ARGOLID TODAY

AN INTRODUCTION TO THE REGION

Our journey into the Argolid has also been a journey into the past. Mycenae, Argos, Epidaurus, Nauplion have been landmarks on the way, and their monuments have carried us back in time. Now, in the second part of our travels we shall become acquainted with the region which provided the backdrop against which the skein of history unwound.

The Argolid, just south of Attica, in mainland Greece, is a mountainous region, its largest level area being the Argolic plain, which lies at its southwestern end. It is bounded on the east, the south and the southwest by the sea, which, since antiquity, has linked the region with Piraeus and with the islands of the Aegean. Its winding coastline forms a succession of bays and small coves, fringed with fine beaches and ending in barren headlands.

The eastern shores of the prefecture are washed by the waters of the Saronic gulf and are for the most part rugged and mountainous, with small coves in between. The southern shores, embraced by the Argolic Gulf, are tranquil, dotted with picturesque settlements, cosmopolitan resorts and sheltered beaches. Along this coast have sprung up the most important tourist centres - Tolo, Porto Heli, Costa, Hermione.

Tolo, with its golden sands and shallow waters, is one of the renowned summer resorts of the Argolid.

The main towns of the Argolid are Nauplion, the capital of the prefecture, and Argos. Both lie in the Argolic plain , Nauplion nestling deep within the curve of the Argolic gulf, and Argos situated inland and further north.

Much of the agricultural produce of the Argolid - vegetables, citrus and other fruit - comes from the plain of Argos. The melons of Argos are renowned for their aroma and, famous too, are the oranges produced in the small plain of Epidaurus and the oil from the olive groves of Kranidi. Also prized is the feta cheese from the area of Tracheia and the savoury fish of the Argolic gulf.

The Argolid attracts large numbers of Greek and foreign visitors each year, thanks to its important historical monuments, its natural beauty, and its temperate climate with its mild winters and warm summers. Other advantages are the proximity to Athens, the good road network and the ample accommodation ranging from camping sites to luxury hotels.

Two different itineraries are offered to us for our journey through the Argolid. One route will take us along the road linking Corinth to Nauplion, while the other will follow the eastern coast of the prefecture towards Epidaurus.

ITINERARY 1

We enter the prefecture of the Argolid after passing through the historic town of Dervenakia, where, during the Greek War of Independence, the famous general of the War,Theodore Kolokotronis, routed the Turkish army led by Dramali in 1822.

About 9.5 kilometres after Dervenakia, at the point where we meet the village of Fichti, we take the road which turns left (east). Two kilometres further on we come to the famous citadel of Mycenae. After Fichti, the road winds through orange groves, passing through small villages, to arrive finally at Argos, the commercial and agricultural centre of the prefecture.

Of interest, apart from the archaeological monuments of the town, are the Museum and the churches - the cathedral of St. Peter and the church of St. John, in the courtyard of which was held, in 1821, the first National Assembly of the modern Greek state.

Places worth visiting in the vicinity of Argos are the sanctuary of Hera - the Heraeon - and Midea, where there are ruins of a Mycenean acropolis near the village of Dentra. On the road to Dentra we find a Byzantine church worthy of note: it is dedicated to the Holy Virgin, was built in the 12th century, and waq- complemented in the 15th and 16th centuries with further additions

We leave Argos behind and continue southwards. About five kilometres further on, we come to a branch of the road on the right which takes us, after 2.5 kilometres, to Kephalari and from there to Helleniko. At Kephalari among the shady trees, we find the abundant springs of the Erasinus stream, gushing out of a rock at the foot of a cliff. Two caves, about 30 metres deep, opening up above the springs, were inhabited in prehistoric times. Above the springs stands the church of Zoodochos Pighi (the Virgin the Life-giving Source), in front of which flow the waters of the stream. At Kephalari we can stop for a meal and a rest at one of the tavernas, under the cool shade of the trees. Here, in antiquity, were held festivities in honour of Dionysus and of Pan. Today, a fair is held on the the feast-day of the Zoodochos Pighi, the Friday after Easter Sunday.

About 2.5 or 3 kms beyond Kephalari, on the way to Helleniko, at the eastern limits of the village, we can see the ruins of an ancient "pyramid" (a similar one exists outside the village of Lygourio). Constructions such as this were once thought to have been burial monuments, but recent research has led scholars to the conclusion that they were most probably wayside fortifications.

We now return to the main road and continue southwards, arriving, after a drive of about five kilometres, at Myloi, a village that owes its name to the water mills which once stood here and used the abundant waters in the area. This village played an important role during the Greek War of Independance, due to its strategic position controlling the passage from Tripolis to Argos, and to its

Kephalari. The church of the Zoodochos Pighi is built above the springs of the Erasinos river.

choice by General Theodore Kolokotronis for his headquarters, in 1822. It was also the seat of the revolutionary government of the Greeks, in 1824, during the siege of Nauplion. Finally, it was here that, in 1825, Dimitrios Ypsilantis, with other Greek chieftains and about 250 men, repulsed the army of Ibrahim.

Two kilometres past Myloi the road branches out into two directions. The right branch leads to the ruins of the prehistoric settlement of Lerna, while the left one brings us to Kiveri with its lovely beach. This is the largest village of the plain which extends south of Myloi. From here the road continues further south, towards the fishing villages of the prefecture of Arcadia - Xeropighado, Astros, Tyros.

We return to Myloi and from there take the right branch. After 5 kilometres we come to Nea Kios, a coastal town with a sandy beach and shallow sea. We continue eastwards, and after 7 kms arrive at Nauplion.

A stroll in the narrow streets of the picturesque town and a coffee in the attractive coffee-shop in the old railway station, situated in the small park of the town, will leave us rested and refreshed before we start off again for the continuation of our journey.

At a short distance from Nauplion, taking a northerly direction, we shall come upon the Mycenean citadel of Tiryns. We may also visit, to the northeast, the monastery of St. Theodosios and, 4 kms east, in the village of Aria, the monastery of Zoodochos Pighi or "Hagia Moni", founded in 1143 by the bishop of Argos and Nauplion, Leon Atzas. Its *katholikon* (main church) is considered to be a representative example of Byzantine art. During the period of Frankish rule (1212-1389), the monastery was granted privileges by the Latin bishop of Argos. It remained in the hands of Greek Orthodox monks during the first period of Venetian rule (1385-1540). During the period of Ottoman rule it was ceded, in 1679, to the Patriarchate of Jerusalem and became a dependency of the Church of the Holy

Above: A "pyramid" outside Kephalari.

Below: Close to Nauplion, lies the golden beach of Karathonas.

Tolo (aerial photograph). →

The modern settlement of Palaia (old) Epidavros (aerial photograph).

Sepulchre. East of Nauplion we will find picturesque fishing villages with tavernas and ouzeries and beautiful beaches, some of which are very popular while others are quiet and less well known, where we can enjoy a dip in the sea or a rest. We will also find places with modern hotels, bars, restaurants, discos and cafeterias.

Outside Nauplion lies the town of Karathonas with its lovely beach of golden sand.

Southeast of Aria, outside the village of Lefkakia, we will follow a branch of the road which takes us in a southwesterly direction. After a drive of two kilometres we will come to Asine with its Mycenean citadel and its beautiful beach, and from there our road takes us to Tolo, a cosmopolitan resort with many hotels, restaurants, and tavernas, and a sandy beach with shallow waters.

Four and a half kilometres east of Tolo we come to Drepano, built among orange groves and by a lovely beach. Near Drepano lies the picturesque village of Vivari with its fish tavernas, facing the sheltered cove, and further to the southeast lie Candia and the beach of Iria.

From Nauplion a good road traverses the inland area to the northeast and, passing through orange groves and small villages, reaches Lygourio, or Asclepieio (25 kms), a town very popular with tourists in the summer. Shortly before we come to Lygourio, quite close to Kazarma, we shall encounter a Mycenean bridge, a vestige of a road of Mycenean times. Surrounded by mountains in a verdant environment, Lygourio is well known for its tavernas serving a variety of tasty dishes and charcoal grilled food. In the area of Lygourio there are many Byzantine churches. Among the most important are the 11th-century church of St. John Eleemon and the 14th-century church of the Holy Virgin, in which there are noteworthy wall paintings. From Lygourio the road branches out in two directions - one to the northeast and one to the southeast. The northeasterly branch leads to the settlements of Palaia and Nea Epidavros, while the southeasterly one traverses the inland area of the prefecture to end up at Porto Heli and Costa, at its southern tip. We will visit these sites on our second journey.

ITINERARY 2

This itinerary will complete our tour of the Argolid. This time we will discover the eastern coast of the prefecture and reach its easternmost and southernmost ends.

We leave the Athens to Corinth national road immediately after the Isthmus and follow the road which takes a left (southeasterly) direction towards Epidaurus.

After we pass the coastal tourist resorts of the prefecture of Corinthia - Kenchreae (Kechries), Loutro Elenis and Almyri - we turn away from the sea and begin to climb into pine-clad hills. In the background is the wide expanse of the Saronic Gulf curving in to form coves and beautiful beaches. After the village of Korfos we find, on our left, the Byzantine monastery of Agnous, containing fine 18th-century wall paintings. Four kilometres further on, climbing to the foothills of Mt. Akros, is the settlement of Nea Epidavros, with its port-town of Paralia nestling among the dense orange groves.

Eight and a half kilometres south of Nea Epidavros, a branch in the road leads to the picturesque fishing village of old (Palaia) Epidavros. Here, against the jetty, yachts lie at anchor and fishing boats rock gently on the quiet waters of the small bay, along which we can find tavernas serving fresh fish and other tasty dishes, as well as pastry shops.

To the right of the harbour have been preserved a small theatre and parts of the fortification of the city of Classical times, while south of the village stretches the long beach of Yialassi with its fine pebbles and sand. Here the orange trees and olive trees come all the way down to the sea. On the horizon we can see the islets of the bay of Epidaurus - Anghistri, Moni and Kyra.

We return to the main road. A branch leading west takes us to Lygourio and from there to Nauplion or to the archaeological site of the Asclepieion. We shall take the road which winds and twists southwards. The view from up here down towards the sea, the village and the beach of Palaia Epidavros is enchanting.

About 10 kms further along we find ourselves in the mountainous area of Tracheia. From here we continue south-

Paralia, the port town of Nea Epidavros, with its delightful beach and orange trees growing almost to the water's edge.

Porto Heli attracts a great number of visitors, who come to enjoy the beautiful beaches and the amenities offered by the comfortable modern hotels.

wards and come to the village of Didyma ("Twins"), outside of which are the twin caves known as "Dolines".
We return again to the main road. A branch brings us to coastal Saladi with its lovely beach. About ten kilometres further on, another branch takes us to Koilada, a fishing village built in the crook of a sheltered bay. Outside the village lies the Francthi cave, in which have come to light palaeontological finds.
Twelve kilometres south of Didyma lies Kranidi, a town built amphitheatrically and surrounded by olive groves. Here there are many Byzantine monasteries and churches - the Monastery of Aghioi Anargyroi with its beautiful wood-carved iconostasis, the monastery of St. Anne and the little church of the Holy Trinity (Hagia Triada). After Kranidi the road ends up on the southern coast of the prefecture.
Porto Heli is a popular resort, on the northern side of a sheltered bay, and in its natural harbour every kind of pleasure boat weighs anchor alongside the quay, while enticing smells of cooked

food waft from the row of tavernas on the waterfront.

Opposite the village, on the south side of the bay, had stood in antiquity the city of Alieis or Alike, founded by Tirynthians who had left their city when it was taken by the Argives. Today we can still see the walls of the ancient city, while in the waters of the harbour can be seen the submerged foundations of edifices and harbour installations.

South of Porto Heli we come to Costa, also a very popular tourist resort. Across the water, at a distance of only

ΕΣΤΙΑΤΟΡΙΟ
SELF SERVICE

1.3 n.m. lies the island of Spetses, one of the lovely islands of the Argosaronic Gulf. It is linked to Costa by a frequent service of small boats which make the trip in about 10 minutes. All around us are sheltered, pine-clad coves with shallow waters and golden sands.

Before Costa a branch in the road turns eastwards and follows the southern coast of the prefecture, dotted with coastal settlements.

Our first stop will be in Hermione, built in a sheltered verdant cove among a profusion of orange, lemon and olive trees. The present-day settlement has developed on the site of ancient Hermione, of which still visible are the ruins of the wall on the northern coast of the peninsula and the foundations of a large temple in its centre. The ancient walls had been restored and extended in medieval times. Opposite the settlement lies the islet of Dokos on which can be seen the ruins of a castle. Ten kilometres east of Hermione we come to Thermesia, a coastal settlement popular with tourists. North of the settlement stands a medieval fort which, in 1537, fell into the hands of the Turks, while in the 17th and 18th centuries it was alternatively taken by the Venetians and the Turks.

Left, and above right: A lovely beach at Costa.

Below: Hermione.

Above: Hermione. Kouverta beach.

Below: Another view of lovely Hermione.

Right: Views of ancient Troezen.

Our next stops are Plepi, Pighadia and Metochi, with their fine beaches for swimming. After Metochi the road leaves the sea and turns northwards. We come to verdant Galatas with its famous lemon groves, which cover the hillside and come all the way down to the sea. In the spring the whole area is redolent with the scent of lemon blossoms.

Just opposite Galatas is the pine-clad island of Poros, to which it is linked by frequent boat services throughout the day and night, the trip across only taking 5 to 10 minutes.

Northwest of Galatas is Troizene, where one can see the ruins of a city which flourished in antiquity. At Troizene, at the site known as Phleba, the 3rd National Assembly of the new Greek state took place in 1827, and elected Ioannes Capodistrias as the first governor of Greece.

Ancient Troizene, believed to be the birthplace of Theseus, was built to the west and north-west of the present-day settlement. Foundations of its walls can be seen 300 to 400 metres north-west of the village, while 1 km further to the north-west lie the ruins of the sanctuary of Hippolytus.

West of Troizene we find Castro, where an ancient citadel once stood. Its walls, as was the case with such fortifications elsewhere, were restored in medieval times for use in the defence of the settlement.

We will now return to the main road, and, north of Troizene, will encounter Methana, lying on the eastern coast of a mountainous peninsula and renowned for its mineral springs.

On the western coast of the peninsula, near Megalochori, stood the ancient city of Methana, part of which is now submerged. The fortified summit of a small hill known as the Castro of Megalochori served as the city's citadel. Its walls, built in the 4th century BC and restored in medieval times, have been preserved in relatively good condition

Modern Methana has been built near the sulphurous springs, known as Vromolimni, which have been well known for their medicinal properties since antiquity.

At the site known as Gozdiza, in the southern part of the peninsula, lies the cave known as "Peristeri" of Megalochori. After we have entered the cave, a small boat awaiting us there will take us across a little lake, known as the "dream lake", and beyond it, into the interior of the cave, where we may admire the breathtaking spectacle of the stalactites and stalagmites which adorn it.

The crater of Methana's now extinct volcano is situated at a place called "Kameni Chora". Pausanias speaks of the last explosion of the volcano as having occurred in 276 AD.

Here ends our journey into the Argolid, a region rich in precious memories of both the distant and the more recent past, and happily enjoying, in the present, the gifts with which nature has lavishly endowed it: the brilliant sun, the shimmering sea and the verdant mountains.

ARCADIA

Land of shepherds and nymphs, breathing an atmosphere of bucolic and idyllic serenity, such was Arcadia for Theocritus, for Ovid and for the intellectuals of 16th- and 17th-century Europe. In fact, Arcadia is a mountainous region, in which nestle small villages; a well-watered region, where high plateaux alternate with small but fertile valleys. According to mythology, it was here that winged Hermes, the messenger of the gods, was born. Pan, too, the shaggy-coated god with the heels and horns of a goat, and the pointed ears, the companion of Cybele and of Dionysus, the patron of shepherds and hunters, and inventor of the shepherd's pipe, was a resident of these parts. Easy-going and boisterous, Pan was said to have lived in the mountains and streams of Mt. Maenalon. Swift-footed Atalante, too, the fearless maiden who was the equal of any man in bravery and hunting skills, lived among the mountains and forests of Mt. Parthenion, east of Tegea.

Pausanias, speaking of the mythical past of Arcadia, tells us that its first king was Pelasgus, who also gave the region the name it held at the time. Pelasgus first discovered the nutritional value of the fruit of the oak tree and thus contributed to the improvement of the inhabitants' life.

Pelasgus was succeeded by his son Lycaon, who founded the first Arcadian city, Lycosura. Legend has it that Lycosura was the first city in the world and that it served as a model for the creation of other cities. Lycaon introduced the worship of Zeus Lycaeos, in whose honour human sacrifices were performed on the altar on the summit of Mt. Lycaeon, in order to pacify the god in times of prolonged drought.

Myths concerning Lycaon refer to his fifty sons and one daughter, Callisto. Some of the most important cities of the region were founded by his sons - Mantineus founded Mantineia, Tegeus founded Tegea, Maenalos the city of Maenalon. Callisto was loved by Zeus, and of their union was born Arcas. When Callisto gave birth, Lycaon invited the god to a meal, and offered him his own son on a plate. Zeus understood, and in his anger changed Lycaon into a wolf. He then brought the young child back to life. Arcas thus lived to become the eponymous founder of the tribe of the Arcadians.

Left: The Leonidian ravine in Cynuria.

Above: The sanctuary of Despoina, the goddess of growing vegetation, at Lycosura.

HISTORY

Arcadia, in ancient times, had no access to the sea, but was limited to the interior of the Peloponnese. However, it occupied a larger area than it does today. It included lands to the north and west which today belong to Corinthia, Achaea and Elis. The cities of Stymphalos and Pheneos then belonged to Arcadia, as did the region around the Aroanian mountains and Phigaleia.

Although a mountainous area, Arcadia was inhabited very early on, as is attested by the ruins of prehistoric settlements which have been brought to light. In the northern part of the prefecture, in the community of Kamenitsa, was uncovered a settlement which has been dated to 4500-2800 BC. This settlement continued to be inhabited after 2800 BC and was abandoned in 1200 BC, at the same time as the other Mycenean centres.

To the east of Tripolis, in the region known as Aghiorghitika, a metallurgical and copper-processing works flourished in 2500-

1700 BC, while, at Asea, southwest of Tripolis, have been discovered ruins of a settlement of the Neolithic, Proto-Helladic and Meso-Helladic periods.
The Arcadians first appeared as a united people at the time of their participation in the Trojan expedition, under their king, Agapenor. The 60 ships with which they joined the expedition were ceded to them by Agamemnon, since Arcadia, being as we have said a landlocked region, did not have a fleet of its own.
In historic times were founded the important Arcadian cities of Mantinea, Tegea, Gortyna, Orchomenos and Megalopolis. The year 371 BC was an important one in the history of Arcadia, as this was when the battle of Leuctra took place between the Spartans and the Thebans. After the defeat of the Spartans the Arcadians entered into an alliance with the Thebans. They founded the *Koinon* of the Arcadians, centred on Megalopolis, a city created by the synoecism,– the joining together,– of 39 smaller cities, an event which is believed to have occurred in 371 BC or in 368 BC after the "tearless battle", in which the Arcadians, together with the Argives and the Messenians, fought against the Spartans.

In the centre of the town, near the theatre - which, according to Pausanias, was the largest in Greece - was built the *Thersilion,* where the representatives of the Arcadian League held their meetings. On matters of war and peace it was the group of the Ten Thousand citizens who made the decisions, while the business of government, including the minting of coins, was in the hands of the generals. Finally, 5,000 select Arcadian men were entrusted with the defence of the cities.
The Arcadian League soon took on a Pan-Arcadian character, as other cities joined-it,, and an attempt was made to shake off the control of the Thebans. However, the *Koinon* of the Arcadians was not destined to last very long. The first conflicts arose from the refusal of the Mantineans to use the treasures of the sanctuary in Olympia for the payment of the soldiers of the Arcadian League. In order to restore order, Thebes mounted an expedition against the Arcadians, who in the meantime had made peace with the Elians and called for the assistance of the Athenians and of the Spartans.
In 362 BC, at the battle of Mantinea, the Thebans and their allies fought against the Arcadians, the Achaeans, the Elians, the

Athenians, the Phliasians and the Spartans. The battle ended in a Theban victory, but the Theban general Epaminondas was killed, and his death created a great void. A "common peace" was then signed between the Greek cities, but this was upset by the desire of the citizens of the smaller communities which had joined together in the synoecism of Megalopolis, to return to their old homes.

In 344 BC Megalopolis allied herself with Philip II of Macedon, and in 311 BC Arcadia, together with the rest of the Peloponnese, came under the dominion of Cassander. In 303 BC all of Arcadia, with the exception of Mantinea, was seized by Demetrius Poliorcetes.

There followed a period during which the Arcadian cities at various times either entered into an alliance with Macedonia, or joined the side of Pyrrhus, king of Epirus, or came under the sway of the Achaean or of the Aetolian confederation.

In 235 BC the Aetolians ceded the Arcadian cities they held to Sparta and its king Cleomenes III, while in 223 BC Tegea, Orchomenos and Mantinea passed into the possession of the Macedonian king Antigonus Doson.

With the Roman conquest of Greece began the decline of Arcadia. In 395 AD it was ravaged by the Visigoths under Alaric and in the 7th century AD it suffered the invasions of the Slavs. In 1205 it was conquered by the Franks and under the name of Messarea was divided into five baronies. It was liberated in 1330 by Andronicus Palaeologus.

From 1458/1460 to 1687 it was in Turkish hands and constituted part of the *vilayet* of the Morea. In 1687 it was recaptured by the Franks and remained in their possession until 1715, when it was taken for the second time by the Turks. Tripolis now became the seat of the pasha of the Morea and the commercial and administrative centre of the entire Peloponnese. In 1764 was founded the famous School of Dimitsana, which developed into an important intellectual and cultural centre for the area.

After the outbreak of the Greek War of Independence in 1821, many of the clashes between the Greeks – mostly under the leadership of Theodore Kolokotronis – and the Turks took place on Arcadian territory. In 1821 Kolokotronis besieged Tripolis and in September of the same year took the town. In 1825 Tripolis was captured by Ibrahim Pasha , who ravaged and devastated Arcadia three times until 1828, at which time the Turks were finally driven out of the region.

GETTING TO KNOW ARCADIA

As we set out to explore Arcadia today we shall follow the roads up into the high wooded mountains, through forests of fir trees and across fertile plateaux; we shall discover traditional mountain villages with narrow cobbled streets, attractive squares, and simple and austere stone houses with tiled roofs. We may stop for a while in some picturesque fishing village with little tavernas facing the sea and enjoy a dip in the clear waters of a quiet beach. Wherever we go, we will find the mountains and the sea, the various shades of green and blue, blending together in perfect harmony.

As we continue on our way, we shall encounter Byzantine monasteries, medieval castles and the ruins of ancient cities.

On our tour we shall first explore the northern part of the prefecture, after which we shall visit the southern part, and we will end our journey with a tour of the eastern parts and the coasts washed by the waters of the Argolic Gulf.

TRIPOLIS

Girded by mountains, on the edge of the plateau of the same name and at an altitude of 650 metres, lies the town of Tripolis. Its history starts from the middle of the 15th century, when the castle of Drobolitsa stood, tall and proud, on the site. Later, the inhabitants of the surrounding villages settled around the castle, which had by then fallen into ruin, but which gave the small town its name, Hydropolitsa or Dropolitsa, which later became Tripolitsa. Up until 1715 it was a small and insignifi-

Tegea: Ancient Tegea was the most important city of Arcadia, before the foundation of Megalopolis. In medieval times, the fortress of Mouchli was one of the strongest in the Peloponnese.

Tripolis, lying on the edge of a fertile plateau.

cant town. In 1769-1770 its inhabitants took part in the revolution of the Russian admiral Orloff against the Turks, following the failure of which they were subjected to severe punishment. In 1785 the Turks fortified the town and used it as their base of operations until 1821, at which time it was captured by Kolokotronis. In 1825 it fell into the hands of Ibrahim Pasha, who set fire to it and razed it to the ground as he withdrew.

After its liberation from the Turks, Tripolis was rebuilt and soon began to grow and flourish. Today it constitutes an important agricultural, administrative and commercial centre of the Peloponnese, as well as an important junction in the road network leading towards the central, southern, southwestern and southeastern Peloponnese.

The town's centre is Ares square, on which stands the neo-classical building of the Law Courts and an equestrian statue of Kolokotronis. Of interest is the Byzantine church of St. Basil, now the cathedral of Tripolis, and worth a visit, too, is the Archaeological Museum (6, Evangelistrias Street, tel.:071/239406), which is housed in a double-storied neo-classical building designed by the famous architect Ernest Ziller, and among the exhibits of which are a collection of votive figurines of the Proto-Helladic period from Sakovouni, and finds from Mantinea, Palaeokastro, Gortyna, etc.

NORTHERN ARCADIA

Twelve kilometres north of Tripolis lie the ruins of ancient Mantinea - "pleasant Mantinea", as Homer calls it in the second rhapsody of the *Iliad,* and "a most ancient and great city of the Arcadians", according to Polybius. The history of Mantinea starts

before historic times, when it consisted of four or five rural communities, which by historic times had united to form the city of Mantinea.

The river Ophis flowed through the town which, because it was built on a plain, had to be defended by strong walls, the foundations of which were made of stone, while the rest of the structure was made of brick. In 385 BC, during a clash between Sparta and Mantinea, the Spartans demanded that the Mantineans pull down their walls. When the latter refused, the king of Sparta, Agesilaos, dammed the river, so that its waters rose and undermined the structure of the walls and houses, which began to crumble. The Mantineans were thus obliged to surrender to the Spartans. They had to abandon their destroyed city and scatter in the surrounding villages.

In 370 BC the Theban general, Epaminondas, invited the Mantineans to return to their abandoned city.

The old settlement was given new fortifications. Around the city was dug a moat and the waters of the river were channelled into it.

At first, Mantinea joined the Achean League but soon afterwards transferred its allegiance to the Aetolian League. In 226 BC, Aratus, a general of the Achaean League, took the city, but the Mantineans, having killed the guard installed by Aratus, joined the Spartans in the Aetolian League.

Antigonus III Doson and the Achaeans, captured the city in 222 BC, plundered it and killed many of its citizens.

Colonists from Argos gave the city the

Above: Mantinea. The church of Aghia Photini, built with ancient building material.

Left: The ancient theatre of Mantinea.

name of Antigoneia, which it kept until the 2nd century AD, at which time Hadrian gave it back its original name. Pausanias, who visited it in the 2nd century AD, refers to the great number of temples and sanctuaries which existed in Mantinea. Among them, of particular importance was the temple of Asclepius, housing the statue of the god created in the 5th century BC by the Athenian sculptor Alkamenes, the sanctuary of Leto and her children, whose statues were carved by the famous sculptor Praxiteles, the shrine of Alea and the temple of Antinoos, in whose honour were held the Antinoan games, whose fame extended beyond the borders of Mantinea itself.

Today, among the ruins of the ancient city, which mostly date from the Roman period, we can easily identify the foundations of the *skene* of the theatre and some seats of the lower tiers, around the orchestra.

To the east of the *skene* lie the ruins of two temples. The larger one is thought to have been dedicated to Hera, while the other was perhaps dedicated to Zeus Soter. East of the theatre lay the agora with the public buildings which surrounded it - the stoa of Eurycles, the *exedra* of Epigone (on the northwestern side, on the site of the older agora), and to the south the *bouleterion* (assembly house).

Also visible are ruins of the city's walls, some four kilometres in circumference and 4.20 metres in width, with their 122 towers and 10 gates, to which led an equal number of roads.

At Mantinea there is also a monument to the war dead and a modern church, dedicated to St. Photini. Ancient building material has been used in the construction of both these monuments.

East of Mantinea, nestling in the mountains surrounding the small valley known in antiquity as the *Argon pedion*, lies the picturesque village of Nestani. The hill of Panigyritsa, to the northwest of the village, was fortified in antiquity and served as the citadel of the small city which belonged to the Mantineans. The entrance

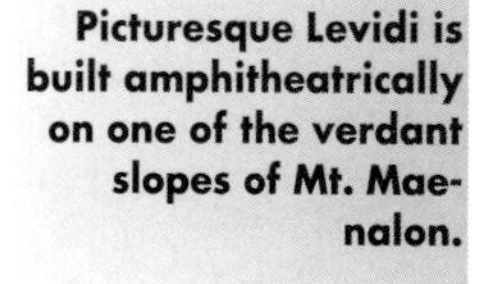

Picturesque Levidi is built amphitheatrically on one of the verdant slopes of Mt. Maenalon.

to the fortified citadel is the same as that used today. Of the ancient city parts of the fortifications and the gate have survived, while ancient slabs and an inscription of the 1st century AD have been used in the construction of a fountain in the village. East of Nestani and at an altitude of 640 m we find the monastery of the Virgin Gorgoepikoos, which dates from the 10th century and is adorned with 16th-century frescoes.

We now continue our journey in a northwesterly direction. Nine kilometres after the almost abandoned village of Kardara and having passed through forests of tall green firs, we come to the plateau of Ostrakina at an altitude of 1600 metres, where there is a skiing centre..

We continue to drive in a northerly direction. The picturesque village of Levidi, built on a verdant slope of Mt. Maenalon, appears before us. Here, in a room of the town hall, is housed a museum dedicated to Alexander Papanastasiou (1876-1936), in which are exhibited personal items belonging to the statesman, sociologist and prime minister who proclaimed the first Greek Republic.

Northeast of Levidi, surrounded by mountains, lie the ruins of ancient Orchomenos. The village of today (formerly known as Kalpaki) has been built on the site of a settlement which flourished in Roman times. Of the Roman period only a few traces have survived. Before the Roman period, Orchomenos, which Homer refers to as "rich in sheep", was built on a plateau on top of a nearby hill. The position of the "upper city" as Pausanias calls it, allowed the king to control the political life of Arcadia in Archaic times. After the Persian wars Orchomenos began to decline. Of the buildings of the agora in the "upper city", just below the top of the hill, can be seen part of the seating area of the theatre, with the steps leading up between the tiers, a cylindrical stone platform and two stone thrones. A great colonnade of the 4th century BC bounding the agora to the north, the foundations of another colonnade and of the temple of Artemis, as well as parts of the fortified enceinte of the city, have also come to light.

After Orchomenos we continue our journey along the verdant slopes of Mt. Maenalon. About 20 kms west of Levidi we meet the Byzantine monastery of the Virgin Kernitsa, clinging to the peak of a rock, which seems to survey the surrounding countryside.

Further south, at a height of 1060 m, in a mountain valley unfolding between the fir-covered slopes of Mt. Maenalon and by the side of cool flowing streams, lies

Orchomenos. The ancient theatre.

Vytina, one of the most beautiful of the Arcadian villages. Woodcarving is an old tradition here, and the inhabitants are still occupied with the creation of various objects of popular art as well as everyday utensils.

In the nearby attractive village of Valtesiniko, we will stop and admire the carved wooden iconostasis of the churches. Northwest of Valtesiniko (1 km) stands the church of the Dormition of the Virgin, the frescoes of which are partially destroyed. This used to be the *katholikon* of a monastery founded in 1625.

From Vytina we may, if we wish, return to Tripolis driving through the beautiful mountain scenery to its south, where lie the picturesque villages of Alonistaina, Piana with its ruined medieval castle and folk art collection, and Davia. We can also continue towards the south-west, to Karkalou and then to Langadia, with its cobbled streets and grand two-storied and three-storied houses, built in stone in the traditional style, and disposed amphitheatrically on a steep slope.

Northwest of Langadia we see yet another attractive village, that of Tropaia. About 3 kms east of the village, on a height, are preserved the ruins of the medieval castle

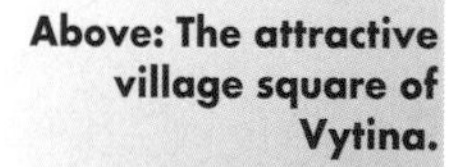

Above: The attractive village square of Vytina.

Below: Vytina. In its narrow streets we shall see traditional houses arrayed in all the colours of nature.

of Akova, built in the 13th century, and the seat of one of the five baronies of the Morea.

From Tropaia we continue northwards. Nine kilometres further along we encounter the dam of the artificial lake on the river Ladon, set in a lovely landscape at an altitude of 420 metres.

We leave Mt Maenalon behind us and follow the Ladon river, in a southerly direction. As we descend the valley towards Elis, about 31 kms south of Tropaia, we find, on the banks of the Ladon, and in a vertily valley, the baths of Heraea, with their sulphurous springs.

South of the baths, and west of the village of Aghios Ioannis, on the slope of a hill near the right bank of the Alpheios river stood, in antiquity, the thriving town of Heraea. Only a few ruins of the ancient settlement have survived. Heraea, situated near the boundary between Arcadia and Elis, was the largest of the Arcadian cities, and was adorned with temples dedicated to Hera, to Dionysus and to Pan. Its founder, according to Pausanias, was the son of Lycaon, Heraieus. The city was a friend and ally of Sparta.

We return once again to the slopes of Mt. Maenalon, to the crossroads at the village of Karkalou, and taking the road that leads southwards, arrive, 7 kms further along, at the historic village of Dimitsana. Clinging to the slopes of the mountain, at an altitude of about 950 metres above the river Lousios, it looks out over the plain of Megalopolis. It was the birthplace of the bishop of Old Patras, Germanos, who proclaimed the start of the Revolution, as well as of the martyred Patriarch Gregory V,

Above: Vytina is one of the loveliest villages in Arcadia.

Below: Langadia, one of the important villages of the region, renowned for its traditional stone houses, built by its famous master-masons.

and played an important role during the Greek War of Independence of 1821. The powder mills of Dimitsana are of particular interest for having supplied gunpowder to the insurgent Greeks.

The village, with its traditional two-storied, three-storied and even five-storied houses with their tiled roofs, its attractive squares and churches – St. George (17th century), St. Kyriaki (1834) and St. Charalambos (1832),– presents a particularly picturesque aspect. Its School was built in 1845, and the similar building erected next to it in 1851 houses a library containing many rare books. A small local archaeological and folk art collection are also

Right: Alonistaina. Another picturesque mountain village.

Centre: Traditional buildings at Dimitsana.

Below: Dimitsana. Amid the luxuriant vegetation, on one of Maenalon's slopes, rise the two- and three-storied houses of Dimitsana.

housed in the same building. Dimitsana is believed to have been built on the site of ancient Teuthis, a view supported by the ruins of an ancient wall, which can be discerned among the houses of the village. The rocky outcrop that rises above the neighbourhood of the "Castro" was the citadel of the ancient city, which was thriving before the time of Pausanias. Medieval ruins show that the settlement also flourished during the Christian era and continued to do so during the period of Ottoman rule, until the middle of the 19th century.

Left: Charming Zatouna lies in a verdant setting, at an altitude of 900 metres.

Below: The Philosophou monastery, perched on a steep cliff above the bed of the Lousios river.

Four kilometres west of Dimitsana, on a verdant, well-watered slope, is built the beautiful village of Zatouna, and further south the monastery of Philosophou, standing in a gorge, on the western bank of the Lousios river. The monastery, of which only the *katholikon* still survives, was probably founded in the 10th century by Ioannes Lambardopoulos, nicknamed the Philosopher. The monastery had originally been built on a steep rock, but in the 17th century it was moved to a more accessible spot.

Southeast of Dimitsana (4 kms) stands the Aimilianon monastery with frescoes painted in 1608 by the brothers Dimitrios and Georgios Moschos, while further south the monastery of St. John the Baptist is situated in an idyllic spot, wedged between the rocks of the breathtakingly beautiful gorge of the Lousios river. According to tradition, the monastery was built in 1167 by the emperor Manuel Comnene.

Northeast of the monastery lies the traditional village of Stemnitsa or Hypsous, a summer resort built at an altitude of 1100 metres on the site of ancient Hypsous. It has beautiful stone houses and a folk art museum and its people have long been renowned as silver- and goldsmiths.

East of Stemnitsa lie the charming mountain villages of Chryssovitsi, built at an altitude of 1150 metres, and Tselepako, and !7 kms south of Stemnitsa we come to Karytaina, built on the site of the ancient town of Brenthe. Its impressive castle, one of the most important in the Peloponnese

Left page: The impressive gorge of the Lousios river.

Left: The monastery of St. John the Baptist.

Right: The Aimilianon monastery.

Below: Stemnitsa, a traditional mountain village built at an altitude of 1100 metres.

Above: An impressive castle crowns the hill above the charming village of Karytaina.

Below: The Frankish bridge spanning the Alpheios, outside Karytaina.

in medieval times and during the Ottoman occupation, stands on the summit of a high rocky hill, to the slopes of which clings the settlement of today, while down below the Alpheios river flows among lush vegetation. The castle was built in 1254 by the Franks, who used building material from the walls and public edifices of the ancient city. Karytaina reached the height of its prosperity during the time of Frankish rule. In 1320 its castle was purchased by Andronicus Palaeologus, and it was then that were built the Byzantine churches and monasteries of Karytaina. In 1458 the castle fell into Venetian hands, only to be seized in the middle of the 15th century by the Turks, retaken by the Venetians in 1685, and recaptured by the Turks in 1715. In 1821 it finally came under the control of general Kolokotronis. Today, all that is left in good condition of the once mighty fortress, are the exterior walls.

At Karytaina, apart from the castle, worth visiting is the church of the Virgin Zoodochos Pighi. Outside the village, over the Alpheios river, still stands an arched Frankish bridge, against which a tiny church resting on a platform seems to lean.

Northwest of Karytaina has come to light another ancient city, that of Gortyn. It is built on the right bank of the Lousios river, on a site of strategic importance for the defence of the Arcadian League. The ruins of the ancient city can be reached

Above: Lithograph of Karytaina.

Left: Ancient Gortyn.

from Atsilocho (north of Karytaina) or from Helleniko, which lies on the road between Karytaina and Dimitsana.
At Gortyn we can see ruins of fortifications of the Macedonian period, foundations of houses and public buildings, as well as a few ruins from a sanctuary of Asclepius that was renowned throughout the Peloponnese. According to Pausanias, the statues of Asclepius and of Hygieia in the Asclepieion were created by the famous sculptor Scopas.

SOUTHERN ARCADIA

Ten kilometres south-east of Tripolis have been uncovered the ruins of ancient Tegea, the most important city in Arcadia before the founding of Megalopolis. Ancient Tegea ruled over the southeastern part of Arcadia, which was known as Tegeatis. According to tradition, the city was founded by Aleus, who formed it by uniting nine small *demes*. It stood on a plain, which is why it was soon fortified by a strong wall, of which today only a few traces survive.

Right: Drums of columns and the platform of the temple of Athena Alea, at Tegea.

Below: Head of a maiden from the temple of Athena, Alea, at Tegea. It has been identified as the head of the cult statue of the goddess Hygieia, while other scholars believe it to be the head of Atalanta from the eastern pediment of the temple at Tegea. Athens, National Archaeological Museum.

The citizens of Tegea took part in the Argonautic Expedition and in the Trojan War. They also fought in the Persian Wars and were allies of the Spartans during the Peloponnesian Wars. They participated in the "*Koinon*" of the Arcadians, but in 235 BC became members of the Achaean League.

In 31 BC, after the battle of Actium, Octavian visited the city and, to punish the inhabitants for having offered their assistance to his opponent, Mark Antony, he carried off the statue of Athena Alea from her temple and took it to Rome. After the destruction of the town by the Goths, it was rebuilt in Byzantine times and became the see of the bishop of Amykles (Nyklion). In 1209 it passed into Frankish hands and in 1295 it was retaken by Andronicus Palaeologus.

Later, near the old city, on a hill, was built the fortified castle of Mouchli, which became one of the most important strongholds in the Peloponnese.

Pausanias tells us that in ancient Tegea, apart from the temple of Alea, which was one of the most venerated in the Peloponnese, there was also a temple dedicated to Athena Poliatis, while in the agora of the city there stood temples of Aphrodite, of the goddess Eileithyia, as well as altars to Zeus Teleios, to Gaia and to Ares. The goddess worshipped in the temple of Alea since Mycenean times, was identified, already before 600 BC, with Athena. She was worshipped in a wooden temple that was destroyed by fire in 395 BC. Around 370 BC or at some time in the second half of the 4th century BC, a marble temple was erected, consisting of a *pronaos*, a *sekos* and an *opisthodomus*. It was a Doric peripteral temple and was designed by the famous Parian architect Scopas. The sculpted decoration of the pediments represented mythological themes - on the eastern pediment was depicted the hunt of the Calydonian boar, in which Atalanta took part, and on the western pediment the combat between Telephos, son of Heracles, and Achilles. The ruins which

have been excavated at Alea belong to a later marble temple.
In the small museum of Alea (tel. 071/556540) are exhibited architectural elements of the temple, parts of the two pedimental compositions and other sculptures.

Megalopolis. The ruins of the ancient theatre. Before it may be seen the ruins of the Thersilion.

At Episkopi, Tegea, excavations have brought to light parts of the agora of the ancient city, and sections of the retaining wall of the seating area of the Hellenistic theatre built in 174 BC by Antiochus III Epiphanes. Within the area of the ancient theatre today stands the church of the Dormition of the Virgin, erected in 1888 to replace the ruined 6th-century Christian basilica, which had served as the cathedral of medieval Nyklion. The present church is cruciform with a dome. The decoration of the interior is modern. Near the church, traces of medieval walls and a mosaic floor from the old Christian basilica can still be seen.
We leave Tegea and take a southwesterly direction, towards Megalopolis, the second largest town in the prefecture. On either side of the road are planted apple and cherry orchards, from which come the delicious cherries and the sweet-scented apples of Tripolis.
On the way to Megalopolis we may wish to make a short halt in the historic village of Valtetsi, built on the slopes of Mt. Maenalon and famous for the two battles won here by the Greeks against the Turks.
Further south we come to Asea. At a short distance from the village have come to light some ruins of the ancient city of Asea, dating mostly from Hellenistic times. We arrive at Megalopolis, the administrative and commercial centre of the surrounding rural area. It stands in the middle of a fertile plain, surrounded by mountains. Megalopolis - the "Great City" - was founded in 371 or 368 BC by the Arcadians, on the initiative of the Theban general Epaminondas.
It became the centre of a large area of Arcadia (the Megalopolitis), which bordered on the south and the west with Laconia, Messenia and Elis, while to the north it reached all the way to Orchomenos and east to Mantinea and Tegea. In 222 BC Megalopolis was destroyed by the Spartans. After the battle of Sellasia and the fall of the Spartan king Cleomenes III, the town was rebuilt but never again regained its former prestige.
The ruins of ancient Megalopolis lie about one kilometre northwest of the present-day town, on the road to Karytaina. The

Above right: Ancient Lycosura. The foundations of the temple of Despoina and the stone steps where the initiates sat during the celebration of the mysteries.

Below left: The marble "sacred cloth" belonging to Despoina and adorned with relief decorations, which was found on the site of the sanctuary of the goddess, at ancient Lycosura.

city of ancient times was divided in half by the Hellison river. On the southern bank stood the theatre and the bouleuterion of the Ten Thousand (the Thersilion) and on the northern bank the agora and the sanctuaries.

Today, of the temples, the sanctuaries and the other public buildings of Megalopolis all that survives are some vestiges of the temple of Zeus Soter and remains of a building believed to have been the gymnasium. Of the theatre have survived only the orchestra, the proscenium, the lower tiers of the seating area and the stone seats with backs that were reserved for distinguished spectators. The theatre of Megalopolis was the largest in ancient Greece, accommodating 20,000 spectators. It had a movable *skene*. It was here that were held the assemblies of the representatives of the Arcadian cities that had joined together in synoecism at Megalopolis.

In front of the theatre stood the *Thersilion*, the assembly hall of the representatives of the united settlements. The Thersilion, which could accommodate 6,000 people,

had a tribune for the orator and most probably wooden seats for the public. The roof was also wooden and covered with tiles.

At Megalopolis, on Stathopoulou Street, there is a small archaeological museum containing finds from the excavations at Megalopolis and the surrounding area.

Fifteen kilometres southwest of Megalopolis, on the slopes of Mt. Lycaeon, stood Lycosura which, as Pausanias says, was the "most ancient of all the cities which ever existed on mainland or island".

Near the spot where ancient Lycosura once flourished stands the village of Stala, which now bears the name of Lycosura. We shall get there by way of the villages of Choremi or Apiditsa. Of the ancient city have been preserved parts of the fortified enclosure of its citadel, which stands on the slopes of a hill.

On its eastern and southern edges there stood a group of buildings belonging to the sanctuary of Despoina. To the west lay a complex of rooms, which may have been a hostel. A road with a propylon on the northern side led to the main sanctuary, which extended towards the northeast. In the narrow area of the sanctuary proper extended, from west to east, the Doric temple of Despoina, with its façade facing the east. In the cella of the temple stood a sculpted group including Artemis, Demeter, Despoina and Anytos, a work created by Domophon. Along the southern side were ten steps, which may have served as seats from which the initiates could follow the secret rituals.

East of the temple stood three altars dedicated to the Great Mother, to Despoina and to Demeter. Further east of these lay a large stoa. South, and further up, stood a monumental altar, the "megaron" of Despoina.

Of the above have been preserved the foundations of the complex of buildings, west of the sanctuary; the foundations of the temple of Despoina, those of the great stoa, as well as ruins of the three altars and of the megaron.

Further west, on the hill, there is a small museum, in which are exhibited finds from the excavations in the area of the sanctuary.

North of Lycosura we come upon the vil-

Left page, below: Ancient Lycosura. The temple of Despoina. We can see the opening for the door, on the south side of the cella.

Below: Mt. Lycaeon.

Right: Leondari. The castle and the town flourished in the 14th c.

Below: The particulary picturesque cherch of St. Theodora Vasta, near Isari.

lage of Lykaio and immediately after it emerges, amid the walnut trees, the village of Ano Karyies. Further up, on the summit of Mt. Lycaeon, on the small plateau formed at an altitude of 1200 metres, are scattered the ruins of the sanctuary of Pan, of the stadium and of the hippodrome. Here were held the Lycaean games, in honour of Zeus Lycaeus. A little higher up, there was an altar at which sacrifices were offered to the god.
South of Lycosura, among the forest-clad mountains, clinging to a steep slope at an altitude of 850 metres, we find the village of Isari. Just outside the village is the small church of Aghia Theodora, the frescoes of which date to the 11th century. Seventeen huge trees have sprung up from among the slabs of the roof.
Twelve kilometres south of Megalopolis stands the village of Leondari, which flourished in the 14th century. The ruins of its castle, on the neighbouring hill, and the interesting Byzantine church of the Holy Apostles, are worth a visit.
Finally, our last stop in southern Arcadia, near its borders with Messenia, is Dyrrachion, a mountain village lying at an altitude of about 800 metres, amid walnut and apple trees and blessed with abundant waters.

EASTERN ARCADIA (CYNURIA)

Last but not least on our journey through Arcadia is its eastern part, consisting of the district of Cynuria. Lying to the east of the Parnon mountain range, whose imposing bulk contributed, in the past, to its isolation, the region has always been distinguished for its particularity in relation to the rest of the Peloponnese.
The capital of the district, Leonidion, is built in the southeastern part, not far from the sea, in a small fertile plain.
Stock raising is an important activity in the mountainous part of Cynuria, while the cultivation of olives, vines and maize are the main activities in the lowlands. Tourism is also now developing in the

coastal settlements of the region. Included in Cynuria is the area of Tsakonia, the land of the Tsakones. The inhabitants of this area have retained their cultural particularities and their own dialect, which has its roots in the language of the Dorians. Here we will discover the picturesque traditional villages of Prastos and Platanos, admire the old fortified houses, dating from the 18th century, with their machicolations over the entrances, the very few openings in the walls, the cylindrical turrets and the embrasures in the corners. Such houses are the "tower of the Agha" in the village of Aghios Petros, the Skarbounis house in Leonidion etc.

We will visit the verdant mountain village of Kastri, built at an altitude of 950 m. We will go as far as the 12th-century monastery of St. John the Baptist, the *katholikon* of which is adorned with frescoes dating from the 18th century. Further south, we shall see, on a hill, the scant remains of the famed castle of Orea, the subject of many a Greek folk song, and will drive up to the village of Aghios Petros, a large and well-watered village built on the slopes of Mt. Parnon, among forests of plane and chestnut trees and orchards of apple, pear and cherry trees. To its west rises the mountain, with wonderful forests of black pine and fir, while to the east lies the plain of Astros, known in antiquity as Thyreatis.

Five kilometres northeast of Aghios Petros stands the monastery of the Virgin of Malevi, which is believed to have been built on the present site around 1600.

Northeast of Aghios Petros and of the Monastery of Malevi we might like to visit the monastery of the Virgin of Luku, founded in the 12th century. It is set in a verdant landscape, and in its katholikon there are frescoes of the 17th and 18th century. In antiquity, north of the monastery stood Eua, the largest settlement of the Thyreatis. The city had an Asclepieion which, as the archaeological finds prove, stood on the site of the present monastery. It would seem that, at this Asclepieion along with Asclepius, was also honoured, his grandson Polemocrates while, by the time of Pausanias' visit the whole sanctuary was dedicated to the latter.

Leonidion. The Tsakonian capital lies at the foot of the precipitous cliffs of Mt. Parnon.

Above left: The monastery of Luku.

Below left: Archaeological finds from Eua in Cynuria.

Above right: Paralion Astros

Below right: Tyros. The Golden Coast.

In the area around the monastery have been found a piece of Asclepius' staff, with the serpents entwined around it, belonging to the statue of the god, and a 4th-century votive relief representing Asclepius, his two sons and three daughters.
In the vicinity of Eua stood the villa belonging to Herodes Atticus. The excavations which are being carried out there have uncovered marvellous objects dating to Hellenistic times and the large mosaic-paved floor of the villa. Herodes was also connected with the region in another way. He had contributed to the embellishment of the Asclepieion, employing for this some of the most famous craftsmen of his time. Many pieces belonging to the decoration of the sanctuary are today preserved in the courtyard of the monastery, while others, such as Corinthian capitals, cymatia and the capitals of pilasters are set in the walls of the church and of the other later edifices.
In the courtyard of the monastery can also be seen architectural remains of an early Christian basilica, attesting to the continuous use of the site as a place of worship.
Our next stop is Astros. This was where the Second National Assembly of the new Greek state took place in 1823. In the small museum of the town, which is housed in a traditional 19th-century building, are exhibited finds from the villa of Herodes Atticus and from other excavations in the district of Cynuria.
The town of Paralion Astros lies at a distance of 4 kms from Astros, on the coast. It is built amphitheatrically on the

slopes of a hill opposite the sea, on the site of the ancient coastal city of Thyrea.

On the top of a hill above the town there is a picturesque medieval castle, which we might like to visit. It was restored during the Greek War of Independence (1824-1825) by the Zaphiropoulos brothers. On the same hill we shall also see parts of a wall dating from Classical times.

Alternatively, we may enjoy a quiet rest on the waterfront, or a swim in the crystal-clear turquoise waters of one of the beaches or creeks which lie to the north, between the village, and the place called Xeropighado.

Leaving Paralion Astros we shall continue our drive southwards along the coast of the Argolic Gulf, towards the borders of Laconia. Each bend in the road presents us with another view of the lovely landscape around us. On our left shimmer the cool waters of the faithful companion of this part of our journey, the sea. We pass the picturesque fishing villages of Aghios Andreas, Paralia Tyrou, Sabatiki. At

Above left: Sabatiki.

Below left: Plaka.

Above right: Poulithra.

Below right: The monastery of Elona.

Aghios Andreas, where a small church of the same name stands on a rise known as Nissi, ruins of ancient fortifications may be seen.
Further south, on the summit of the hill of Profitis Ilias, which rises above Tyros, was worshipped Apollo Tyritas together with Apollo Maleatas. Excavations carried out in the area have brought to light the ruins of the two temples. A relief representation which has been found suggests that Apollo Tyritas was a local divinity and the patron of dairy farmers (tyros = cheese).
After Tyros we come to picturesque Livadi, and to Pragmateftis - built on a hill with a view towards the sea - and, finally, to Sabatiki. Looking down on it as we drive along the road, its small pebbly beach and blue waters look most inviting.
We arrive at Leonidion, the capital of the area of Tsakonia, with its traditional stone houses and characteristic chimneys. To its left rise the red rocks of the Parnon, while rugged mountains enclose it on another two sides, so that its only opening is towards the sea, on which side lies a small verdant plain.
From 1845 on, many inhabitants of the surrounding mountain villages, such as Prastos, came to settle in Leonidion, thus

contributing to the town's development. In the small museum of Leonidion are housed finds from the ancient town of Prasiae.

Picturesque Plaka is the port of Leonidion. Its long pebbly beach and its seafront are lined with tavernas and ouzeries. Our drive therre will take us through groves of olive and fruit trees. Here at Plaka, stood in antiquity, the town of Brasiae or Prasiae, one of the seven cities making up the amphictyony of Calauria. The city submitted to the Spartans shortly after the year 550 BC.

On the mountain which rises above the coastal settlement are preserved parts of the fortified enceinte of the citadel, while parts of the walls of the ancient city can still be seen on the slopes of the mountain along the road which leads from Leonidion to Plaka.

South of Plaka lies the last coastal village in Arcadia, picturesque Poulithra. Peaceful and serene, with its attractive stone houses lining the beach, along the blue waters of the Argolic Gulf, it is an ideal place for a quiet and restful holiday. Near the village, on Vigla ("lookout") hill, which served as the citadel of ancient Polichna, survive parts of the city wall.

Northwest of Leonidion, the 17th-century monastery of St. Nicholas Sintzas is worth a visit, while 17 kms southwest of Leonidion we should see the 16th-century monastery of Elona, clinging to a sheer red rock. A guesthouse, at the monastery, welcomes visitors. Here, in this delightful region of Cynuria, ends our tour of fascinating Arcadia.

LACONIA

HISTORY

ANCIENT SPARTA

LEONIDAION - ACROPOLIS - SANCTUARY OF ORTHIA

MENELAEION

SANCTUARY OF APOLLO

VAPHEIO TOMB

MYSTRAS - MONEMVASIA

THE SURROUNDING AREA

(NEAPOLIS-ELAPHONISSOS - KYTHERA)

ZARAKAS AREA - THE MANI

Our tour through the Peloponnese will now take us through a barren but enthralling landscape. Here, great boulders clad only in wild holm-oak and prickly pear, tumble down into the blue waters of the Mediterranean, Byzantine and Frankish castles cling to the grey rock and proud towers stand watch over humble homes. We shall wander in ancient, deserted fortress towns, girded by walls enclosing silent palaces and little gems of Byzantine churches decorated with beautiful frescoes. We will discover villages lying on the slopes of hills or perched on small plateaux, from where open up magnificent views towards the sea. We will admire the decor of stalactites and stalagmites in fairyland caves with underground lakes, explore the valley of the Eurotas river, where the ancient Spartans used to train daily so as to be always ready for war if the need arose. We will wander in the land where the Dioscuri were born, and their sister, Helen the Fair, for whose sake the Greeks set out to besiege Troy. All these we shall discover, as we explore beautiful Laconia.

HISTORY

According to archaeological finds, the region between Mt. Parnon and Mt. Taygetus was probably inhabited between 6000 and 3000 BC. The Neolithic settlements were succeeded by Bronze Age settlements (3000/2800-1100 BC) - Phari, Amyclae, Therapne in the upper valley of the Eurotas, Pellana further north, and further south, coastal Elos - the harbour-town of Amyclae - Boiae, Las, etc. According to mythology, the first inhabitants of Laconia were the Leleges, under their king Lelegas, who later mixed with the Achaeans of Argos. In 1100 BC, at the time of the descent of the Dorians into the Peloponnese, a small Dorian group of about 2000 warriors, under their leader

Aristodemos, settled in the northernmost part of the Eurotas valley, on the site where Sparta was later founded.

A number of the older, Achaean inhabitants abandoned their homeland, while others remained as serfs (Helots). The Dorians of Laconia, determined to retain their racial purity, lived in a state of constant preparedness for war, in military camps, and obliged the local population, by which they were not absorbed, to till the land for them, thus creating the class of helots. In the following centuries, the new colonists waged a series of wars against their northern neighbours (8th century), in order to secure their borders against their enemies the Arcadians and the Argives, while the increase in their population towards the middle of the 8th century made it necessary for them to annex other fertile areas. Their military expeditions resulted in the conquest of the fruitful valleys of neighbouring Messenia, and Sparta finally came to control two fifths of the Peloponnese, making it one of the largest of the Greek states of that period. It occupied the entire southern part of the Peloponnese, which included - besides the Laconian area - the districts of Messene to the west and of Thyreatis (the plain of Argos) to the east. Sparta was the centre of this state, which comprised the independent rural settlements of Pitane, Limnae, Mesoa and Cynosura, which were later joined by Amyclae. Gytheion, was the port of Sparta while on the promontory of Taenaron was established a "*psychopompeion*"; a place where departed souls were evoked and manifested themselves to the living.

Sparta's mode of life and government was based on what was known as the laws of Lycurgus, expressed in the *Great Rhetra*. The system was strictly aristocratic, and authority was exercised by the two kings who represented the two royal houses of Sparta, that of the Agiadae and that of the Eurypontidae; by the Senate - that is the Council of Elders, composed of 28 members of sixty years of age and over; the Assembly of Citizens (the *Apella*), which represented the people of Sparta; and finally, after 754/3 BC, by the five Ephors (overseers), one for each of Sparta's *demes*.

Spartan society was composed of three classes - that of the Spartan citizens, that of the *perioeci*, (the "dwellers round about") and that of the helots or serfs. Devotion to the state was taught to the young from an early age. Spartan boys lived at home until they were seven, but thereafter lived together until the age of twenty in groups or "packs", undergoing rigorous training to defend the state, for which, and for the common good, they had to be prepared to sacrifice themselves. They hardened and disciplined their bodies, ate simple meals of the "*melas zomos*" (black broth) and were also taught to read and write, to learn patriotic poems by heart, and to express themselves briefly and concisely (which thenceforth became known as "laconic" speech). They were also taught music and dancing. The attacks of the Spartan army were always carried out to the accom-

Sparta. The view from the hill of the Menelaeion towards the city and the valley of the Eurotas, where the ancient Spartans used to exercise, is magnificent.

On the summit of the hill of Mystras still stands the mighty fortress, while on its slopes can be seen the impressive ruins of the famous Byzantine city.

paniment of the flute. Spartan discipline extended to the women as well, who also underwent state training, to prepare them physically and mentally to become the mothers of good soldiers.
During the 7th and at the beginning of the 6th century BC, Sparta was open to every kind of communication with the outside world. It was an artistic centre, producing vases which soon became well known outside Laconia. Along the coastal areas and in the hinterland of Asia Minor, in Rhodes, in Samos, in northern Africa, Italy and Sicily, works of Spartan craftsmen have been uncovered by archaeological excavations.
The city developed commercial relations with other regions. Its sanctuaries were adorned with works of art made of materials such as ivory, imported from Egypt and the East. Its young people took part in pan-Hellenic games.
Towards the middle of the 6th century BC the power of the five ephors increased in relation to that of the kings. From that time on the Ephorate became a stumbling block, impeding any attempted reforms.
The helots were controlled by means of the institution of the *Krypteia*, or secret police. During the *xenilasia* all non-Spartans were expelled. The circulation of gold and silver coins was prohibited. Sparta turned to isolationism. Life became totally oriented towards military ideals.
Sparta did not take part in the first war of the Persians against the Greeks, but during the second Persian expedition, Sparta assumed the general command of the land army as well as the leadership of the Greek navy. Thanks to the self-sacrifice of the Spartan king, Leonidas, and of his three hundred men, at the battle of Thermopylae, and to the role of Pausanias at the battle of Plateae, Sparta contributed greatly in averting the Persian danger.
After 431-404 BC the Spartans became involved in wars against Athens, known as the Peloponnesian Wars, from which they emerged victorious, but after 395 BC and after a series of military expeditions, the power of the Spartans began to wane. Following the defeat of the Spartans at Leuctra in 370/369 BC at the hands of the Thebans, the coastal towns became increasingly autonomous and, from the beginning of the 2nd century BC, with Roman support, formed the "*koinon*" of the Lacedaemonians, which was later renamed the Koinon of the Free Laconians.
There followed the destructive earthquakes of 375 AD, and a series of barbarian raids - that of the Erulians in 276 AD, of the Visigoths led by Alaric in 396 AD, of the Slavs in the 6th century AD. It was at this time (6th century AD) that the fortress of Monemvasia was established by the Laconians, who sought refuge there from the invaders. In the 6th/7th century AD was built the castle at Tigani, on the southwestern coast of the Mani, and a Byzantine guard installed.
In the 7th and 8th centuries AD the raids of the Arabs continued from the sea, as well

as Slav invasions from the north. In the 10th century, during the lifetime of the famous missionary, St. Nikon (Nikon *o Metanoeite*), the ancient acropolis of Sparta was fortified and became the centre of the region of Lacedaemonia.

In 1248 the Frank, William II de Villehardouin, with Venetian help, seized the town of Monemvasia and became the master of the region of Laconia, including the Mani. In 1249 Villehardouin built Mystras and made it his headquarters. Immediately after the building of Mystras the Franks erected the fortress of Passavas, in 1251 that of Yisterna or Beaufort (at Leuctron in Messenia), and restored the Byzantine castle of the Great Maine or Maina at Tigani. In 1262 William II de Villehardouin was obliged, after the battle of Pelagonia (1259), to cede to the Greek emperor of Nicaea, Michael Palaeologus, the fortresses of Mystras, of Monemvasia, of Maina and of Beaufort. From that time on Mystras became the seat of a Byzantine *kephalé* (head) and from 1348 the capital of the Despotate of the Morea. The inhabitants of Sparta (or Lacedaemonia), moved for safety to Mystras, where the Palaeologan capital was also transported before the end of the 13th century. The period from 1350 until 1460 was the heyday of Mystras. Here dwelt also the neo-Platonic philosopher Georgios (*Plethon*) Gemistos. In 1460, after consecutive Turkish invasions, Mystras was finally taken, as were, in 1481, the castles of Passavas and Zarnata, which controlled the access to the Mani. In 1540 the fortified town of Monemvasia also fell.

In 1605 the Maniots revolted against the Turks and in 1687 Mystras, Monemvasia (in 1690) and the remainder of the Peloponnese passed into the hands of the Venetian general Francesco Morosini. Monemvasia became the seat of the administration of the eparchy of Laconia.

In 1715 the region was taken by the Turks for the second time. In 1821 the clarion call for freedom was sounded in the Mani, to which the entire region eagerly responded. In the early years of the rule of the first king of Greece, Otho, (1831) Mystras was abandoned and Sparta became the capital of Laconia. The town plan was laid out, and the modern town began to be built on the site of the ancient and the early Christian town, on the right bank of the Eurotas river.

SPARTA AND THE SURROUNDING REGION

Modern Sparta is a well laid out and attractive town, spread out below the snow-clad peaks of Mt. Taygetus, the highest mountain of the Peloponnese.

ARCHAEOLOGICAL MUSEUM OF SPARTA

The museum is situated in the centre of the town, in a neo-classical building built in 1875/76 on the designs of the Bavarian architect Hansen. Among its exhibits are votive offerings to the goddess Artemis Orthia, bronze Archaic figurines, sculptures of Archaic and Classical times, mosaic floors of the Roman period etc. (Dionysiou Dafni street, tel.: 0731/28575).

View of Sparta, with the Taygetus in the background.

Above: Geraki, lying at the foot of Mt. Parnon.

Below: Visible, on the hillside, are the ruins of the mighty fortress of Geraki.

To its west, on the road to Kalamata, we find verdant Trypi, at an altitude of 600 m, rich in flowing streams. Near the village is a precipitous rock, which has been identified as the famous Caiadas, from which any Spartan child found to be physically defective or weak was hurled into the ravine. Further south, on one of the many peaks of Mt. Taygetus, at the site of Varvara (1600 m altitude), among verdant fields and forests of tall black pine and fir trees we will find a well-organised mountain refuge, reached from the village of Anogeia.

Southeast of Sparta, at a distance of about 40 kms, lies Geraki, built on the slopes of Mt. Parnon. On the site of the present-day village there stood in antiquity the city of Geronthrae which, as the finds of excavations prove, was inhabited since the Bronze Age. The ruins of the settlement of historic times are more numerous in the lower town where, as Pausanias says, stood the agora. Today, we will find ancient building material set in the masonry of the old churches of the village - Aghios Athanasios and Aghios Ioannis.

East of the village of today, on the summit of a hill, stand the ruins of the castle of Geraki, built in the early 13th century by Guy de Nivelet, baron of the Tsakones, to whom had been ceded in 1209 one of the twelve baronies of the Principality of Achaea, as the Frankish domains in the Peloponnese were called. The castle of Geraki was larger than that of Mystras; it had the shape of an irregular parallelogram and boasted strong towers with projecting parapets and with cisterns for storing water in the event of a siege. Today, besides the walls, can also be seen the ruins of houses and churches. Of these, the best preserved, within the castle, are the churches of St. George and of St. Paraskevi, while in the village can be seen the Byzantine churches of the Evangelistria, of St. Nicholas, of St. John Chrysostom, of the SS Theodore and of the Prophet Elijah.

Northeast of Sparta, on Mt. Parnon, the mountain with the splendid forests and the profusion of wild flowers, we will find at the site of Arnomoussa (1400 m altitude), yet another well-organised mountain refuge, the George Pierce refuge. We will get to it from the village of Vamvakou (49 kms from Sparta) from where a drive of 26 kms along a forest road in good condition will bring us to the refuge.

ANCIENT SPARTA

Of ancient Sparta only a few parts of the foundations of the walls which surrounded the city survive. The walls were built for the first time in 320 BC after the battle of Leuctra in order to protect the city from a possible attack from the north and from the west.

The most clearly distinguishable foundations are to be found to the west, near the new bridge over the river Eurotas, and north, on Klaraki hill. The walls had stone foundations, while the upper structure was of brick and was topped by a kind of covering of well-baked tiles.

According to Polybius, the perimeter of the walls measured 9 kms and, thanks to the tiles which have been found, we know the line they followed.

THE ACROPOLIS

To the north of the present-day town rises the acropolis of ancient Sparta, which was also encircled by a wall dating from the late Roman period.

Of the temples on the citadel described by Pausanias, only a few remains have come to light. Parts of the sanctuary of Athena Chalkioikos, who owes her epithet to the bronze plaques adorning the interior of the temple, have been excavated. It was previously known as the temple of Athena Poliouchos, since the goddess was presumably the patroness of the city. The temple of Athena stood on the summit of the hill of the acropolis and it is believed to have flourished in the 6th and the 5th centuries BC. The parts which have been uncovered are made of large, almost completely unworked stones, without any binding material between them. Exactly below the temple, on the southwestern slope of the hill, stand the ruins of the theatre, almost all of which belong to the Roman period. Only a few traces have survived of an older theatre dating to 200 BC.

Sparta. The sanctuary of Orthia was the place where the children of ancient Sparta received their civic training.

East of the temple of Athena can be seen the ruins of a large church dedicated to Christ Soter, and dating to the 10th century. Here St. Nikon, who, having preached Christianity in Laconia, spent the last years of his life in Sparta, lived the life of a hermit.

SANCTUARY OF ARTEMIS ORTHIA

Southeast of the acropolis and east of the road which leads from Tripolis to Sparta have come to light the ruins of the sanctuary of Artemis Orthia. It stands on the site of the settlement of Limnae, which is why the goddess was also known as Limnatis.

LEONIDAEON

Northwest of the present-day town of Sparta has come to light the Leonidaeon or Tomb of Leonidas. This is an impressive temple-shaped structure of two rooms, built of rectangular, well-dressed stones. Its foundations measure a total of 12.5 m in length and 8.5 m in width.

According to Pausanias, the remains of the famous Spartan general Leonidas were brought here to be buried, forty years after the battle of Thermopylae. Each year memorial speeches were delivered here and games were organised in which only Spartan athletes could take part.

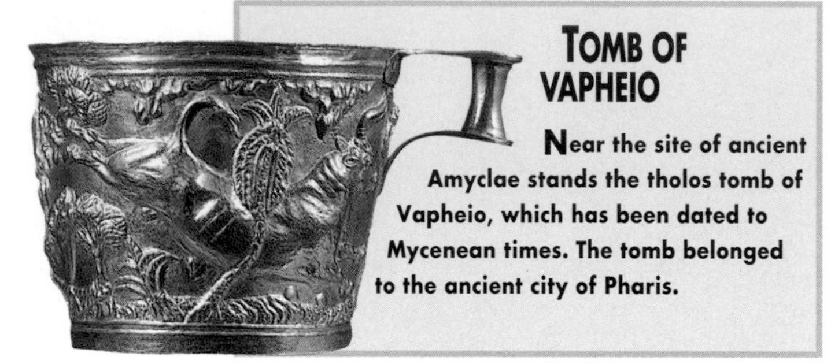

TOMB OF VAPHEIO

Near the site of ancient Amyclae stands the tholos tomb of Vapheio, which has been dated to Mycenean times. The tomb belonged to the ancient city of Pharis.

According to a commentator on Pindar, Orthia was the goddess of salvation of humankind as well as the goddess of fertility. Inscriptions of later years identified her with Artemis. She had a close connection with the children and youth of Sparta. At the age of seven years, when boys left their families, as they were henceforth considered to belong to their city, their state training began, which took place at the sanctuary of Orthia. The younger children took part in three contests, while the youths were subjected, on the altar of the goddess, to the ordeal of flagellation. Of the sanctuary today survive the foundations of the Archaic temple of the early 6th century BC, which underwent a series of restorations until the 3rd century AD, the ruins of two altars - one of them dating from the Archaic period, and the other from the 3rd century AD - as well as the foundations of a Roman horseshoe-shaped amphitheatre, which surrounded the temple on three of its sides.

MENELAEION

Opposite Sparta, on the left bank of the Eurotas, have been preserved traces of the Menelaeion, the temple of Menelaos and his beautiful wife Helen. It is a large pyramid-shaped platform set on top of a hill. On the level ground formed by the platform was found a small edifice, possibly a small temple.

SANCTUARY OF APOLLO

South of Sparta at a distance of 5 kms, on the hill of Aghia Kyriaki, where stands the church of the same name, we shall see the supporting wall and the precinct of the sanctuary of Amyclaean Apollo. The sanctuary belonged to Amyclae, the oldest pre-Doric settlement renowned for the high level of its culture. Amyclae and Pharis were the main centres of the Achaean kingdom of Lacedaemon.

MYSTRAS

THE BYZANTINE CITY

We leave Sparta behind and drive in the direction of the mighty Taygetus, the "masculine" mountain, as the poet Nikephoros Vrettakos calls it.

As we drive along, the first silhouettes of the ruined houses, palaces and castle of Mystras begin to take shape. As we approach, these shapes become more clearly defined. By the tall cypress trees we can make out the red domes of the churches, the walls, the remains of the resplendent palaces which housed the courts of Villehardouin, of the Cantacuzenes and the Palaeologues.

Soon we shall be following the narrow cobblestone paths along which, six or so centuries ago, the great neo-Platonic philosopher George *Plethon* Gemistos would have wandered, deep in thought, devising the methods he would propose to the lords of the Despotat as to how they could better face the invaders - proposals which, in the event, were not taken into account. On the fateful day of the 30th May, 1460, the impregnable castle, after a series of internal conflicts, squabbles and intrigues, fell into the hands of the Turks. No longer would the lovely princesses - the Frankish wives of the Byzantine nobles - look out over the valley from their balconies. Silence fell over the rooms of the castle, and another bastion of Hellenism was lost. Today, with a thrill of emotion and awe, we can still admire the beautiful churches of Mystras, with their superb frescoes depicting Christ and the Holy Virgin, companies of

venerable saints and hosts of angels. We shall climb up the steep slope to visit the palace, threading our way through ruined mansions. We shall even reach the top of the hill, where the battlements and towers of the once mighty citadel still stand.
The history of Mystras begins in 1249, when the Frankish prince William II de Villehardouin decided to build a fortress from which he could control the Morea. His choice fell upon the hill known as Myzithras, west of Sparta - a site of crucial importance, because from there he could protect the area from invasion by the Slav tribes which had settled on Mt. Taygetus. On the plateau on the summit of the hill he erected a mighty castle which today, after a series of interventions by the Byzantines and the Turks, bears only a slight resemblance to Villehardouin's stronghold.
Below the castle, on a plateau on the north side of the hill, Villehardouin built his own palace, while, around the square in front of it were erected the first houses of the town. The palace of William and of the later rulers, as well as the houses around it, were encircled by strong walls, which started west of the castle. On this side the walls are reinforced by a series of towers, and have two entrance gates, which are also protected by towers. The walls come down to the north edge of the plateau, continue to the east, pass by the monastery of the Pantanassa and end up at the gorge which opens up on the south side of the hill.
The settlement surrounded by these walls is known as the Upper Town, and to it led two gates, the eastern one being the Nauplion gate and the western one the Monemvasia gate. The two gates were connected by a three-metres-wide avenue that passed in front of the palace and divided the town into two. On the northern side were the palace and the noblemen's houses, and on the southern side those of

View of Mystras. Standing out on the hilltop is the imposing castle.

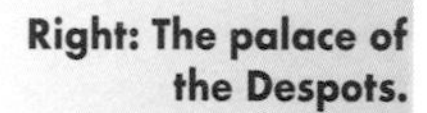

Right: The palace of the Despots.

Below: The church of the Hodegetria (Aphendiko)

the middle-class families. As the years went by, the Upper Town grew and houses and churches began to be built outside the walls as well. Thus was created the "Middle" or "Lower Town", which was in turn surrounded by a new wall starting from the west, from the church of the Hodegetria (also known as Aphendiko), coming down east and, passing by the Metropolis or cathedral, ending up at the monastery of the Peribleptos. In 1262 Mystras passed into Byzantine hands and became the seat of the annually appointed military governor of the Morea. As the town grew in importance, the post of governor became a permanent one from 1308 on, the first governor being a member of the Cantacuzene family. His successor, Andronicus Palaeologus (1316-1321), extended the domination of Mystras all the way to Akova and Karytaina.

In 1348 the emperor John VI Cantacuzene created the Despotat of Mystras under the leadership of his son Manuel. In 1384, Theodore, the son of the reigning emperor of the time, John V Palaeologus, overthrew the Despot Demetrius Cantacuzene and the suzerainty of Mystras passed into the hands of the family of the Palaeologues. Thus, the relationship between Constantinople and the Despotat - which at that time extended over al-

most the entire Peloponnese - became a closer one. Between the 13th and the 15th centuries, Mystras was the city which was in closest contact with Constantinople and the Imperial Palace.

The brothers of Theodore Palaeologus, Constantine and Thomas, became despots of other despotats founded in the Morea. The seat of Constantine was at Glarentza (1429) and that of Thomas at Kalavryta (1430).

Following a succession of Turkish raids and internal quarrels among the despots of the Morea, the Despot of Mystras, Demetrius, surrendered Mystras to the Ottoman sultan Mohammed II in May 1460. The town began to decline. From time to time it was used as the seat of a pasha, while it was also the permanent administrative centre of a *vilayet*. In 1687 it was seized by the Venetian, Francesco Morosini. In 1715 it was recaptured by the Turks. In 1770 it enjoyed a short period of freedom, but was shortly afterwards destroyed by the Albanians. It was liberated again in 1821, but in 1825 was once more burned down by Ibrahim Pasha.

After the foundation of Sparta in 1831, Mystras gradually began to be abandoned by its inhabitants. Those that did not move to the new town settled in the village of Neos Mystras, in the fertile valley south of the Byzantine citadel.

We shall now begin our climb up the narrow streets of the once mighty capital. On our right we see the Metropolis of St. Demetrius. The church, which was initially a basilica divided into three aisles, has not retained its original form. This was altered in the 15th century, and today it is a three-aisled basilica on the ground floor and a cross-in square church with a dome on the upper storey.

Set in the floor, beneath the dome, is a slab carved with a double-headed eagle - the symbol of the Palaeologan dynasty - on which, according to tradition, Constantine, the last of the Palaeologan emperors, stood when he was crowned.

The frescoes of the church, executed in a variety of styles, belong to the late 13th and the early 14th centuries. The fresco in the *diakonikon* depicts a host of angels worshipping God and lauding him. Their billowing mantles delineate their graceful forms. In the south aisle is portrayed St. Anne, the mother of the Virgin, resting after giving birth and receiving the care of her handmaidens. In the northern aisle St. Demetrius and St. Nestor are shown being

The Metropolis (St. Demetrius). The interior is decorated with frescoes of the last quarter of the 13th century.

found in Mystras, epistyles of iconostases and other architectural elements similar to those we shall see in the churches we shall be visiting.
On our left, as we leave the Metropolis, we see the ruins of Byzantine houses and also another church, that of the Evangelistria.
Throughout the two centuries during which Mystras was the Byzantine capital of the Peloponnese, many churches, monasteries and chapels were erected, which have been restored with laborious and loving care. They were adorned with frescoes which represent all the tendencies of the art of their period in the capital of Byzantium. The church of the Evangelistria is a two-column cross-in-square type of church, like the Peribleptos and St. Sophia, and is believed to have been built in the 14th or the 15th century.
We now climb towards the northern side of the enclosure. Here we find the two most impressive churches of Mystras - the church of the Saints Theodore and that of the Virgin Hodegetria, known as Aphendiko, both of them belonging to the monastery of the Brontochion.
The church of the SS Theodore, one of the oldest of Mystras, is an octagonal church, a type which is found in grand Byzantine

cruelly tortured, to earn the crown of martyrdom. In the narthex are shown sinners suffering the fires of hell, in a grandiose Second Coming. The decoration of the church is complemented by sculptured compositions of various periods and styles, on the capitals and on the iconostasis.
In one wing of the church there is a museum, in which are housed capitals, representative of the various types usually

Left page, above: The Saints Theodore.

Left page, below: The Evangelistria.

Left: The Pantanassa.

monuments. Its construction was probably begun in 1290, under its abbot Daniel, and completed by the abbot Pachomios in 1296. In the north-eastern chapel there is a tomb opposite the representation of Manuel Palaeologus, who is portrayed wearing a blue robe girded by a yellow sash, and kneeling in supplication before the Virgin and Child. Legend has it that the tomb belonged to the emperor Manuel II Paleologus himself, although we know that he died in 1425 and was buried in the monastery of the Pantocrator in Constantinople.

Aphendiko began to be built by Pachomios in 1310. The ground floor is a basilica divided into three aisles and the upper storey a cross-in-square church with five domes. In the northern chapel there are two tombs: one is that of the Despot Theodore II Palaeologus, who, in the last years of his life, became a monk. On the wall above the tomb, Theodore is represented twice -on the left in the sumptuous robes of a despot, and on the right in the simple habit of a monk. The other tomb belongs to Pachomios. On the wall is depicted the abbot himself, on his knees, offering the church to the Virgin.

In the northwestern chapel, which has no windows, all the walls are covered with inscriptions copied from imperial decrees (*chrysobulls*) of the first decades of the 14th century, recording the goods and privileges granted to the monastery. As we enter the church, we are impressed by the grandeur of the place and the well-thought-out disposition of the painted cycles and scenes which lead the gaze all the way up to the dome. Imposing prophets with burning eyes, serene martyrs, and angels in lively motion, holding the mandorla surrounding the figure of Christ the Lord are part of the mural decoration of Aphendiko.

East of the church of Aghioi Theodoroi an uphill path leads to the church of the Pantanassa, while, passing under the gate which led to Monemvasia, we come to the Lower Town and the palaces.

The buildings constituting the residence of

The Peribleptos, built under the rock.

the despots stand on level ground on the western side of the hill. They consist of two wings joined at right angles to each other on the northern part of the small plateau, thus closing the western and eastern sides and forming a sheltered square. In the wide space created, large public gatherings were held during the period of Frankish and Byzantine rule, while the area was used as a market place during Ottoman rule.

The edifices on the southern side belong to a later period, and date from the Ottoman occupation.

Of the palace buildings, the oldest is the eastern wing. It is thought to have been built by Villehardouin between 1249 and 1261. The pointed arched windows lining the façade and the narrow balcony, evidence Western European influences.

Adjoining this building was built in later years (1350-1400), perhaps in the years of the Cantacuzenes, a wing in which are to be found the apartments of the despots. It had large rooms and on the second floor an oratory decorated with frescoes. In the northern part of the building there was an open porch, supported by five square piers and decorated with the small arches characteristic of the architecture of Mystras. The roof of the porch formed a balcony with a splendid view over the entire valley. The adjacent northwest wing of the palace was built in the time of the Palaeologi (1400-1460) and consists of a single large edifice. On its façade it had a double-storied porch, of which only the bases of the piers can be seen. This porch also formed a balcony.

The Palaeologan wing consisted of a semi-basement level and of two storeys.

On the first floor there were eight vaulted rooms which did not communicate with each other and were perhaps offices. The entire second floor formed a single large space measuring 36 x 10 metres. On the wall of the eastern side one can still see the alcove where stood the throne and, above, the points which supported the canopy. A low bench runs along the walls of the room; here used to sit the fine noblemen and gentle princesses who were invited to the formal gatherings. The room was very well lit, because a row of arched windows were set in the long eastern façade, while just above them was a second row of openings. Along the western wall there were eight fireplaces which heated the room and the whole palace in the cold winter days. Southwest of the palace we see the church of St. Sophia. We are now near the highest gate leading to the castle.

St. Sophia was the palace church and the *Katholikon* of the monastery of Christ Zoödotes, founded by the first despot of Mystras, Manuel Cantacuzene. It belongs to the simple two-column type of church. Colonnades run along two of its sides (north and south). At the end of the northern colonnade rises the bell tower. Of its three storeys only two have survived as well as the narrow inside stairway. The building with the many openings on the northwestern side of the bell tower was the refectory of the monastery.

West of St. Sophia we find the gate leading up to the castle. From the top the view is superb. Our gaze reaches all the way to the range of Mt. Parnon, down to the Eurotas flowing among the reeds and poplars and surrounded by the fertile plain of Sparta. We pass through the entrance of the citadel and find ourselves inside it.

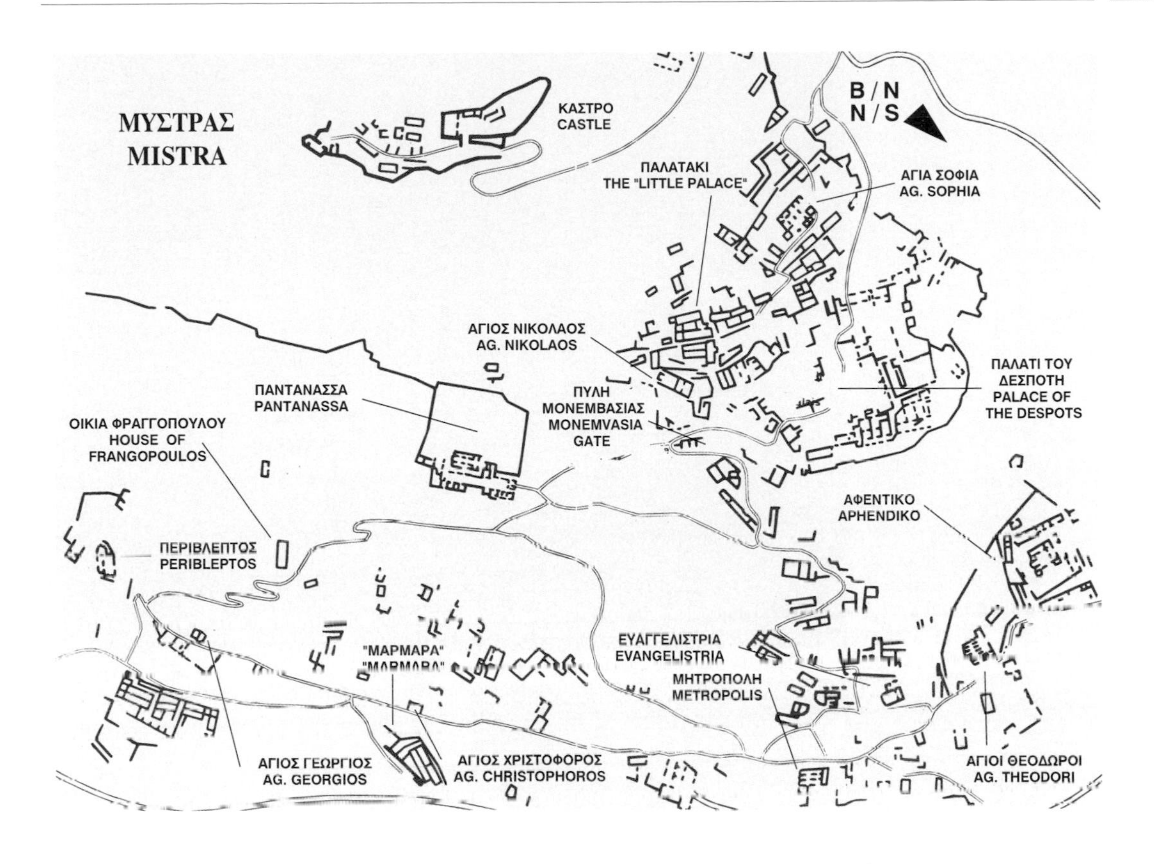

As we see it today, the impregnable castle has a double wall. In the space between the two enclosures, which is the largest space, we see ruins of houses of the Turkish period and a lookout tower on the southern end of the wall where the sentry could command a wide view over the southern approaches to the citadel.
The interior enclosure occupies the highest point of the hill (at an altitude of 621 m). Here stood the residence of the governor of the citadel. Northwest of it have survived the ruins of a chapel, while on the western edge of the plateau another lookout tower allows the sentry to command the view to the west.
We leave the citadel and begin our descent. On our right and left are the ruins of Byzantine houses, among which are some noble mansions. The houses of the Byzantine period were two-storied and had a gabled roof. Some had a balcony on their façade, with a view over the valley, while the houses of the nobles also had a strong tower for protection. The ground floor was the stable or storeroom. It had no windows, only narrow openings. Part of the ground floor was often vaulted and served as a covered passageway for passers-by. On the upper floor there was a spacious room with large windows and niches in the walls which served as cupboards. The arch is a characteristic element of the architecture of Mystras. All the windows of the houses were either arched or surmounted by an arch.
East of St. Sophia and just before we get to the 17th-century chapel of St. Nicholas we come to the ruins of the largest of the houses of Mystras and the most complex, the so-called "Palataki" (little palace). It consisted of two buildings. The northern one, which incorporated a three-storied tower, dates from around 1300, while the southern one was built later, in the 14th century. We continue to wind our way down eastwards. From above we can see the monastery of the Pantanassa, founded by John Frangopoulos, the chief minister of the Despotat. We come to the

Right: The Metropolis. Northern aisle: The Martyrdom of St. Demetrius.

Below; The Peribleptos. North apse. The Touching of Thomas.

church, which stands on a piece of level ground. Built in the early 15th century, it impresses one with its elegance and grace. It belongs to the type of the three-aisled basilica on the lower part, with a five-domed cross-in-square above. There are porches on its northern and eastern sides. From one, which has survived in its entirety, we have a view over the valley. It is supported by three columns and is covered by narrow barrel vaults with a dome in the centre. Of the other porch outside the narthex only traces of the base of the wall have been preserved. Arches, windows and garlands in relief grace the exterior surfaces of the church. However, it is in the tall four-storied bell-tower in the northwestern corner that the Frankish influence is most apparent. On the walls of the lower floor of the church we can see illustrated the 24 *Oikoi* (strophes)of the *Akathistos* Hymn, painted in later years (17th-18th centuries). Of the original frescoes, the Annunciation, the Entry into Jerusalem, the Ascension, are painted in glowing colours and are full of movement. The Pantanassa today is a hospitable monastery inhabited by kindly nuns, the only living presence in Mystras.

All about us, as we walk along the narrow streets and pass by the vaulted passages with their round or pointed arches, wild ivy and weeds entwine themselves around these time-worn ruins and cover them, mindful only of their own natural laws.

Leaving behind us the mansion of the Frangopouloi built in the 15th century, whose balcony with its arched windows looking out over the Eurotas valley is still in place, we come to the monastery of the Peribleptos, built against the steep rock. Today all that survives is the church of the monastery, with its chapels and the Frankish-type tower, which served as the refectory. The church is cruciform and domed, but it presents certain particularities due to the form of the terrain. The main entrance faces north instead of west and the shape of the church is not the usual rectangular one. What is most impressive as we gaze on the frescoes of the Peribleptos, is the richness of the scenes embracing large groups of figures. The three cycles of representations (the Eucharistic cycle, the cycle of the Passion and the Mariological cycle) are intermingled. In the representation of the Nativity we note the refined grace of the Virgin resting, under the gaze of the lauding angels. The fresco, evincing a wonderful feeling for colour and rich in emotion, is one of the most technically perfect compositions in Mystras.

Descending from the Peribleptos we make our way towards the site known as Marmara. On our left are the ruins of a two-storied mansion belonging to the Lascaris family, one of the most illustrious families of Mystras. Near the Lascaris house we can still see a fountain, crowned by a pointed arch and adorned with a decorative marble band, dating from the period of Turkish rule. From here begins a paved path which winds up the hill and reaches the Pantanassa. Here ends our ramble along the narrow streets of the "impregnable citadel" and its long-lost world. For a moment we seemed to catch the rustle of brocaded Byzantine robes and the clatter of horses' hooves on cobbled pavements, as, through the castle gates, passed the retinue of Constantine Palaeologus accompanying their sovereign on his journey to the Capital, where he would become the last emperor, and the most tragic of them all.

The Pantanassa. East apse: The Entry into Jerusalem.

MONEMVASIA

On the edge of the peninsula which faces the Myrtoön sea and ends at Cape Maleas, stands the proud citadel of Monemvasia clinging to its formidable rock.
In the time of Pausanias, this rocky promontory, rising to a height of 300 metres, was called *Minoa akra*. Later was built here the Byzantine citadel, inaccessible from the north, east and south, which in time became still another impregnable fortress of medieval times. It was called Monemvasia or Monovasia, from the words *moni* (only) and *embasia* (entrance or access), because it was only accessible from the west, on which side a narrow causeway linked it to the mainland. This narrow strip of land, part of which was taken up by an arched stone bridge measuring 130 m in length, was well protected by a tower standing on the citadel end. In the 6th century AD, during the reign of the emperor Mauricius, inhabitants of the town of Sparta fleeing from the Slav invaders came to settle on the plateau on the summit of the rock.
Soon, a second settlement was established lower down, in the concave southern side of the rock. Shortly, thanks to the commercial activities of its inhabitants, this settlement quickly developed into an important harbour and into a Byzantine site of strategic importance, on account of which the Byzantine emperors granted the town a number of privileges.
In the 12th century the castle of Monemvasia controlled the area of the southeast-

The rock of Monemvasia as it appears from the mainland opposite.

ern Peloponnese. In 1248, after a siege lasting three years, it was taken by Villehardouin, who held it until 1262, when he was forced to cede it to the Byzantines.
The 14th century was a period of great economic prosperity, due partly to the particular privileges granted to the town by the Byzantine emperor, partly to the successful commercial activities of the inhabitants and partly to the town's merchant fleet. Among the basic products carried by the Monemvasian ships was the famous "Malmsey" wine produced in the area - the "Monemvasitis" of the Byzantines, or the "Malvasia" of the Venetians.
From 1460 to 1464 Monemvasia was under papal domination, and in 1464 it was taken by the Venetians for the first time. Commerce suffered from the Turko-Venetian wars, and this in turn affected the economy of Monemvasia.
In 1540 Monemvasia surrendered to the Turks. Many noble families abandoned their town, some settling in Venice, others in Corfu or Crete. In 1690, after a lengthy siege, the town once again surrendered to the Venetians and became the capital of one of the four *eparchies* (districts) of the Kingdom of the Morea.
Many descendants of the inhabitants who had abandoned the town during the first period of Turkish occupation, now returned to their family homes, and with

Monemvasia: The lower town encircled by its defensive wall.

Coloured lithograph of Monemvasia. Théodore de Moncel. *Excursion par terre d'Athènes à Nauplie.* Paris (1845). Gennadius Library. →

TTA DI MALVASIA IN MOREA
3
2
1

them came many Cretans. In 1715 the town once again fell into Turkish hands. During the second period of Turkish occupation the town began to decline. Many of its inhabitants left. Finally, in 1823, it was liberated from the Turks after an arduous siege.

A wall fortified by towers, which was restored at various times, surrounded the town built on the summit of the rock (Pano Polis or Goulas). At first, access to the

The church of St. Sophia, built by Andronicus Paleaologus, still stands on the edge of the cliff.

goulas was from the north, where ended a walled path starting from the bridge which linked the rock to the coast opposite. This entrance was closed by a wall during the first period of Turkish rule.

The upper town was the seat of the governor of the town. Besides the buildings destined for military use, here, in Byzantine times, were also the residences of the nobles. There were also churches and chapels and a Roman Catholic monastery which, during the period of Turkish rule, was converted into a mosque. Many small cistems supplied the town with water. Of the public and private edifices of the upper town only ruins have survived, but these still testify to the glorious past of the Byzantine and Venetian citadel.

Right page, below: The church of the Christ "Helkomenos" ("being dragged to Calvary").

In the lower town, the existence of which is recorded for the first time in the 10th century, were the homes of the sailors. This town was also surrounded by walls. To the south were the sea walls with jutting towers and a gate leading to a quay. On the western and eastern sides, the upper end of two fortified parallel walls running vertically to the sea wall, reached the level of the rock which rises sharply above the lower town. The lower town communicated with the upper town by means of a fortified way (the *voltes*).

The lack of space is manifest in the lower town. The houses are built very close to each other. There are no squares other than the square in front of the cathedral, which in medieval times was smaller. The roads were narrow, with as few steps as possible, so that the mules, which were the main means of transport, could easily negotiate them. The houses often extended over the streets forming vaulted archways, the so-called *dromikès*.

Our walk through the streets of the medieval town is enchanting - narrow cobblestone streets, churches, two-storied and three-storied houses with arched doors and windows, with verandas looking out over the wide expanse of the Aegean and with tiled roofs and characteristic Venetian chimney-pots, delight us at each turn of the road.

Of the churches it is worth visiting the Byzantine church of St. Sophia in the upper town, built on the edge of the rock at the end of the 13th century by Andronicus II Palaeologus. In the lower town, the church of the same period (13th century) also built by Andronicus and dedicated to Christ Helkomenos, is today the cathedral of the town. It belongs to the type of the domed basilica. Other interesting churches are those of St. Nicholas (18th century) and Panaghia Kritikia. In the building of the

Left: View of the lower town from the castle.

Below: In the evenings the narrow streets and tiny square of the town offer a different picture.

mosque, which stands opposite the cathedral, is housed a small museum.
On the mainland opposite the rock, near the bridge, has sprung up the modern coastal settlement of Gephyra.

THE SURROUNDING REGION

At a distance of 6 kms from Monemvasia lies the coastal town of Neapolis. It is situated on the southwestern coast of the Maleas peninsula, on the side washed by the waters of the Laconian Gulf. The town was built by inhabitants of the village of Farakla, on the site of the ancient city of Boeae, an important Spartan port. Boeae reached the height of its prosperity when it was a member of the *Koinon* of the Eleutherolakones (Free Laconians).
Vestiges of the ancient city are still to be seen in the innermost part of the bay on which has been built the new town of Neapolis. On the western side, the gulf is closed by the island of Elaphonissos (Deer Island), which in ancient times formed a peninsula known as *Onou Gnathos* (Ass's Jaw). The strip of land linking the peninsula to the mainland was, eventually, covered by the sea and thus was formed the small island with its marvellous sandy beaches. Its northernmost point lies at a distance of approximately 500 metres from the Peloponnesian coast, to which it is linked by boats plying between the island and Neapolis.
A little further south lies the island of Kythera, the isle of love and fabled birthplace of Aphrodite. The Phoenicians who came to the island named it Porphyroussa, or Porphyris, after the many marine snails of the same name found in abundance along its shores, from which the famous Tyrian purple dye was extracted.
Around 2000 BC the Minoans founded a settlement at the place called Kastri, which flourished until the 15th century BC. After the Minoans, came the Phoenicians, who established trading posts. They were followed, in the 10th to the 8th century, by Dorians of Argos, and later, in the 6th century, by the Spartans, who took Kythera and established a permanent guard there. In antiquity the capital of the island was the city of Cythera, which was situated at

Above: The bridge and the rock of Monemvasia.

Right, above: Kythera, the fortress and the Chora.

Right, below: Kapsali, the port of Chora.

the place called Palaiokastro, on the southern slope of the hill, on the top of which was the acropolis of the city. The whitewashed houses and white bell-towers blend harmoniously with the grey pile of the castle which watches over them. In the distance, within the deepest curve of the bay, can be made out its port town, Kapsali.

The strong fortress was built in 1503 over an older Byzantine fort. In the distance stretches the Cretan Sea, while the delicate tracery of the coasts forms sheltered inlets with attractive beaches. At a short distance from the village of Mylopotamos, on the western side of the island, we may visit the cave of Aghia Sophia - where there is a little church of the same name - with its small lakes adorned with multicoloured clusters of stalactites and stalagmites.

THE ZARAKAS REGION

North of Monemvasia we shall encounter the ruins of the ancient city of Epidaurus Limera, today known as Palaia Monemvasia. The city was inhabited since ancient times, as is proven by the discovery in the area of chamber tombs of the Mycenean period.

The city was particularly prosperous in the 5th or 4th century BC, from which time date the imposing polygonal walls which surrounded the city and its acropolis.

North of Epidaurus Limera stretches the region of Zarakas. Here, in ancient times, stood the coastal city of Zarakas (today's Gerakas) and, a little further to the north, on the site of present-day Kyparissi, that of Cyphanta.

In Pausanias' time, Zarakas was a member of the *Koinon* of the Eleutherolaconians. The remains of the walls which are visible today date from the end of the 5th or 4th century.

The picturesque modern settlement of the harbour of Gerakas, built to the north of the closed bay, on the site of ancient Zarakas, serves today as a "landing stage" for the villages of the interior: Gerakas, Aghios Ioannis, Reichia and the other mountain settlements.

In this lovely mountainous region, dominated by the fir-clad peaks of Chionovouni and fringed by a steep rocky coastline, interrupted by the beaches of Gerakas and Kochylas, we shall visit the picturesque villages of Gerakas, Aghios Ioannis, Reichia, Harakas and Kyparissi, with their traditional stone houses with the tiled roofs and the doors and windows surrounded by coloured frames, offering intense chromatic contrasts, mostly in combinations of indigo and ochre.

ARCHAEOLOGICAL MUSEUM OF KYTHERA

Among its exhibits are Minoan vases, Mycenean pottery, amphorae and sculptures of the Archaic and Classical periods. Tel. 0735/31739.

THE MANI

Grey, bare rocks punctuating the thirsty landscape, stunted, tortured olive trees, struggling to survive in this barren land, dry-stone walls in irregular shapes, prickly pear, kermes oak and thorn bushes lending a bit of variety to the stony plains- this is the Mani.

Tall towers, built of stone - the only material found here in abundance - defend what for the Maniots was always the greatest good: freedom.

Speaking of the Mani, D. Vassiliadis says: "...The region is narrow, meagre, dry and barren, the land unable to feed its people, water in short supply and collected in cisterns, grass is scarcer still. The inhabitants are crowded together in a thirsty, stony, rugged, narrow space. They must jostle in order to survive."

The daily struggle for survival against unfavourable conditions is marked on the spare figures of the people of the Mani. Rebellious, strict and uncompromising, they remind one of the ancient Spartans, who could not tolerate weaklings and who sent off their youth going to the wars with the injunction that they return "with their shield or upon it", victorious or dead. Endemic in the Mani was also the vendetta, the unwritten law which determined human relations. The defence of one's honour was a paramount duty, a duty which was translated into revenge and subsequently into a vendetta.

The vendetta would go on for years. One death, one injustice, was repaid with another death. New links were added to the bloody chain, which only broke when the score was even on both sides. Then only could there be peace and reconciliation, when all debts had been paid.

And when death knocked at the door, the departed soul was sped on its way to the nether world by women in starkest mourning, singing their laments. Because, as they said, "*grief breaks out in doleful moans, and moans in lamentations*", and also: "*smoke causes eyes to weep and storms bring lamentations*". Beating their breasts as they sang their interminable improvised dirges, they expressed their sorrow in eloquent tones, as they sat around in a circle, speaking in verse and pouring out all their pent-up emotions: *"O Georgie lad, how mourns your home, and how laments your courtyard, while from the tiles above your roof a poisoned streamlet trickles; and I am thirsty and will drink and for your love will perish."**

All this world, living by its own rules, was isolated and buttressed, as were the towers of the Mani. Tall, shuttered, inaccessible, with only a few small windows and a good number of embrasures, these strongholds, the like of which is found nowhere else in Greece, were always ready to confront the Turk or any other invader. Impregnable, they lifted up their three, four, or even five storeys, putting up an obstinate resistance against anyone who attempted to reduce them. The approaching enemy was met with a bullet or with scalding water or boiling oil poured from its machicolations. The tower, which was both a residence and a fortified stronghold, might be standing alone or in a group with others. No conqueror ever set foot in the villages the Maniots founded. The Mani did not submit to the Turks, as did the rest of Laconia. By paying a yearly tribute, its inhabitants managed to maintain a peculiar status, which ensured the region's autonomy and allowed them to carry arms.

On March 17, 1821, the start of the revolution was proclaimed in the town of Areopolis and, in 1826- a critical year in the struggle for independence- the Maniots took part in the battles waged on their territory and contributed to their victorious outcome.

The special landscape of the Mani is in perfect harmony with the particular towers and fortified houses, which are a characteristic feature of the region, and the size of which corresponded to the power and position within the community held by the family that owned them. Up until 1840 the fortified houses were single-storied or double-storied. The primary concern in their construction was that of safety, after which care was taken to satisfy the essential needs of the inhabitants.

In the two-storey houses, the ground floor was reserved for the livestock, while the upper floor served as the habitation of the family. Later, outbuildings were added in the courtyard, which were used as storerooms, the oven for baking bread and food, stables and pens for the animals.

From 1840 to 1870 more storeys were added to these fortress-like houses, while from 1890 to 1915 newer houses of one or two stories were also built. The houses were protected by fortified towers, built at strategic points in the settlement, or further afield. In the beginning, the towers were two- or three-storied square or rectangular structures. They controlled and defended the region in the case of an enemy attack. Their construction is believed to date from between 1770 and 1830, while in the southern Mani they continued to be built until 1880.

Besides the military towers and the fortified houses, the settlements contained churches, streets and small squares known as "rougés". As the cultivation of the olive-tree and the processing of the product spread, from 1880 on, oil-presses were also added to the settlements.

At strategic points, either by the sea or inland, rose fortified complexes, such as those belonging to the Kapetanakis family at Trikotsovo, or to the Petreas and Mourtzinos clans in Pano Kardamyli, etc. These comprised, besides the residence, a fortified tower and other ancillary buildings. They were surrounded by a defensive enceinte and belonged to chieftains or beys. In the construction of these Maniot buildings, the use of wood was limited to floors and ceilings. Stone was used for the walls and vaults, while slate was used for the roofs.

Particularly interesting is the social structure of the Maniot communities in the 18th and 19th centuries. Each settlement was made up of the members of one group- the clan- united by their descent, through the father, from a common ancestor, and

***By Costas Parsayiannis, "Maniot laments and songs" (Athens 1928). From the book by D. Vassiliadis, "Οδοιπορία στον ελληνικό χώρο", Athens 1979.**

The traditional settlement of Vathia, in the Mani. The houses here, as in the other Maniot settlements, combined the characteristics of a house and a fortress. They were tall, closed in and inaccessible. They had more than one storey, small windows and many loopholes.

divided into smaller groups, the last in the pyramid being the family. These groups were very closely knit and were characterised by very strong solidarity among their members. Most important to the development and dominance of the clan was the production of male children - "guns", as men able to bear arms were called. On matters concerning the action of the group or its relations with other groups, competent to make decisions was a council made up of adult males, the "*gherontiki*" (council of elders).

Our first stop on our journey of exploration of the Mani, which is divided into two regions - the Deep Mani or Laconian Mani and the Outer Mani or Messenian Mani - is the port of Gytheion, the harbour town of Sparta. Here, the green of the olive groves, alleviates the roughness of the landscape. The town is built amphitheatrically along the slopes and at the foot of Koumaro hill. The two- and three-storied brick-tiled houses lined along the quay are reflected in the calm blue waters of the Laconian gulf, while caiques and fishing boats rock gently in the harbour.

Tavernas along the sea-front offer fresh, succulent, charcoal-grilled fish and seafood. A causeway links the shore to what was once the islet of Cranae, now known as Marathonissi (Fennel island). The pine trees that cover it are all bent, following the course of the wind. In its centre stands the Tzannetakis tower, restored by the National Tourism Organisation, and now a Historical and Folk Art Museum. It was built in 1829 by the general of the War of Independence, Tzannetakis Grigorakis. It consists of a three-storied tower with a terrace, battlements and four circular corner turrets. Adjacent to the imposing edifice on its northern side, is a long and narrow two-storied residence. North of the modern town lay the ancient city of Gytheion. Among the ruins that have come to light, those of the ancient theatre stand out.

The Archaeological and Byzantine Collection of Gytheion is housed in rooms of the city's town hall (tel. 0733/22427). The exhibits date from various periods

Left page: Gytheion and Cranae. We can see the lighthouse and the Tzannetakis tower.

Left: View of Gytheion from Cranae.

Below: The ancient theatre of Gytheion.

and have come from excavations carried out in the surrounding area.

Further south, on the road leading to Areopolis, crowning a steep hill, stand the lead-grey walls of the castle of Passava (from the French military command "passe avant"). It was built by the French nobleman Jean de Neuilly in 1254. At the foot of the hill lay the ancient city of Las.

The castle of Passava, which controlled the eastern pass to the Mani, changed masters several times. In 1262 it was occupied by the Byzantines, in 1480 it was seized by the Turks, and in 1685 by the Venetians. In 1715 it was recaptured by the Turks and in 1780 it was taken by the Maniots. This stronghold, as is the case

Below: View of Areopolis.

Right: Areopolis. The church of the Holy Taxiarchs, with its tower-like belfry.

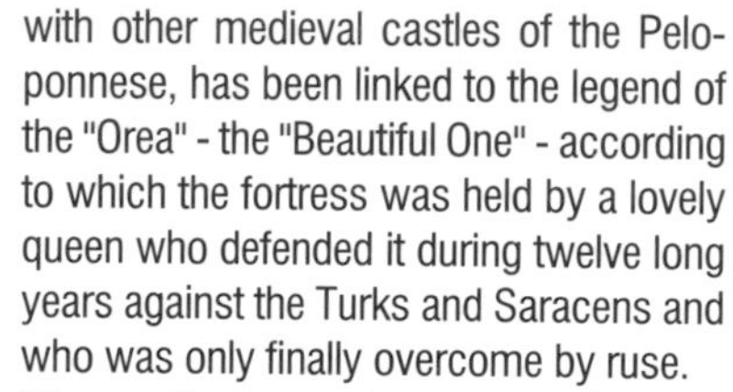

with other medieval castles of the Peloponnese, has been linked to the legend of the "Orea" - the "Beautiful One" - according to which the fortress was held by a lovely queen who defended it during twelve long years against the Turks and Saracens and who was only finally overcome by ruse.

We continue our journey south-westwards. The landscape now changes; bare rocks now replace the earth, the olive trees give way to dry-stone walls and prickly pear.

Twenty-six kilometres north-west of Gytheion we come to Areopolis, the city of Ares, the god of War, lying in the shadow of the grey mountain. Worth seeing is the church of the Holy Taxiarchs (the Archangels), with its tower-like belfry. Old Maniot towers, stone houses with tiled roofs and the Kapetanakos tower, which has been restored by the National Tourism Organisation and now functions as a guest house, adorn the town.

To the south-west of Areopolis, lying on the coast by the Laconian Gulf, we find Kotronas, a picturesque traditional village. As we move southwards we come across more and more towers. The grey mountains succeed one another, as do the small settlements. Along the coast we encounter small coves with deep blue waters and sparkling white pebbles.

We come to Porto Kayio, on the south-eastern end of the Taenaron peninsula. Here the red rock forms a striking contrast with the clear blue of the sea. On the mountain slope, the scant ruins of a castle, probably built by William de Villehardouin to defend the coast from pirate raids, look down over the bay. It is identified by many as Villehardouin's castle of Maina.

Further south the land ends at its southernmost point at Cape Taenaron or Matapan. On the summit of the rock which rises above the sea, stands a tall white lighthouse.

By the small cove of Porto Sternes or Asomatos, the Spartans or the Taenarians, in the 4th century BC, established a small sanctuary dedicated to the Taenarian Poseidon as well as a place where departed souls were evoked. A cave nearby was believed by the ancients to be the entrance to Hades.

Above: Porto Kayio. On the slope of the mountain survive the ruins of the castle built by William de Villehardouin.

Left; The lovely beach at Porto Kayio.

Below: The picturesque seaside settlement of Kotronas.

Left page: View of Vatheia, with the sea in the distance.

Left: Beach at Kyparissi.

below: Kyparissi, one of the picturesque villages of Zarakas.

We now continue our journey northwards. On the top of a hill, proudly overlooking the sea, stands Vatheia, a characteristic example of a Maniot settlement. Most of the houses have been restored by the National Tourism Organisation and operate as guest houses. One of them has been disposed in such a way as to represent a typical Maniot house. The settlement of Vatheia was probably established in the 18th century, flourished in the 19th and began to decline at the beginning of the 20th century.

Further north we come to Kyparissos. On the site of the modern village stood in antiquity the city of Kainipolis, in which were temples of Aphrodite and Demeter, parts of which were used as building materials for the construction of the churches of the village of today. Here have been excavated the remains of the basilica of St. Peter, probably dating from the 5th or 6th century AD. The next village on our route is Yerolimenas, a traditional Maniot settlement lying along the shore, its beach of white pebbles encircling the limpid waters of a small bay. Pano and Kato Boularioi contains important Byzantine churches, those of Ai-Stratigos, Agios Panteleimon and Agios Georgios, relics - as are so many others - of the numerous Byzantine settlements established in the Deep Mani during Byzantine times.

We come now to Kitta, with its ruined towers and fortified houses. Not far from Kitta we shall find one of the most important churches of the Deep Mani, the church of the Saints Sergius and Bacchus (*Trouloti*) built at the beginning of the 12th century.

On cape Tigani are preserved the ruins of the castle of Maina, near the ancient city of Messa, on the southern side of the bay of Mezapos. The castle was built by William de Villehardouin in the 13th century.

Our drive continues through the barren country, typical of the Deep Mani. Ten

kilometres further on, we come to Pyrgos Dyrou and to the wonderful caves of Dyros. There are two of them: one is that of Glyphada or Vlychada ("brackish water"), and the other is known as Alepotrypa ("foxhole"). Both are very spectacular.
The cave of Glyphada is considered to be one of the three most beautiful lacustrene caves in the world. It was first explored by the speliologist John Petrocheilos and his wife Anna, and later by Anna Petrocheilos alone. The itinerary followed by visitors to the cave comprises a part on dry land and a part on the water of the underground lake. Stalactites and stalagmites of amaz-

Above: Pyrgos Dyrou.

Below and right: Pictures of the breathtakingly beautiful caves of Dyros.

ing shapes and colours adorn the various chambers and galleries of the cave. The temperature of the cave is constant - about 16-20 degrees Celsius - while the temperature of the water is about 12 degrees Celsius.

Two hundred and twenty metres to the east of the Glyphada cave we find the Alepotrypa. Here, too, the stalactites and stalagmites offer a wonderful sight. The constant temperature of the cave is 19 degrees Celsius. Within the cave as well as outside had grown an important prehistoric settlement. Human skeletons have been found, as well as stone weapons and tools and Neolithic vessels.

North of Dyros lies coastal Limeni by a turquoise-blue sea, and also the "palace" of the Maniot chieftain Petrobey Mavromichalis. Here is preserved a small cave, which served as a hiding place and a lookout. It is known as the "katafyngi", the "refuge".

As we move northwards, the landscape changes. The grey stone recedes: nature assumes a milder aspect.

We come to Oitylon. The two-storey castle-houses no longer have the grim and austere look of those of the Deep Mani. The doors and window frames are painted and the roofs are tiled. On the site of the modern settlement stood, in antiquity, the ancient city of Oitylon, one of the nine cities of the Achaeans mentioned by Homer in his *"Catalogue of Ships"*. Opposite the village, beyond the ravine which opens up towards the south-east, amid grey boulders and clumps of thorny broom, rises the fortress of Kelephas. It must have been built in the 17th century by the Turks to protect Oitylon, which was an important commercial port, against raiders. In 1685 the fortress was taken by the Venetians and recaptured in 1715 by the Turks. With Oitylon, which is the last stop on our tour of the Laconian or Deep Mani, we end our journey of acquaintance with the prefecture of Laconia.

Above: Opposite the village of Oitylon lie the ruins of the castle of Kelephas.

Below: Lithograph of the castle of Kelephas.

MESSENIA

HISTORY

KALAMATA

THE MESSENIAN MANI

CENTRAL MESSENIA

ANCIENT MESSENE

THE SURROUNDING REGION

WESTERN MESSENIA (METHONE-CORONE-PYLOS)

West of Laconia and of the imposing mass of the Taygetus range, which constitutes a natural boundary between the prefectures of Laconia and Messenia, lies the wide Messenian plain, which witnessed the development of two important centres of antiquity: "sandy" ("*amoessa*") Pylos and powerful Messene. This particularly fertile plain makes Messenia self-sufficient in agricultural products. The small rivers which flow through it (Pamissus, Nedas), contribute to the fertility of the soil. The hillsides are covered with vineyards, olive and fig-trees, as well as with vegetable gardens. The coasts of Messenia end in long sandy beaches, in white pebbly coves and small inlets of crystalline waters. On Mt. Taygetus and on the lower mountains in the region are perched picturesque villages of various sizes.

HISTORY

According to legend the province owes its name to Messene, who was the daughter of Triops, a king of Argos, and who became the wife of Polykaon, the first king of the region.

Messenia began to be inhabited at a very early date. It flourished in the Bronze Age (3200-1050 BC), as is evidenced by the sites excavated by archaeologists: those of the early Helladic "Megaron" at Akovitika near Kalamata (2500-2300BC), the middle Helladic settlement at Malthe (2000-1800BC) and the Mycenean palace of Nestor at Pano Englianos (13th century BC). In 1184 BC the cities of Messenia took part in the Trojan expedition under the leadership of the king of Pylos, Nestor.

From the end of the 8th century BC until the 5th century BC Sparta attempted to gain control of the fertile Messenian plain. This long period is marked by the two great Messenian wars (the 1st Messenian war from 735 to 715 BC, the 2nd Messenian war from 669 to 657 BC), the result of which was the total subjugation of the Messenians to the Spartans in 657 BC.

Driven out of their land, but retaining their own identity, the Messenians accepted the invitation of Epaminondas, in 370/369 BC, after the defeat of the Spartans at the battle of Leuctra, to settle in the new town founded by the Theban general.

Between Messenia and neighbouring Laconia rise the impressive peaks of the mighty Taygetus.

The region lying along the southern slopes of Mt. Ithome, on the summit of which stands the sanctuary of Zeus Ithomatas, was chosen as the most suitable site for the new city of the Messenians. The surrounding area and the towns on the Messenian coast also belonged to Messene. In 338 BC its boundaries, as they were defined by Philip II of Macedonia, extended as far as the river Nedas in the north and up to the Pamissus river in the east, thus including the towns of

Thouria, Asine, Methone, Pharae and Avia.

In 146 BC Messene became a Roman eparchy, while after the 4th century AD it suffered the raids of the Visigoths under Alaric and later those of the Slavs. In 1204 the region fell into the hands of the Franks, while after 1460 it was gradually overrun by the Turks, except for the towns of Methone and Corone, which had been in the possession of the Venetians since 1209. On the 23rd March 1821, the start of the War of Independence was proclaimed in Kalamata, and the region was liberated in 1828.

KALAMATA

The attractive town of Kalamata, famous for its sesame sweets and its silk kerchiefs, is the capital and harbour town of Messenia. It is built in the crook of the wide Messenian gulf. The ruins of a Frankish castle stand on the site of the ancient city of Pharae, mentioned by Homer in the *Iliad* and the *Odyssey*. Homer says of Pharae that it belonged to the kingdom of Agamemnon and was one of the seven cities which the commander-in-chief of the Achaeans had promised to Achilles, if he rejoined the combat. At the time of the

Right: The sea front of Kalamata with the Taygetus in the background. Along the waterfront we shall find modern hotels and a string of tavernas.

Below: The gate with the Venetian lion in the castle of Kalamata.

Trojan expedition, Diocles was king of Pharae. He had two sons, who were both killed in Troy by Aeneas.

In the later Middle Ages the town was renamed Kalamata. A widely held view is that the name derives from an icon in one of the churches in the citadel, known as the "Virgin Kalomata" ("good-eyed"). According to others, the town owes its name to the many reeds (kalamia = reeds) growing in the area. When, in 1205, the Franks under Geoffrey I de Villehardouin set foot in Kalamata, the fortifications built by the Byzantines on the castle were in a state of neglect.

Although the seat of the domain was in Andravida, Kalamata became the favourite town of Geoffrey de Villehardouin. This is where his younger son, William, was born and grew up. William de Villehardouin, who was to become one of the better-loved foreign rulers, was also known as "Kalomatis" ("of the good eye"). In 1245 William became prince of Achaea and had the castle's fortifications rebuilt. It was in the halls and courtyards of this castle that roamed William's daughter, Isabel, known

to Greek readers as the heroine of Angelos Terzakis' novel *The Princess Isabeau*. In 1685 a large part of this castle was destroyed by the Venetians, who themselves repaired it just before 1700.

As we enter the castle precinct, we see over the gate the half-effaced relief of a Venetian lion. The view from up here is enchanting. Our gaze sweeps over the southern part of the verdant plain, with its olive groves and luxuriant vegetation, known in antiquity as "Makaria" ("Blessed"). A little further along rises the mighty range of the Taygetus and in the distance shimmers the deep blue sea.

Below, at our feet, lies the old town with the tiled roofs of its buildings, among which stand out the Byzantine church of Ypapanti, which houses a venerated icon of the Virgin, and the Monastery of Kalograion. In this monastery, built in the 18th century, the nuns weave the famous silk

KALAMATA MUSEUMS

BENAKEION ARCHAEOLOGICAL MUSEUM

This houses finds from the surrounding area (Benaki and Papazoglou Streets no. 6, tel. 0721/26209).

FOLK MUSEUM

Here are exhibited memorabilia from the Greek war of Independence and other objects (Kyriakou and Agiou Ioannou 20, tel. 0721/28449).

LIBRARY

Manuscripts, papyri and rare editions (Cultural Centre, tel. 0721/28449).

PANTAZOPOULEION PNEVMATIKO KENTRO (CULTURAL CENTRE)

Here are displayed finds from excavations carried out in the surrounding area (Aristomenous 33, tel. 0721/86550).

On the road from Kalamata to Sparta, on the slopes of Mt. Taygetus, lies Alagonia in its nest of verdure.

Kalamata kerchiefs. In the centre of the old market still stands the historic church of the Holy Apostles, built in 1317, in which Petrobey Mavromichalis proclaimed the start of the Greek War of Independence.

Kalamata, through which the Nedon river flows, is an attractive town, with many modern buildings. Along the coast can be seen some of the few surviving two-storey neo-classical buildings which once graced the town. It is a very lively place, throughout the day and the night, especially along the waterfront. Here, all along the four kilometres of its length, we will find cafeterias, tavernas serving grilled meat and tasty fish, fried cod with a delicious garlic sauce, seafood, and a whole range of other savoury dishes, accompanied by wine drawn straight out of the barrel. On the small quay of the marina, to the west of the harbour, the ouzeries serve a variety of appetising snacks to go with a glass of ouzo or raki.

The road linking Kalamata to Sparta winds away from the town to the northeast. The scenery along the way is breathtaking, as the road follows the steep slopes of Mt. Taygetus, running above deep ravines, through dense forests of fir, beech and chestnut trees, and passing through the picturesque village of Artemisia, lying within a ring of high peaks, on a site on which is believed to have stood in antiquity the city of Dentheliatis.

Northeast of Artemisia lies the verdant village of Alagonia, while on the northwest stood a sanctuary dedicated to Artemis Limnatis. On the site of the temple was built in 1910 the church of the Virgin Volymniotissa, in the construction of which ancient building material was used. From Artemisia the road continues on, ending up at Sparta.

THE MESSENIAN MANI

Our journey into the Messenian Mani starts out from Kalamata. Outside the town stretches the long beach which reaches all the way to Almyros, the coastal settlement opposite Kalamata. Here are the boundaries of the Messenian or Outer

The ruins of the castle of Zarnata, by the village of Kambos. The fertile valley stretches as far as the eye can see.

Mani. On our right sparkle the deep blue waters of the Messenian gulf, and on our left, clinging to the slopes of Mt. Taygetus, lie the villages of Pano and Kato Verga, offering a fantastic view over the Messenian plain. The road branches out here into two directions. The right branch continues along the coast. It passes through small coastal settlements (Paliochora, Avia, Kato Mantineia), which are very popular in the summer months, and skirts a succession of coves and inlets with clear waters and clean, pebbly beaches, until it reaches the last fishing village of Kitriés.

It is worth walking down to the small beach on which stand an old castle-house and a number of tavernas, their tables and chairs invitingly set out beside the sea. We might like to try some grilled octopus or squid, and, if we are lucky, we might be able to sample the fried, unsweetened doughnuts known as "lalangia".

On our left, there is a small beach hidden by the rocks, where the bushes spill down from the mountainside all the way into the sea, turning its colour into a deep bluish-green. The left branch of the road, at Almyros, will lead us to Kardamyli and to Aghios Nikon, the last village of the Messenian Mani. After we pass through the verdant village of Kambos, we will see, on the summit of the conical hill in the middle of the plain, the ruins of the castle of Zarnata.

We do not know when and by whom the small fortress, which was also in use after the Greek War of Independence, was built. Seventeenth-century sources mention it as being Turkish. Today, all we can see of it is a ruined three-storied tower with arched windows and battlements and a fortified half-ruined house.

As we continue on our way, we find that the scenery is constantly changing. Small plains alternate with deep ravines and steep mountains. We arrive at the lovely village of Kardamyli, situated beside a long beach. Opposite the village, only a few metres away from the coast, lies the islet of Merope. On either side of the road running through the village stand the two-storey stone houses with their brick-tiled roofs. At

Views of Kardamyli, the popular centre of the Messenian Mani, with its church of St. Spyridon and the tiny island of Merope lying just off the coast.

Pano Kardamyli there are still old towers and fortified houses. A fountain, built in the 18th century and restored in the 19th, can also be seen. To the northeast of the village are preserved a few scant ruins of the medieval castle of Kardamyli. Worth visiting is the Byzantine church of Aghios Spyridon, with its belfry, adorned with carvings in relief. Behind the village rise the jagged peaks of the Taygetus range. There, between the folds of the mountain, just outside the village, begins the dramatic Vyros gorge, which can compete with the famous Samaria gorge in Crete as regards the beauty of its scenery.

South of Kardamyli lies Stoupa, with its marvellous beach. Between Stoupa and Leuktro, on a low but steep hill, we can see the ruins of the castle of Gisterna, or Beaufort castle, built around 1251 by the Franks. Our route is dotted with villages, some built on the coast, others perched on the sides of the mountain. Here the scenery is gentle, not grey and bare, as in the area known as the "Mesa Mani" (the Deep Mani). The villages are surrounded by greenery. Among the stone houses with their tiled roofs rise towers and fortified houses with the characteristic cylindrical loopholed "cages" in the corners. Our next stop is Aghios Nikolaos. Here, the houses are built right on the water's edge. By the road leading to Aghios Dimitrios lies the Katafyngi cave. The route is a spectacular one. On our left rises the bare mountain. On our right the sheer cliffs fall steeply into the dark waters. A path from our road leads to the huge flat, perpendicular rocks, which appear to have been carved by some master sculptor. Here is the entrance to the cave, which is adorned with fantastic formations of stalactites and stalagmites. When the cave was explored, in its interior were found black potsherds and human bones.

Further south lies the coastal village of Aghios Dimitrios, followed by Platsa and Thalames (Koutifari), picturesque villages with their stone houses and towers perched on the sides of the mountain. The last villages of the Messenian Mani are Trachila and Aghios Nikon, both built along the shore.

Messenian Mani. Stoupa is renowned for its marvellous beach.

CENTRAL MESSENIA

ANCIENT MESSENE

North of Kalamata, and after we have driven through part of the Messenian plain, we come to Mavrommati, a name the village owes to the spring (mavro mati =

black eye) around which it was built. The hamlet, perched on the foothills of Mt. Ithomi, is also known as Vulcano. On the summit there stood a sanctuary dedicated to Zeus Ithomatas, whose worship is believed by many scholars to present similarities with that of Zeus Lycaeus in Arcadia. According to local tradition, when Rhea, in order to protect the young Zeus from his father Cronus, entrusted the infant to the Couretes, the latter hid him in Ithome, where he was looked after by the two nymphs of the region, Ithome and Neda.

In the centre of the village, near the coffee-shops, grill-house and other shops, underneath the tall plane trees, flow the cool, crystalline waters of the Callirhoe fountain, from the spring often identified as the Clepshydra of antiquity. It was in these waters gushing out of the mountain that, according to the myth, the two nymphs bathed the baby Zeus.

Below the stone houses of the village, in the plain planted with olives and vineyards, lie the ruins of ancient Messene, the most important city of the ancient Messenian state, which was founded by the Theban general Epaminondas.

The city was built after the battle of Leuctra in 370/369 BC, at the same time as Megalopolis. The purpose behind the founding of these two cities was to limit Sparta to the Laconian region. In the new town were invited to come and settle the

Messenians who had been obliged to abandon their land after it had been seized by the Spartans, and who were living in other places, such as Sicily and Cyrenaica. The city was built under the supervision of the Argive general Epiteles, with money derived from the spoils of the expedition against Laconia. It was fortified by a strong wall built entirely of stone, from the foundations all the way up to the battlements, and became an important centre and the capital of the free Messenian state.

During the periods of Macedonian and Roman rule, the town continued to flourish, until the beginning of the 4th century AD. It was gradually abandoned after the invasion of the Visigoths in 395 AD. The inhabitants of Messene settled in safer areas and the place lay desolate for a great many years. Life only returned to the region in recent times, when the village of Mavrommati was established.

When Pausanias visited Messene in the 2nd century AD, the town was still an important political and cultural centre. The famous traveller speaks with admiration of the walls surrounding the city, noting that, in comparison with the walls of the best fortified towns of his own time, the fortifications of Messene were much stronger. He also mentions the agora of the city - the fountain of Arsinoe, the stadium and the theatre, the sanctuaries dedicated to Asclepius, to Poseidon, to Aphrodite, to Demeter, to Sarapis and to Isis, and the temples of Eileithyia and Messene. He also refers in detail to the statues adorning the Asclepieion, the other sanctuaries and the various other parts of the agora, making special mention of the statues of the mother of the gods and of Artemis Laphria, works of the Messenian sculptor Damophon.

Excavations in the area where once flourished ancient Messene, conducted by the Archaeological Society, began in 1895 under Themistocles Sophoulis. In 1909 they were continued by George Economou and in the period between 1957 and 1974 by the academician and archaeologist Anastasios Orlandos. After the death of the latter, Petros Themelis became the director of the excavations. New finds are continually coming to light as excavations continue, finds which accord with the descriptions of Pausanias in his *Travels*. The large number of inscriptions

Above left: Messenian Mani. Aghios Nikolaos.

Left below: Trachela, one of the last villages of the Messenian Mani, on its borders with Laconia.

Below: Mavrommati is built on the site of ancient Messene, on the slopes of Mt. Ithome.

Above: Ancient Messene. The northern portico of the Asclepieion and the small theatre or odeon.

Right: A square defensive tower, part of the wall of ancient Messene.

Above: Ancient Messene. The east side and propylon of the sanctuary of Asclepius.

Left: Section of the frieze of the temple of Asclepius at ancient Messene.

Below: The Arcadian gate, outside the village of Mavrommati.

Right: Ruins of walls and a tower, parts of the strong defensive wall of ancient Messene, clamber up the slopes of Mt. Ithome.

and coins uncovered by the archaeologists' pick constitute an important source of information concerning the periods they represent.
The older excavations conducted in the area of ancient Messene had already brought to light the remains of the sanctuary of Asclepius and of the buildings surrounding it.
The wide, rectangular outdoor area, in the centre of which rose the temple of the god, was surrounded by four colonnades. The temple, which stood on a low, three-stepped platform, was a peripteral Doric temple and consisted of a porch, a cella and a rear porch. A ramp led to the entrance to the shrine.
To the east and at a small distance from the temple stood a large rectangular altar. In the outdoor area around the temple there were many bases of votive statues.
The entrance to the open-air interior area of the complex was made through a monumental propylon which was situated in the centre of the eastern side.
The propylon consisted of two porticoes which communicated through a door. To the south of the propylon has been preserved the *bouleuterion*, a large hall with four pillars in the middle and an entrance with six openings on the western side. Along the three walls we can still see a continuous stone bench, on which used to sit the representatives of the cities of autonomous Messenia. In front of the fourth, western wall, there must have stood a platform, from which the speaker addressed the audience.
North of the propylon lay a small theatre or odeon, which is thought to have been used by the Messenians for theatrical and musical performances and for oratorical competitions, as well as for meetings when the number of the participants was large and the area of the bouleuterion was not big enough to accommodate them.
On the south side of the theatre or odeon was a built stage and a high proscenium. The entrance to the area was effected through three doors. The orchestra forms a circle which adjoins the stage.
The seats of the theatre are made of stone and most of them survive to this day. On the rectangular base, which is situated beside the eastern entrance passage, stood, in the 2nd century AD, the statue of Tiberius Claudius Saethedas a member of the Roman family of the Saethedae, who were benefactors of the city.
A grand stairway, in the middle of the northern side of the peristyle courtyard, led from the interior outdoor area of the complex to the upper section of seats. To this upper section also led the two smaller L-shaped stairs, which were situated to the right and left of the central stairway.
Near the eastern end of the northern portico there was a deep niche, the *oikos*, facing the south side, with a rectangular base and two columns between the pilasters. This may have been an area dedicated in Roman times to the worship of some ruler.
On the western side of the complex and near its northern end a built stairway has been uncovered, which led to a courtyard surrounded by a colonnade. South of the stairway has come to light a small temple dedicated to Artemis. The altar of the goddess stands in the interior open space. The temple consisted of a cella on the eastern side, facing the courtyard.
It was divided into three parts by two rows of columns, one on the left and one on the right of the entrance. At the back, between the two rows of columns, there was a pedestal on which stood the cult statue of the goddess, and in front of this pedestal an offertory table and a hollow receptacle for liquid offerings. Around it were found smaller bases on which stood statues of the priestesses who had served the goddess. Along the walls of the side areas ran benches to accommodate those participating in secret rituals.
South of the temple of Artemis there are another four spaces. In the last one to the south there was an entrance from the west into the area of the sanctuary of Asclepius.
On the eastern end of the southern side of the complex, and outside the wall of the southern portico, there was a small structure which has been identified as a *heroön*, a monument in which members of a family whom the Messenians wished to honour were buried.

Recent excavations in the area of ancient Messene continue to bring to light public buildings and sanctuaries of the ancient city, among which the following:
On the northern side of the agora a double stoa and a fountain which has been identified as the fountain of Arsinoe; the sanctuary of Demeter and of the Dioscuri, the first building phase of which has been dated to the Archaic period and in which were found two bronze shields, one of which was dedicated to Polydeuces, one of the Dioscuri. The sanctuary of Artemis Orthia between the sanctuary of Demeter and the Asclepieion. Artemis Orthia was the goddess protectress of infants. The sanctuary comprises a small prostyle temple, a stoa and bases of votive statues.
In the northern raised area of the agora, two rectangular buildings lying to the east and west of the monumental stairway are thought to have been connected with a *sevasteion*, that is a place where the emperor Augustus and the city of Rome were honoured.
In the area of the Asclepieion, were discovered architectural vestiges of an earlier Asclepieion, votive statues and parts of marble compositions which have been attributed to Damophon and which represent Asclepius with his sons Machaon and Podaleirius, Apollo and the Muses, the Theban Heracles with a personification of the city of Thebes, and also the goddess Tyche and Artemis Phosphorus. East of the Asclepieion are two adjoining areas which in Roman times may have been libraries. South of the Asclepieion are public baths with a hypocaust, dating from the 3rd to the 1st centuries BC.
South of the public baths there is a sacrificial area, a square edifice with an interior peristyle, which served for ritual banquets.
In the southwestern corner of the ancient city, adjoining the fortified precinct,lie the stadium and the gymnasium.
The horseshoe-shaped *sphendone* of the stadium with 15 tiers of seats and another 19 rows separated by stairs, was encircled on the northern side by a double colonnade in Doric style, while on the east and west sides simple Doric porticoes extended up to the southern end of the track.
West of the western portico of the stadi-

ary of the river-god Acheloös, have also been found behind the reservoir of the fountain. Epaminondas initially fortified Messene with a wall of which only some small sections have survived, at the "Laconian" gate and the north-western (Aghios Basilios - Mt. Eva) side.
Later, in Macedonian times (3rd c. BC) was built the impressive wall measuring 3 metres in width and 9 kilometres in length, which is considered to be one of the most perfect examples of the art of fortification ever created. Of the walls of ancient Messene, best preserved is the northern section around the "Arcadian" gate, while its exact perimeter has been traced by following the parts which have survived at various points. Its shape is irregular, while at various intervals stood two-storey square or round towers. The garrison was

um was found a sanctuary dedicated to Heracles and Hermes. The heroön uncovered at the southern end of the stadium is a Doric prostyle temple which constituted the mausoleum of some eminent Messenian who was honoured as a hero during the games. To the northeast of the stadium, the western retaining wall of the seating area of the theatre, the western passage into it and part of the stage have come to light.
The Clepshydra fountain and the sanctu-

housed on the upper floor of the towers.
Rectangular blocks of local grey stone, quarried at Ithome, were used in the construction of the wall.
Today, along the road leading from Mavrommati to the new monastery of Voulkanos. we can see parts of the "Laconian" gate, through which passed the road which led from Messene to Sparta and Pharae. Better preserved is the "Arcadian" gate through which passed the road to Megalopolis and which must

have been the main gate of Messene. A paved way led from the one which opened into Messene to the agora of the ancient city.
From Mavrommati a path brings us to the top of Ithome, the mountain which Homer calls "ladder-like", because of its stony and steep stepped slope. Up here, within the walls, stood the sanctuary of Zeus Ithomatas. Later, in Byzantine times (13th c), the emperor Andronicus Palaeologus built, near the sanctuary, a monastery dedicated to the Virgin - the old monastery of Voulkanos, known as the "Katholikon".
In the little church on the summit, which leans against a huge rock, there are half-effaced murals, works of the Moschos brothers.
Here again, ancient building material was used in the construction of the monastery.
Halfway along the path leading from the top of Voulkanos to the village, have come to light the foundations of a small Ionic temple of the 3rd century BC, belonging to a sanctuary dedicated to Artemis Limnatis or Laphria, as well as a second sanctuary dedicated to an unknown deity.
To the south-east of the two sanctuaries, on the saddle between Mt. Voulkanos (Ithome) and Aghios Vasilios (Mt. Eva), beyond the "Laconian" gate, on a shady plateau with tall plane trees and cool running waters, we find the later monastery of Voulkanos, in which there is an icon of the Virgin which has been brought from the monastery on the summit.
The view from up here is unique. Beneath us, and as far as the eye can see, extends the valley with its gardens, vineyards, olive groves and scattered small villages.
The new monastery has a guest house with a few cells for visitors Here, on the day of the Dormition of the Virgin (August 15), is held a village fete, during which the icon of the Virgin Voulkaniotissa is carried in procession to her first home, that is to the old monastery.
The new monastery of Voulkanos is connected to the village of Mavrommati by a tarred road.

THE SURROUNDING AREA

In the region extending to the north of Kalamata we will encounter small villages lying among vegetable gardens, olive groves and vineyards. We will drive up mountains covered with bushes and prickly pear. In the spring a profusion of wild flowers covers the slopes and there are splashes of colour everywhere - mostly purples and yellows.
After the modern town of Messene we encounter, to its north, the picturesque village of Androusa with the ruins of its Frankish castle. North of Androusa lies Hellenoklissia and outside the village, at the place called Kalogherorachi, we might like to visit the church of Samarina, a domed cross-in square church of the 12th century, which celebrates its feast-day on the first Friday after Easter.
Near the village of Zerbissia, northwest of Mavrommati, among the plane trees and the flowing springs, we will find the abandoned monastery of Andromonastiro or Andreiomonastiro, which is said to have been built in the 13th century by Andronicus Palaeologus, to whom it owes its name. Northeast of Mavrommati, driving from Nichori to Meligalas, we pass over the triple bridge of the Mavrozoumaina, which, according to popular legend, is haunted, as is the bridge at Arta on mainland Greece. It is said that the big bridge with its nine arches was built thanks to the sacrifice of the wife of a man named Mavrozoumis, to whom it owes its name of Mavrozoumeno or Mavrozoumaina. The foundations of the bridge date back to antiquity, while the upper portion with the arches was built in the time of the Ottoman occupation.
After we have traversed the plain of Meligalas, the "*Stenyclerion pedion*" of antiquity, we come to Vassiliko and to the hill of Malthe, with the Mycenean tholos tombs at its foot and a prehistoric settlement at the top.
Southeast and above the central road linking Kalamata to Megalopolis, we encounter the village of Aghios Floros, with its tall shady plane trees and the springs of the Pamissos river.

Left, above: the new monastery of Voulkanos.

Left, below: The castle of Androusa.

WESTERN MESSENIA

This itinerary, the last in our tour of Messenia, will take us to the areas west of Kalamata. We will discover beaches with crystal-clear waters, wander through medieval castles and visit Homeric Pylos, the city of Neleus and of Nestor.

Ten kilometres from Kalamata beside the Pamissos river we find Messene, the commercial and agricultural centre of the Messenian plain. Just beyond lies the airport of Kalamata. Four kilometres further along we find the long beach of Bouka, with its fine sand and limpid sea. Further south, within the small inlet beside the sandy beach, lies Petalidi, on the site of ancient Corone.

We continue southwards and come to Corone (medieval Coron), built on the site of ancient Asine. The picturesque town of today with its tiled houses, arched or rectilinear doors and windows, its balconies adorned with lace-like ironwork, clings to the slopes of the low hill on the eastern side of the peninsula, embraced

Right: the golden sands of Bouka.

Below: The beach at Petalidi.

Right page: View of Corone and its castle (aerial photograph).

by the mighty walls of a Venetian castle. The castle, built in 1250, was a veritable eyrie, with strong walls and massive gates. Today, although in ruins, it still looms large and imposing. Corone and Methone (medieval Modon), were taken by the Venetians in 1209 and developed, during the first period of Venetian rule (1209-1250) into important stations for Venetian ships on their way to the East. This was a time of great prosperity for the two towns. They had shipyards for repairing ships, commerce flourished, and the towns' engineers were renowned Jnowned for their skill in the construction of siege engines. During the period between 1500 and 1685 the two towns were subjected to Turkish rule. From 1685 to 1715 they again passed into Venetian hands, to be retaken once again by the Turks in 1715. In 1828 they were liberated by the allied forces (English, French and German), but after 1500 both towns had already begun to show signs of economic and social decline.

After their liberation, they once again began to prosper, this time thanks to agriculture and the trade in oil and currants and to the development of the tile-making industry.

Today, within the precinct of the castle of Corone stands the women's monastery of St. John the Baptist, built in the early 20th century, and the Byzantine church of Saint Sophia, while below the citadel, in a luxuriant garden, stand the church of the Eleestra and a building in which is housed the Historical and Archaeological Collection of Corone.

Our next stop is Phoenikous, the picturesque fishing village built in the safety of a closed bay. It boasts a splendid beach with crystal-clear waters. After Phoenikous we come to Methone, Homer's "Pedasus rich in vines" or Pausanias' "Mothone", the last of the seven cities which Agamemnon offered Achilles to placate him.

Beside the castle lies the small town with its double-storied houses covered with red tiled roofs. Here too there are arched

Left: Pictures of Corone.

Below: View of the castle of Corone.

Above: Picturesque Phoenikous.

Below: Lithograph of Methone.

Right page: Phoenikous. Along the edge of the limpid blue sea runs the marvellous beach.

doors and windows, and balconies adorned with elaborate ironwork. The Venetian castle stands on the edge of the promontory. On the seaward side, the islet of Bourdzi, fortified during the period of Turkish rule, was connected by a causeway to the gate, flanked by two towers, which leads into the mighty fortress.

To enter the castle we must cross a large stone bridge with fourteen arches, which spans the deep Venetian moat and which was built by the French in the 18th century. The fame of Methone as a port dates all the way back to the late years of antiquity.

The city of ancient times was built, as was the medieval one later, on the fortified peninsula. During the Byzantine period, the Venetians cast a covetous eye on the port, which they managed to seize, together with Corone, in 1209. It is at this time that the strong walls were probably built.

In front of the town spreads the shallow sandy beach, an earthly paradise for

FINISSIA

Left page: Methone and its castle (aerial photograph).

Right page: Above left: View of the interior of the castle. Above right: The stone bridge with its fourteen arches. Below: The castle and the tiny fortified island of Bourdzi.

summer visitors of all ages. Opposite Methone, the little islands of Schiza - on which there is an impressive cave - and Sapientza provide stopping places on the course of migrating birds. On Sapientza a tall lighthouse beams its warning to passing ships.

About 12 kms north of Methone lies the small town of present-day Pylos (or Navarino), built amphitheatrically on the southern edge of the bay of Navarino, on plans designed by the French architects accompanying general Maison in 1829.

The double-storied whitewashed houses in the narrow streets, which give the place the air of an island village, start from the waterfront of the small harbour and climb up the gentle slopes of the hill of St. Nicholas.

Tall plane trees shade the main square ringed with pastry shops. Here, between two cannons - a Turkish and a Venetian one - stands the trilateral marble column put up to honour the memory of the three admirals - Codrington, de Rigny and Heyden - who on the 21st of October 1827 annihilated the Turko-Egyptian fleet in the bay of Navarino.

West of the small town stands Niocastro, the "new castle" of Navarino, built by the Turks in 1573, two years after their defeat at the battle of Lepanto. Fortified by a strong wall and mighty towers, it protected Pylos from the south, making the older Frankish fortress known as Palaiocastro, quite redundant.

At the highest point of Niocastro the hexagonal castle, which served as a citadel, is still impressive, with its mighty towers standing on each of its six corners. The section of the wall which rises above the sea has been fortified by two square bastions, one on each of its two corners. The entrance to the citadel is between the hexagonal fortress and the nearby round tower. In 1686 Niocastro passed into Venetian hands, but was retaken in 1715 by the Turks. In 1821 it was seized by the Greeks, who kept it until 1825, at which time it was captured by the forces of Ibrahim pasha. After the victory of the allies on October 10, 1828, the fortress passed into the hands of the French, who restored it.

In the centre of Niocastro stands the church of the Transfiguration. Built by the Franks, it was turned into a mosque by the Turks but was later reconverted into a church by the Greeks.

The large bay of Navarino is closed on the western side by the long and narrow mountainous island of Sphacteria, leaving only two narrow passages, the Sykia passage to the north and the large Thouri passage to the south. During the period of Ottoman rule the Turks, in order to prevent ships from entering the north passage, filled in the sea at that point so that it would be too shallow to allow them to negotiate it safely.

Sphacteria in antiquity was also known as Sphagia. In medieval times the Europeans called in Jonc or Junch or Gioncho, or Avarino-Navarino, a name which was also used for the area of the peninsula of Koryphasion, which lies further north.

Above left: View of Pylos.

Below Left: Niocastro, with Sphacteria in the distance.

Above: The cove of Voidokoilia.

Aerial photograph of Pylos. Beside the town, we can see Nicastro, while, in the distance can be made out the villages of Yialova and Divari. →

Right: Ancient Pylos. The Palace of Nestor. The Throne Room with the circular hearth in the centre.

Above; part of the stairway which led to the upper storey.

Above right: Tholos tomb of the 15th century BC, at Pano Englianos.

At Sphacteria in 425 BC the Athenians surrounded the Spartan hoplites and took them prisoner. The vestiges of an ancient wall in the northern part of the island are thought to have been part of the walls built by the Spartans. Sphacteria can be visited by caique or motor boat.

On this island we will see the Russian memorial, the bust of the Italian philhellene Santarosa, as well as the monument of Prince Paul-Marie Bonaparte, a nephew of Napoleon, who was killed near the island of Spetses at the early age of 18. In the middle of the bay of Navarino there is another rocky islet known as Marathonissi, where can be seen the cenotaph of the British sailors who died in the battle of Navarino, while on another rocky islet has been set a monument to the French.

The north side of the bay is dominated by the rocky headland of Koryphasion, which closes the Voidokoilia ("Ox-belly") bay with its sandy beach on the southern side. To the right of the bay lies the lagoon of Divari, which was only invaded by the waters of the sea in medieval

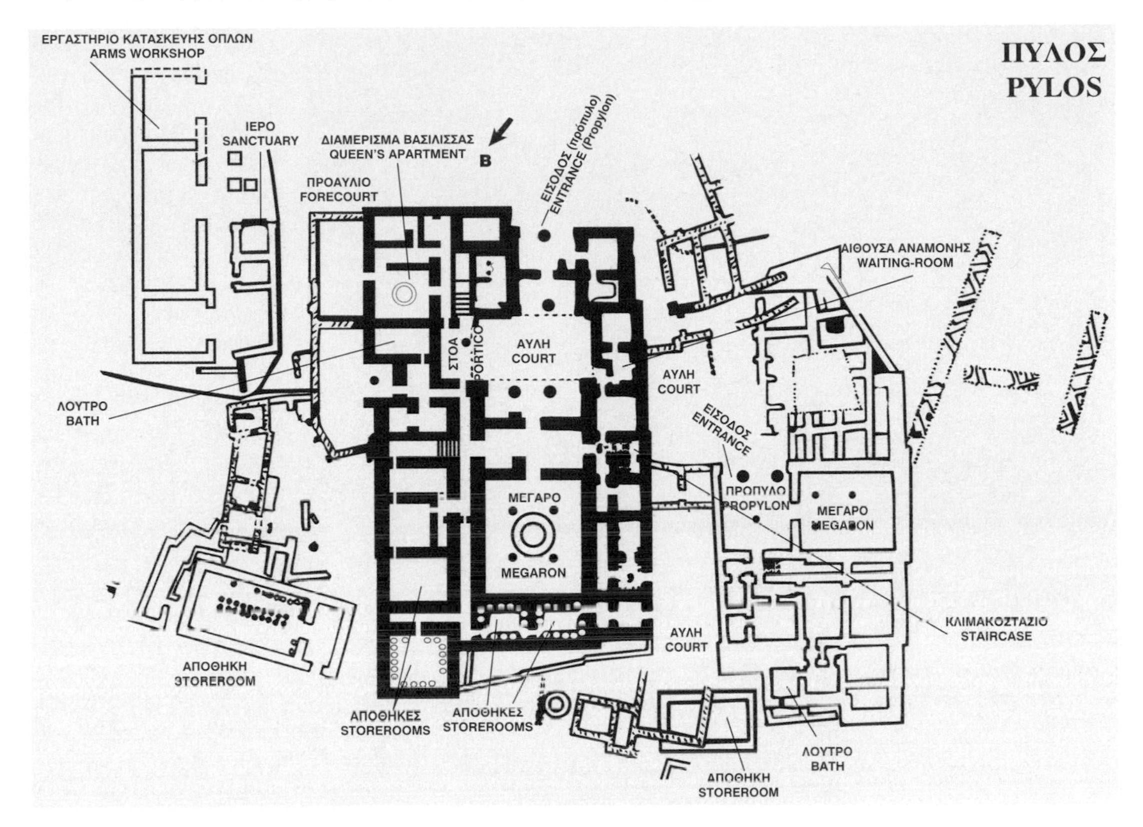

times. Here, in antiquity, was situated the cemetery of the city of Koryphasion. Tombs dating from Classical, Hellenistic and Roman times have been found on the site. The top of the peninsula is crowned by the castle built by the Franks in 1278. The entrance, fortified by a strong tower, was situated on the south side of the walls. On the site of the castle used to stand, in historic times, a small town which already bore the name of Pylos in the 5th century BC.

During the Macedonian and Roman periods, Pylos, which retained its ancient name, was a free Messenian city. When Pausanias visited the area in the 2nd century AD, the inhabitants of Pylos showed him, by the northern opening of the Voidokoilia bay, the Mycenean tholos tomb which they believed belonged to the son of Nestor, Thrasymedes.

On the northern slope under the castle of Palaiocastro, we will see the opening of a cave, which was believed to have served as a cow-shed for Nestor's cows. In Pylos there is a Museum known as the Antonopouleion Museum, in which are housed finds from the surrounding area. Six kilometres north of Pylos, we encounter yet another sandy beach, surrounded by the verdant valley of Yialova. The area of Yialova is the largest wetland area of the district.

Seventeen kilometres north of Pylos is built, on a low hill, the picturesque village of Chora, with tile-roofed houses and narrow streets. In its Archaeological Museum are housed finds from the palace of Nestor and the Mycenean tholos tombs at Peristeria.

Southwest of Chora, at a distance of 4 kms, at Pano Englianos, have been excavated the ruins of a Mycenean palace, known as "the palace of Nestor", king of "sandy Pylos", as Homer calls it in the *Odyssey*. The palace was built in the 13th century BC and was destroyed, as were the other Mycenean centres, in the 12th century BC.

Nestor's kingdom was the most important one in the Peloponnese after that of Agamemnon. In the "Catalogue of Ships"

Above: Lithograph of Pylos.

Below: Kyparissia and its medieval castle.

in the *Iliad* Homer says that of all the Achaeans, it was Agamemnon and Nestor who commanded the greatest number of ships - he attributes one hundred to Agamemnon and ninety to Nestor.

According to legend, Pylos was built by Neleus, son of Poseidon and a distant descendant of Deucalion and Pyrrha, who were the only humans to have survived on earth after the flood. In Heracles' attack against Pylos, all of Neleus' children were killed, except Nestor.

The palace of Pylos presents more similarities to the Minoan palaces than to those of Mycenae and Tiryns. The acropolis of Pylos, in contrast to those of Mycenae and of Tiryns, was not walled. It is situated on the top of a hill and surrounded by a verdant landscape which creates a feeling of tranquillity and peace.

Excavations have brought to light a palace worthy of the fame of Nestor, son of Neleus. Archaeologists have uncovered 1250 clay tablets bearing inscriptions in Linear B script, which have been deciphered and provide very useful information. The palace consists of three complexes: the main residence, the storerooms for wine and oil and the workshops. The entrance to the palace was effected through a propylon, and from there, through a narrow *prodomos* (vestibule) to the *domos*, the main room of the Megaron, where was set a throne. In the centre of the room has been preserved the circular clay hearth and around it the bases of four columns which supported the balcony or clerestory.

The floor of the Megaron was laid out in coloured squares and its walls, as well as those of the other important areas, were decorated with rich frescoes. It is from the Megaron that the fresco with the representation of a lyre player and a bird originates.
In the first two of the rooms west of the Megaron, were found inscribed tablets; the first room appears to have been a storeroom and the second perhaps a waiting room. In the fifth room were found clay vessels. Large jars for the storage of oil were set in the floors of the storerooms, north and east of the Megaron.
The room with the hearth in its centre, east of the Megaron, is thought to have belonged to the queen's apartments. Here was found the fresco with a representation of a griffin and a panther. The next-door room was a bath. The clay bathtub and two jars, which must have held water for the bath, were found in it.
The small room which is situated to the east of the palace apartments must have been a shrine, while the nearby area to its east was a workshop for the construction or repair of chariots and armour.
Northeast of the workshop has been uncovered the largest of the tholos tombs excavated around the palace.
The palace of Pylos was two-storied. Large limestone blocks were used for the construction of the outer walls, while for the inner walls undressed stone was used. Large amounts of wood also went into the construction of the palace - in the columns, the roofs and the door-frames.
We leave Pylos.
On the verdant slope of a hill we see the village of Gargaliani, while by the sea lies its port of Marathoupolis, and opposite it the islet of Proti, on which there are ruins of an ancient wall. Further north lies Filiatra, where there are a number of old churches.
At Aghia Kyriaki, has come to light a five-aisled early Christian basilica of the late 5th or early 6th century. Baths have been found nearby, dating from the 4th or the early 5th century AD.
Kyparissia, to which we come next, was a flourishing town in Macedonian and Hellenistic times. When Pausanias visited it, it was the most important centre of western Messenia. On the hill where today we can see the ruins of a medieval castle, stood, in Hellenistic times, the acropolis of the city. Its fortifications were preserved throughout the pre-Christian and Byzantine periods. At that time Kyparissia was known under the name of Arkadià. In 1205 it was captured by the Franks, who built a castle on the acropolis. The castle was held in the 12th century and around 1700 by the Venetians. Thomas Palaeologus took it in 1459 and Mohammed II seized it in 1460. In 1825 Arkadià (Kyparissia) was destroyed by Ibrahim pasha and, when it was rebuilt, it once more assumed its earlier name of Kyparissia. East of the small town has been excavated a tholos tomb of the late Mycenean period.
Further north, near the village of Myros or Moira, at the site of Peristeria, have come to light a large tholos tomb and two smaller ones, while on the hill were found the foundations of houses.
After Peristeria our road will take us to Elis, in which lies ancient Olympia, the birthplace of the Olympic games.

Mycenean tholos tomb.

ELIS

LEGENDARY KINGS - MYTHS

HISTORICAL TIMES

PYRGOS

ANCIENT OLYMPIA

THE OLYMPIC GAMES

GUIDED TOUR OF THE ARCHAEOLOGICAL SITE

THE HIGHLANDS OF ELIS

(KRESTAINA-ANDRITSAINA-BASSAE-PHIGALEIA)

THE LOWLANDS AND THE COAST

(CAIAPHAS-MONASTERY OF SKAFIDIA-ELIS-ANDRAVIDA-
KYLLENE-MONASTERY OF PANAGHIA BLACHERNA)

Here, we shall hear stories about the great river-god of the region, Alpheius, and of his loves with Artemis; we shall hear about the ancient king of Elis, the arrogant and vainglorious Salmoneus, who believed he was a god and demanded that his subjects honour and worship him as a divinity, until the day that Zeus hurled a thunderbolt at him and struck him dead.
We shall make the acquaintance of the seer, Melampus, whom the god Apollo himself had endowed with the power of divination. We shall hear about another soothsayer, the famous Ianus, born of a secret love-affair of the same god.
We shall learn about King Augeias, who kept thousands of oxen, the dung of which filled his stables until Heracles, in performance of one of his labours, cleaned them out in one day.
We shall read about Oenomaus, son of a god, king of Pisatis and Elis, and father of the fair Hippodamia, who married Pelops, the son of Tantalus, after Pelops had won the chariot race against her father, a victory that Oenomaus had set as a condition to the pretenders to his daughter's hand. Finaly, we shall hear about Pelops himself, who became the master of the whole land south of the isthmus of Corinth, which thereafter was known as Peloponnesus, the island of Pelops.

OTHER LEGENDARY KINGS - TRADITIONS - THE HISTORICAL YEARS

First of the rulers of this land was Aethlius, after whom came his son Endymion, who had four children, three sons, Paeon, Epeius and Aetolus, and a daughter.
After winning a race against his brothers, at Olympia - in games organised by his father - Epeius was offered the throne as a reward. From him his subjects took the name of Epeioi, which is the oldest name by which the inhabitants of this region were known. It is by this name that they are referred to by Homer in the *Iliad*. After the death of Epeius, who produced no male heir, the kingdom fell to his sister's son, Eleias. Eleias changed the name of the inhabitants of the land from Epeians to Eleans, and that of the land itself to Eleia or Elis, a name which still survives today.
Several names of other rulers follow, mentioned by Herodotus, Apollodorus and Strabo, until we come to king Iphitus, a contemporary of king Lycurgus of Sparta, who brought the Olympic games - which

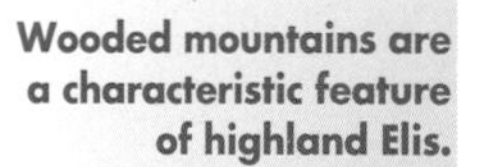

Wooded mountains are a characteristic feature of highland Elis.

Left and below: Views of Pyrgos.

The sanctuary of Olympia (aerial photograph).→

had stopped following the death of king Oxylus - back to Olympia.

The Eleans took part in the Trojan war as well as in battles against the Persians.

During the last years of the Peloponnesian war they joined the alliance of the Athenians, Argives and Mantineans, whereupon Agis, king of Sparta, advanced against them with his army. In the battle which ensued and which took place at Olympia, in 364 BC, the Eleans were victorious and the Lacedaemonians were put to flight.

During the reign of Philip of Macedon the Eleans formed an alliance with the Macedonians and fought by their side in the battles against the Lacedaemonians. However, after the death of Alexander the Great, the Eleans joined the other Greeks in resisting the Macedonians.

In 191 BC Elis, the capital city of the province, became a member of the Achaean confederacy. In 146 BC it surrendered to the Romans. Long years of obscurity followed, until 1210 AD, when the province of Elis was captured by the Franks and made the centre of the Principality of Achaea with Andravida as its capital. In 1452 Elis was taken by the Turks, in whose hands the province remained - except for a short period of Venetian rule - until 1828, when it was liberated.

PYRGOS

The province of Elis stretches out along the western coast of the Peloponnese. It borders with Achaea, Arcadia and Messenia, and is washed, on its western side, by the Ionian Sea. Capital of the prefecture is the town of Pyrgos. Ancient tombs found on the eastern fringes of the city testify to the existence of a settlement on the site of the modern city, during late antiquity. The city owes its name to the tower (pyrgos) built by John Tsernotas between 1512 and 1520. It has retained the same name since 1687.

Of the older city all that remains is the Municipal Market, and the Apollon Municipal Theatre, two beautiful neo-classical edifices, built on plans of the famous architect E. Ziller. Standing on a busy street are also the Municipal Library and the Municipal Gallery.

ANCIENT OLYMPIA

Nineteen kilometres east of Pyrgos stretches a truly enchanting site, that of ancient Olympia. The landscape is idyllic, exuding a kind of tranquil, divine serenity. A little further down flow the waters of the Alpheius and of one of its tributaries, the Cladeus.

ESTABLISHMENT OF THE GAMES

According to legend, the first athletes to run in Olympia were the Curetes, the brothers Heracles, Paeonaeos, Epimedes and Idas, who had come from Mount Ida in Crete, where they had guarded the newborn Zeus. The older Curete, Heracles, bade his brothers run at Olympia and crowned the winner with an olive wreath.

To the Idaean Heracles, then, belongs the glory of having first instituted the Olympic games and having given them their name. And, as they were five brothers, he decided that they should be held every five years.

It was said that it was here that Zeus wrestled with Cronus to determine who would be the ruler of Mount Olympus and that the games were instituted by Zeus when he won the throne. It is also said that Apollo defeated Hermes in a foot race and that he prevailed over Ares in a boxing match.

Another legend relates that, after the flood, in the days of Deucalion, there came from Crete a descendant of the Idaean Heracles named Clymenus, who established the games at Olympia, and raised an altar in honour of the Curetes.

Later, Endymion organised a foot race in which the only contestants were his own sons, and subsequently Pelops instituted

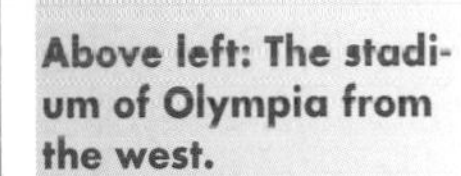

Above left: The stadium of Olympia from the west.

Below left: The Krypte, the arched passageway.

Above: The eastern section of the Gymnasium (2nd century BC) and, in the background, the reconstituted columns of the Palaestra.

Red-figure amphora decorated with a representation of a boxing match between two athletes. By the Pythocles painter. Dated to the beginning of the 5th century BC. Athens, National Archaeological Museum.

ΕΞΕΔΡΑ ΗΡΩΔΟΥ
EXEDRA DES HERODES

contests in honour of Zeus the Olympian. Legend tells us that there were others, too, who held games at Olympia. Among these were Pelias, Neleus, Augeias and Heracles. The Olympic games were interrupted for a time after the death of king Oxylus, and were restarted in 776 BC during the reign of the king of Elis, Iphitus. From then on, it was established that they should be held every four years. Before the games, heralds travelled throughout Greece proclaiming a Sacred Truce for the duration of the festival. Thus every conflict ceased. The various contests included in the programme were established gradually. While, in the first Olympiad, in 776, the only competition was foot racing, in every subsequent Olympiad more events were added. Thus, towards the middle of the 5th century BC (from 480 to 448 BC), and between the 75th and 83rd Olympiads, the games included the following events: the *stadium* (a foot race of 600 Olympic feet or 192.27 m), the *diavlos* (a double-stadium race), the *dolichos* (an endurance race of 20 to 24 stadia or about 5 kms), the *pentathlon* (comprising the long jump, the foot race, wrestling, discus-throwing and javelin-throwing), wrestling, boxing, the *pancration* (a combination of wrestling and boxing), the stadium for young boys, wrestling and boxing for young boys, a hoplite race (an armed race), a chariot race between quadrigas (chariots drawn by four horses) and the *kelis*, a horse race in which the riders rode young colts. At that time the events lasted five days, and the games were held on the eighth month of the Elean calendar, that is in July-August.

The game were organised and supervised by the *hellanodikae* (judges).

The first to arrive in Olympia were the athletes, who came early in order to train. Then began to stream in crowds of merchants, artists, writers, orators and others, who displayed their works and skills, thus ensuring the spread of their fame throughout Greece and the colonies.

Each city-state aspired to producing an Olympic victor. The prize for the winner was an olive branch - the *Kotinos* - always cut from the same wild-olive tree, the *Callistephanos*, which grew within the sacred Altis, by the south-western corner of the temple of Zeus. To honour the victor, his native city would tear down its walls. In 393 AD the Olympic games

Left page: The Nymphaeon, or Exhedra of Herodes Atticus. It was dedicated to Zeus by Herodes' wife, Regilla.

Above left: Black-figure vase, decorated with the representation of a quadriga. By the Amases painter. London, British Museum.

Above: Bronze discus with an incised design inscribed with the name of Poplius Asclepiades, who offered it to Zeus after his victory in the pentathlon. Found at Olympia and dated to 241 BC. Olympia, Archaeological Museum.

Below: Marble weight inscribed with the name of Armatides from Olympia. It was used by jumpers to give impetus to their jump. Olympia, Archaeological Museum.

Above left: The east pediment of the temple of Zeus. It depicts the preparation for the chariot race between Pelops and Oenomaus. In the centre stands Zeus, with Oenomaus on his right and Pelops on his left. Olympia, Archaeological Museum.

Above right: The west pediment of the temple of Zeus. It represents the battle between the Centaurs and the Lapiths. The figure of Apollo dominates the centre of the composition.

Below right: Marble head of Alexander the Great. Copy of a work of the Hellenistic period. Olympia, Archaeological Museum.

were abolished by the emperor Theodosius the Great. They were to be revived in Greece, their natural birthplace, fifteen centuries later, by the French historian and educator, baron Pierre de Coubertin. It was in 1896 in the beautiful marble Panathenaic stadium in Athens that the Olympic Hymn by Greece's national poet, Costis Palamas, set to music by the Corfiot composer Spyros Samaras, was heard for the first time. The Marathon race was won by the Greek water-carrier, Spyros Louis. Ever since that time, every four years, the Olympic flame has been carried by a relay of runners from ancient Olympia to Athens, and thence to the place where the Olympic games are being held. To this purpose was established in 1961 the International Olympic Academy which has its headquarters in Olympia.

A GUIDED TOUR OF THE ARCHAEOLOGICAL SITE

The site of Olympia has been inhabited since very ancient times. Besides other vestiges, there have been found Mycenean vases and potsherds and more than ten Mycenean chamber tombs.

A descending path will lead us to the sacred grove of Zeus, the Altis, enclosed on its western and southern sides by a wall, built in the 4th century BC. On its northern side rises the hill of Cronus. Outside the sacred grove were buildings, providing accommodation for the athletes, visitors and the personnel working in Olympia.

Dominating the Altis was the temple of Zeus, the construction of which took ten years. It was completed in 457 BC. The sculptures that adorned it were made of island marble, but Pentelic marble was also used. It is a peripteral Doric temple built by the local architect, Libon. On either end of the roof was set a gilt cauldron, while a gilt Nike crowned the middle of the pediment. Around the cornice of the temple were twenty-one gilt shields. The pediments were adorned with sculptured representations: the east pediment showed the chariot race between Pelops and Oenomaus, created by Paeonius, while the western side, depicts the combat be-

tween the Centaurs and the Lapiths.
The twelve metopes of the temple represented the labours of Heracles. The columns in the temples formed porticoes through which one came to the statue of Zeus, a work of Phidias.
The god, made of gold and ivory, was seated on a throne. He wore a wreath and held in his right hand a Nike. In his left hand was a carved sceptre. His sandals were of gold, as was the throne which was decorated with precious stones. Two Nikes ornamented each of the legs.
On the base which supported the throne were gold representations of the god Helios and other gods. Above the head of the statue were placed, on one side the three Graces and on the other the three Hours.
In the Altis, besides the temple of Zeus, there was also an altar to the god, the exact position of which is not known. It is conjectured that it lay between the Pelopeion and the Heraion. The Pelopeion, the place of worship dedicated to Pelops, stood between the temples of Zeus and Hera. At the foot of the hill of Cronus, on

the western side, we shall see the remains of the peripteral Doric temple of Hera, built around 600 BC. Here, sixteen women occupied themselves, every four years, with the weaving of a mantle for Hera, and also with the organisation of the Heraea, a foot-race between maidens. Inside the temple stood sculpted portraits of Zeus and Hera as well as statues of other gods, such as that of Hermes, shown holding the infant Dionysus, a work of Praxiteles, found, lying beside its base, in 1877. Also in the temple was the terracotta coffin of the tyrant of Corinth, Cypselus, decorated with wonderful mythological representations.

The early-Christian basilica built in the 5th century AD on the foundations of the workshop of Phidias. We can make out the central nave and the parapet of the sanctuary.

South-west of the Heraion we shall encounter the foundations of a circular edifice, the Philippeion, commissioned by Philip after the battle of Chaironea. Here the sculptor Leochares had carved the figures of Philip and Alexander.

West of the Heraion stood the Metroön, a small Doric temple with a cella, a structure built in the early years of the 4th century BC. Between the Heraion and the Metroön stood the Nymphaeon or Exhedra of Herodes Atticus, a fountain but also a reservoir holding the water brought to Olympia by Herodes. It dates from between 156 and 160 AD.

Lying at the foot of the hill of Cronus are the Zanes, the bases of sixteen bronze statues of Zeus, the cost of which was defrayed from the fines imposed on athletes who were guilty of bribing their opponents.

Inside the Altis, besides the altar of Zeus, there were another 70 altars, among which were those dedicated to Athena, Artemis, Alpheius, Hephaestus, Heracles, Hera Olympia - whose surname seems to have given its name to the site - to Apollo etc.

The Echo Colonnade, or Poekile Stoa, constituted the eastern boundary of the Altis. It owed its first name to the fact that, within it, a sound would be re-echoed seven times, while the name "Poekile" referred to its rich mural decoration. The colonnade measured 98 metres in length and 12.5 metres in width. It was built in the 4th century BC. At the point where the row of Zanes ended, began the *Krypte*, the "hidden entrance", a vaulted passageway through which athletes and *hellanodikae* entered the stadium.

The stadium lies to the north-east of the Altis. It was 500 feet long and was used for foot races. After the earthen embankments had been raised, it could accommodate forty to forty-five thousand spectators. Within the arena of the stadium was built, towards the end of the 4th century, an *exhedra* or tribune, where sat the judges and umpires of the games. On the north embankment was a marble altar from which the priestess of Demeter, Chamyne, could survey the games. To the south-east of the stadium was situated the hippodrome, consisting of embankments of piled-up earth. At the foot of the Cronion, between Herodes' Nymphaeon and the stadium, stretched a row of treasuries. These were small, rectangular cellae, usually adorned with two columns between the door jambs. They strongly resemble temples, which is why they were called *naiskoi* (small temples), or even just "temples". Here were kept the precious votive offerings of the various states.

Above: The Palaestra. Here, the athletes who competed in the wrestling, boxing and long jump events used to train.

Left: The temple of Hera, built on the site of an older temple, which was destroyed by fire.

Right: Terracotta statue of a warrior, produced by a Peloponnesian workshop around 480 BC. Olympia, Archaeological Museum.

Right page: The temple of Zeus (aerial photograph).

To the north-west of the Altis lay the gymnasium,where the athletes taking part in the foot races and the pentathlon trained. Nest to it, to the south, stood a smaller edifice, the palaestra, in which those competing in the wrestling, boxing and long jump events could train and practise. South of the palaestra stood two buildings: to the west the Heroön, a circular edifice with a rectangular room and a porch on its western side and, to the east, the *Theocoleion*, the house of the priests of Olympia. It was a square building arranged around an inner colonnaded court.

Further to the south used to stand the workshop of Phidias, where the great sculptor worked on his statue of Zeus. On the site of the workshop was built, in the 5th century AD, a three-aisled Christian basilica. Of this, today, only the central nave and the lower parapets of the sanctuary survive. Still further south we find the Leonidaeon, a large edifice of the middle of the 4th century BC, intended for the reception of distinguished guests. To the east of the Leonidaeon, just outside the enclosure

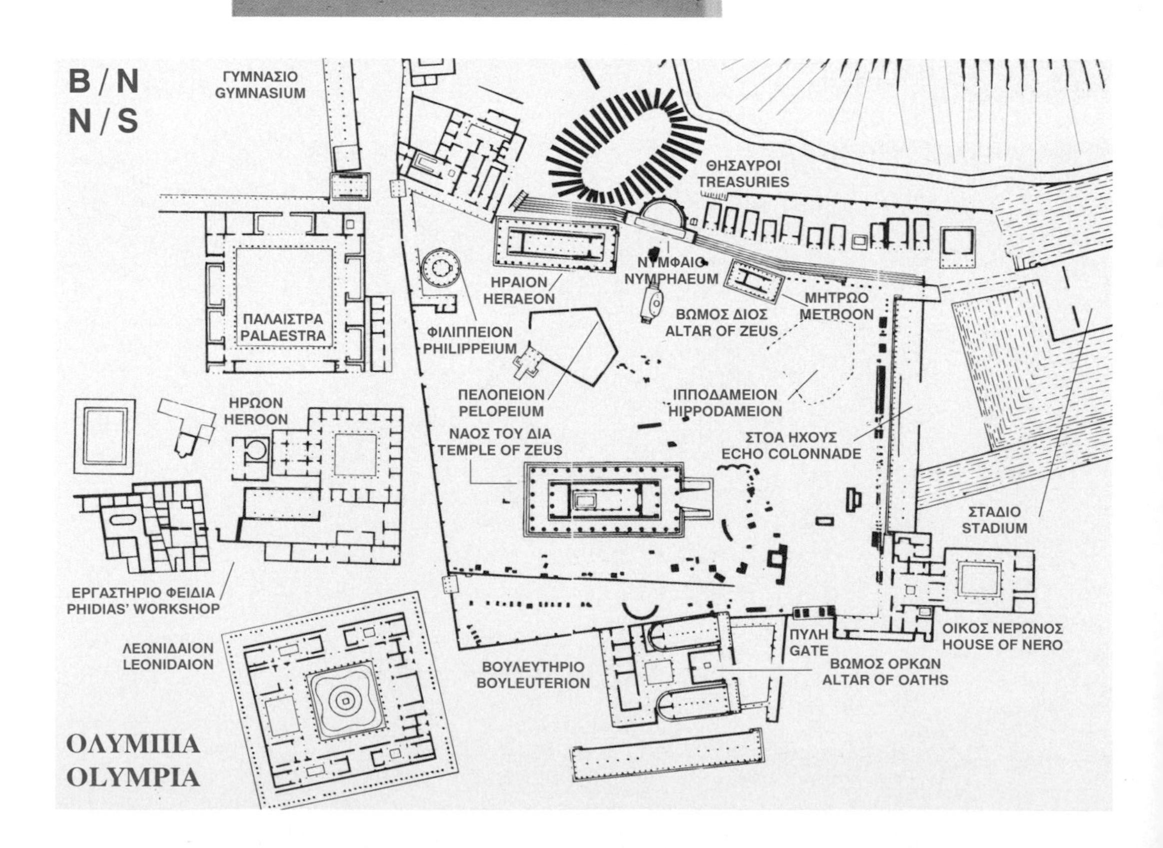

MUSEUM OF THE OLYMPIC GAMES

Not far from ancient Olympia we shall encounter the modern village of Olympia where we shall find the unique Museum of the Olympic Games. Here are displayed memorabilia of the Games, as well as the rare series of stamps by Papastephanakis and Provatakis on the theme of the Olympic Games (tel.0624/22544).

Archaeological Museum of Olympia. Left page, top: The Atlas metope from the temple of Zeus. Below: Statue of the emperor Claudius (left). The Hermes of Praxiteles, 330 BC (right).

Right page, top: Mycenean stirrup cup. Below: Bronze greave (6th century BC). Bronze tripodal cauldron (9th century BC). Ritual vessel from the tumulus of Samikon.

ARCHAEOLOGICAL MUSEUM

In its rooms we shall find disposed in chronological order objects dating from 2800 to 700 BC.
Finds of the Geometric and Archaic periods. Parts of the pediments of the treasuries of Megara and Gela. The helmet of Miltiades. The terracotta statue of Zeus and Ganymede. A lovely terracotta head of Athena and finds from the workshop of Phidias. The sculptures that adorned the pediments and metopes of the temple of Zeus. The marble statue of Nike by Paeonius and the famous statue of Hermes by Praxiteles. We shall also see various weapons, figurines, terracotta vessels and many small works of art (tel. 0624/22742).

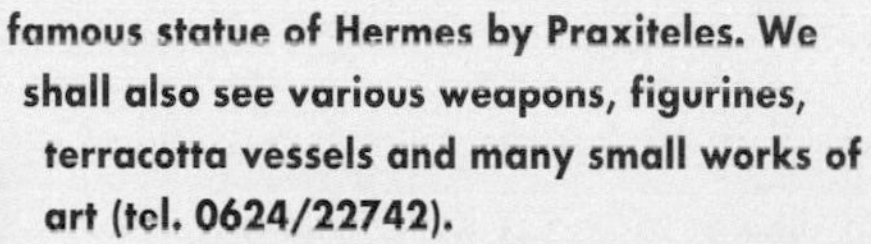

of the Altis, were discovered the foundations of a building complex, known as the *Bouleuterion*, the Council Hall. This was the assembly hall of the representatives of the Eleans, and perhaps also of the *hellanodikae*, when they met to judge the athletes who had broken the rules. It is dated to the middle of the 6th century BC.

To the northwest of the Altis existed a square building, the *Prytaneion*, where the ceremonies accompanying the awarding of the prizes took place. There was also a refectory where one could have a meal.

Baths of various periods have been found between the palaestra, the workshop of Phidias and the Cladeus.

On the hill of Cronus, outside the Altis, were set up sanctuaries of Eileithyia and of Aphrodite Urania.

Opposite the archaeological site and among a grove of trees is situated the new museum of Olympia. As we make our way towards it, we encounter the monument to Pierre de Coubertin, which encloses the heart of the man who worked so zealously to revive the Olympic Games.

GETTING TO KNOW ELIS

THE ELEAN HIGHLANDS

From Olympia a road leads towards Lala and the mountains of Pholoe. Here the sun is king, the grass is luxuriously green and the air is pervaded with the scents of the earth. About us spreads an immense carpet embroidered by a giant hand with trees and flowers and rolling hills. Every nook is connected with some myth or legend.

The first village we encounter is that of Lala, nestling among cherry and walnut trees. The murmur of running waters accompanies us on our way. On the outskirts of the village are the ruins of a Turkish castle. Leaving the village we come to the oak forest of Pholoe, the abode of the kindly centaur, Pholus, from whom the place took its name. Here walked Heracles when he was entertained as a guest by the centaur

Following our ascending route we come to Lambeia (Divre), built at an altitude of 800 metres. The village comprises seven neighbourhoods, each of which has its

own name, its church and its fountain.
The road leads towards Tripotama, which forms the border between Elis, Achaea and Messenia. This is a place of mountains, of ravines, of sheer cliffs and precipices. Down below, rivers wind their serpentine way among the rocks. Up here, we feel as though we were discovering a pristine world, untouched by time and inhabited only by gods and nymphs.
Many of the villages of Elis, whether clinging to mountainsides or hiding among trees, will enchant and delight us.

TOWARDS BASSAE

As we follow the road towards Andritsaina, we come first to Krestaina, an attractive small town in a verdant setting.
A side road leads to a nearby hill, where may be seen the remains of ancient Skillous, a city which was already fairly prosperous in Meso-Helladic times. Here have come to light finds dating from the early Mycenean, Archaic, Classical and early Hellenistic periods. The flourishing state of Skillous is testified by the fact that the city built the ancient temple of Hera at Olympia. Here the Athenians exiled Xenophon, who built a temple to the Ephesian Artemis. At a short distance from here is the village of Makrisia where, on the hill of Profitis Ilias above the village, on which stands a church and a convent, was discovered and excavated a Mycenean tumulus.
We continue on our way towards Andritsaina, which we can see from afar, emerging from among the trees that cover the verdant mountainside. We come to the village square with its huge plane tree, surrounded by coffee-shops and tavernas. This is a favourite place for gourmets who come to taste the famous cooking of Andritsaina. We wander among the cobbled

Left page, top: Head of a terracotta statue of Athena. Dated to c.490 BC. Olympia, Archaeological Museum.

Left page, below: The head of the statue of Apollo, from the west pediment of the temple of Zeus. Olympia, Archaeological Museum.

Above: the picturesque traditional village of Andritsaina.

paths of the village, admiring the sturdy stone houses with their tiled roofs, their latticed windows and the balconies adorned with plants in flower pots.
From time to time a church reminds us of the deep and natural piety of the inhabitants. Everything here speaks of serenity and peace. Andritsaina boasts a library housed in an old school, containing rare editions dating from 1500 and later, and also a notable folk art museum.
Outside the village may be seen the ruins of the monastery of Isova (13th c.) and all that survives of the *katholikon* of St. Nicholas, rare vestiges of Frankish times. Below the monastery, spreading out before us, are green valleys and low hills covered with cypress and pine trees. We now start to ascend towards Bassae.
As we climb upwards, the vegetation recedes. Around us now are nothing but bare rocks, low scrub and naked mountains. The landscape is rugged and wild.
In this awe-inspiring place, dominating the desolate scene, stands the temple of Apollo Epicurius (the Succourer), built in 420 BC on the foundation of an older temple by the inhabitants of neighbouring Phigaleia. It was dedicated to the god Apollo, in thanksgiving for his succour during a great plague. Designed by the architect Ictinus, who was also the designer of the Parthenon, this is the best preserved temple in Greece after the temple of Hephaestus (Theseum) in Athens. The peripteral Doric temple consists of the pronaos, cella and opisthodomos, and has six columns front and back, and fifteen along the sides. Within the cella stood the cult statue of Apollo. Along the top part of the cella ran a frieze depicting scenes from the battles of the Centaurs and of the Amazons, most of which is now in the British Museum.
North of Bassae the road leads to the village of Alipheira where, on a height, may be seen the ruins of a fortified enclosure, the foundations of buildings, as well as the remains of a Doric temple of Athena, dating from the 5th century BC.
For our return journey we may again take the same, comfortable tarred road that brought us here, or we may opt for another road out of Bassae, which is not tarred but which is easily negotiable and worth following. The descent is made through mountainous country and the view is superb. After a series of bends, the first signs of greenery appear which, as we continue our descent, grows thicker.
We come to Phigaleia, a small village in a verdant setting, containing Byzantine churches, two mosques and Turkish houses.
Not far from the village, we find the ruins of ancient Phigaleia. We can make out the remains of fortifications, with towers and battlements, the foundations of a church and architectural members of buildings.
Following the main road, we come to the village of Nea Phigaleia, where is preserved a three-aisled Byzantine basilica. Seven kilometres to the west of Nea Phigaleia lies the village of Lepreon. On a height, at some distance from the village, we can see the ruins of the acropolis of Lepreon, ruined towers, vestiges of a Doric temple consisting of a pronaos, cella and pteron, as well as the remains of buildings of Hellenistic times. A built rectangular altar has been excavated in the vicinity.
We return to Phigaleia. A little below us flows the river Nedas with its waterfalls
If we wish to see them, we must take a small path, running at first through vegetable gardens. It is not an easy hike and there are several natural obstacles along the way. However, when we reach our destination, we shall be richly rewarded for our efforts. From a precipice tumble down a series of cascades, the "white waters", as the locals call them. The spectacle is breathtaking - a fitting climax to our tour of the highlands of Elis.

THE LOWLANDS OF ELIS AND THE COAST

Here the soil is rich and fertile. All around us stretch vineyards, olive-groves, fields of wheat and maize, vegetable gardens... Every so often we come upon a row of greenhouses.
For this journey we shall start out from Zacharo, a small town in a verdant setting, which spreads out on a hill and comes all the way down to the sandy beach that

Bassae: Views of the temple of Apollo Epicurus, above, as it looked some time ago, below, as it appears today.

The lake of Caiaphas (aerial photograph). →

fringes the clear blue waters of the Ionian Sea. After a while we come to Caiaphas, a town known for its mineral springs. It is built on the tiny island of Aghia Aikaterini in the middle of a small lake. On the eastern shore of the lake, under a slope of Mt. Caiaphas, there is a cave, known as the cave of the Anhydrides, the mythical abode of nymphs. Within the cave is a warm sulphurous spring, whose waters are beneficial to those suffering from skin diseases. There are bathhouses on the western side of the lake.

There are also mineral springs in another lake, known as Geraneion cave, situated at a distance of a few hundred metres from the cave of the Anhydrides. The waters of this cave, also the fabled abode of nymphs, have a disagreeable sulphurous odour. However, according to legend, the unpleasant smell is due to the fact that the centaur Nessus used these waters to cleanse the wound he received from the poisonous arrow of Heracles. On the northern edge of Mt. Caiaphas, and not far from the village of Kato Samiko, there are ruins of an ancient city, which Pausanias calls Samia, while Strabo refers to it as Samon, and others call it Samikon. Others believe that this was the Homeric Arene. Surviving here are sections of a wall dating from the Macedonian era. From here the road leads to Epitalion, identified by Strabo as the Homeric Thryon or Thryoessa,

Above left: The Alpheius river.

Below: The monastery of Skafidia.

meaning a place of many rushes. On a site to the north-west of the present village, archaeological excavations have brought to light a Roman bath, workshops, a pottery kiln, a large public edifice, and the foundations of houses.

In the vicinity have been found many vessels of the 4th century BC, and an even greater number of vases of the 2nd and 3rd centuries AD. On the opposite side, across the main road, rise hills where many remains of the Mycenean period have been uncovered.

Continuing our journey, we pass the Alpheius and its dam, and come to "medieval" Katakolon. North-west of the town and at a short distance from it, lies the beach of ancient Pheias, today known as Aghios Andreas.

On the top of the hill, above the beach, may be seen the ruins of the medieval fortress known as Pontikokastro (Mouse Castle). Ancient Pheia, whose name is confirmed by Homer, was the second most important port of Elis, after that of Kyllene. On the hill stood the acropolis of ancient times, the building material of which was used in the construction of the castle.

From here, the road continues on to the village of Skafidia. On an idyllic spot we find the women's monastery of Skafidia. The entrance is through an arched portal. Above the portal rises a square tower. The *katholikon* of the monastery was built in the 12th century, but in 1887 it was converted into a single-nave basilica with a narthex and a fore-porch (*prostoön*). The narthex is covered with murals of the 18th century. Along the southern side of the

monastery lie the cells of the nuns, the museum containing important relics and manuscripts, and a fountain.

The most interesting part of the monastery is the west side, on which stands a strong fortress. It is a two-storey, building, on the four corners of which there are circular bastions. The fortress is built in the western architectural style and is a unique specimen of its kind.

We come to Amalias, in its rich setting of vineyards and olive groves. Just beyond the village we shall encounter the monasteries of Panaghia Frangovilla and St. Nicholas "tou Frangopidimatos".

Continuing northwards, our road leads towards the ruins of ancient Elis, one of the important centres of antiquity, which reached a high peak of prosperity during

Left page: Views of idyllic Katakolon, the port of Pyrgos.

the Roman period. Elis was the largest city of the province of Elis, but also a centre of all of Greece. Recent finds indicate that it was inhabited since very ancient times. It has been ascertained that it existed 1500 years before 471 BC, when it was constituted as a city. In historical times the Eleans considered Elis a sacred city, which is why they never fortified it. It was in Elis that athletes trained, one month before the start of the Olympic games. Accompanying the athletes were members of their family and friends, as a result of which the city was transformed into a cosmopolitan centre. It was flooded with people coming from every corner of Greece, from the islands as well as from the mainland, but also with Greeks from the colonies in Asia Minor, the Pontus, Magna Graecia - Sicily and southern Italy - and Africa.

A GUIDED TOUR OF THE ARCHAEOLOGICAL SITE

Among the most important edifices of ancient Elis was the gymnasium, where the

athletes trained before going to Olympia. Inside the gymnasium were altars to Heracles, Idaeus, to Eros and Anteros, to Demeter and Kore. Adjacent to the gymnasium was another square building, the palaestra, which was where the wrestlers exercised. In this building there was a statue of Zeus which had been paid for with the money exacted from an athlete as a fine for breaking the rules. In Elis, in contrast to Olympia, there was a third gymnasium, which was called *Maltho* (soft), because of the softness of its ground.

In one corner of this gymnasium, there was a bust of Heracles and, in another, a relief representation of Eros and Anteros. This gymnasium also served as an assembly hall where the Eleans met to present improvised talks but also their written works. The edifice was known as *Lalichthum*, after the name of the donor.

To get to the baths, which were outside the gymnasium, one followed the "street of silence" and passed by the altar of Artemis Philomeirax ("friend of youths"), an epithet given to the goddess because of the proximity of her altar to the gymnasium.

As for the "street of silence", it was given this name after a group of Pisatans, who had been spying on the city of Elis, had entered into the city by following this road, without being heard. Another passage led to the agora and to the *Hellanodikaeo*n, the headquarters of the *hellanodikae*.

The agora had porticoes, situated at some distance one from the other and with streets passing in between, and its size was such that it was also called the hippodrome. The portico on the south side of the agora, built in Doric style, was where the hellanodikae spent the day. Another portico nearby was known as the *Kerkyraike Stoa* - the Corcyrean portico - because it had been erected by the Eleans with the booty taken from the Corcyreans. Also in the agora was a temple of Apollo Akesius, the stone statues of Helios and Selene, a sanctuary of the Greeks, a statue of Eros, a temple of Silenus, the grave of Oxylus and the House of the "Sixteen" (women) who wove the mantle of Hera.

Following these was an ancient peripteral temple dedicated to Roman emperors. Behind the Kerkyrean Portico stood the temple of Aphrodite Urania, in which was a gold and ivory statue created by Phidias, and an open-air sanctuary of Aphrodite Pandemus, in which was a statue of the goddess seated on a goat, made by Scopas. Further on stood the temple of Hades, one of the newer sanctuaries of the agora, which the Eleans opened once a year, because men only descended into Hades once. On the northern fringes of the agora was the theatre and the sanctuary of Dionysus containing a statue of the god, by Praxiteles. The theatre had assumed a monumental form in Hellenistic times, which proves that, already then, Elis possessed important edifices. The spectators seated in the theatre had their backs to the agora and faced the river Peneius, which flowed close by, at a little lower level.

Finally, as Pausanias informs us, in the acropolis of Elis, there was a sanctuary of Athena and a gold and ivory statue of the goddess, the work of Phidias. Not far from ancient Elis we can see the Peneius dam, one of the largest earthen dams in Europe. Here, noises are muted and rare is the sound of a human voice. Silence envelops the dam in infinite loneliness.

Two towns surrounded by lush vegetation, close to the river Peneius, are those of Gastouni and Bartholomio. North of Bartholomio lies Andravida and to the west, Kyllene.

Andravida, built in a rich and fertile plain, was a flourishing city in Frankish times. It was the capital of the principality of Achaea and it was visited by considerable numbers of noblemen and knights who came here to practise their horsemanship. Of the Latin church of St. Sophia built in 1236 in Gothic style by the Franks, only the eastern section survives.

The city of Kyllene, which retains its ancient name, was the port town of the city of Elis. It was a harbour of considerable importance during the Peloponnesian Wars and, as Thucydides informs us, it was here at Kyllene that Alcibiades, having defected to the Spartans, landed on his way to Sparta. Today, Kyllene is a small village with a port from which sail the ferry-boats linking the mainland to the Ionian island of Zakyn-

Ruins of buildings at Elis, the largest city of ancient Elis.

thos. In Frankish times the city was called Clarentia - which became Glarentza in local parlance - and it was a thriving trading and financial centre with a busy port.

The medieval town was surrounded by a fortified wall, with battlements and towers. Today, of these mighty fortifications, only ruins remain. It is said that the castle was destroyed in 1430 by the emperor Constantine Palaeologus, to avoid its falling into Turkish hands.

At a distance of 2.5 kms from the village we shall find the Byzantine convent of Panaghia Blacherna (12th c) with its marvellous frescoes.

Six kilometres further north, by the village of Kastro, stands another Frankish castle,

known as Castel Tornese, or Chlemoutsi. It was built in 1220 by Frankish knights and was originally known as Château Tournois. When the Venetians took it, in 1687, they Italianized the name to Tornese. It was later named Chlemoutsi, meaning small hill.
It is the most beautiful and best preserved castle of the Peloponnese. Its shape is roughly hexagonal and it is encircled by strong crenellated walls and towers. Inside the citadel we shall see the central courtyard, large vaulted halls, a chapel and a cistern for storing water.
We now move southwards and come to Loutra Kyllinis, a thermal establishment organised by the National Tourism Organisation. In the wide surrounding pine-clad area, which reaches all the way down to the golden sandy beach, there are two hotels, an organised camping site and mineral springs. Continuing southwards, we come to the fishing villages of Arkouda, Glypha and Bouka, with their sandy beaches lying along the deep blue sea.
The road north leads to Lechaina, the birthplace of the novelist Andreas Karkavitsas, and on to Manolada with its 12th-century frescoed Byzantine church of Palaiopanaghia.
From here, the road runs through a pine forest and comes to the village of Kounoupeli, built on the site of ancient Hyrmina. Right next to the village rises a lofty rock, from the entrails of which gush mineral springs. Further north, on a rocky headland, may be seen the remains of an ancient Mycenean acropolis. Before us stretches the wide, infinite sea, while across the way we can just make out the coast of neighbouring Achaea.

Left page, top: The pine trees come down almost to the water's edge, on the lovely beach of Kyllene.

Left page, below: Chlemoutsi castle on the top of the hill, at the foot of which lies the village of Castro. In the distance, the deep blue waters of the Ionian Sea.

Lithograph of the castle of Tornese, or Chlemoutsi.

ACHAEA

Our tour ends with the prefecture of Achaea, which occupies the north-western part of the Peloponnese.

The contour of the land is mostly mountainous, dominated by the three lofty mountain ranges of the Panachaikon, Mt. Erymanthus and the Aroania or Chelmos. It borders on the east with Corinthia, on the south with Arcadia, on the west with Elis, while its northern side is washed by the waters of the gulfs of Corinth and Patras.

The low, coastal zone of the prefecture stretches from Corinthia to Cape Araxos; it is dotted with charming villages and ends in a fringe of superb beaches. The mountains and highland regions impress us with their own wild or gentle beauty.

In the forests of Mt. Erymanthus lived the terrible boar which continuously ravaged the countryside around, and drove the farmers to despair, until Heracles captured it alive - this being the fourth labour imposed on him.

On the Aroanian mountains, from one of the highest peaks known as the Neraidorrachi, the frozen waters of the Styx - the "calamity-bearing waters", as Strabo called them - tumble down into the deep gorge.

According to mythology, the nymph Styx was the daughter of Oceanus and wife of the giant Pallas. Their children were Cratus (Strength), Bia (Violence), Zelus (Zeal) and Nike (Victory). Another son of Styx, fathered by Erebus, was Charon, the ferryman of Hades.

Gods and men swore by the waters of the river Styx, and woe unto him who broke his oath. It was believed that its frozen waters eventually ended up in the land of the dead, after having run around it nine times.

In the Aroanians, near the village of Kastria, there is a wide gaping cave. Here, it was said, took refuge the daughters of the king of Tiryns, Proetus, who were made mad by Hera because they had boasted that they were more beautiful than she. In their madness, they imagined they were heifers and wandered from place to place, spreading a "mania" among the women of Argolis, until they finally came to the cave in the Aroania.

Here, also , is the monastery of Aghia Lavra in the precinct of which, under the historic plane-tree, was raised in 1821 the standard of the revolution, marking the start of the War of Independence.

The Achaea of today covers a much larger area than the Achaea of antiquity. Its name, at that time, was "Aegialos", mean-

ing seashore, and that of its inhabitants "Aegialeis". It is under this name that they appear in Homer's "Catalogue of Ships", in the *Iliad*. It got its name of Achaea from the Achaeans of Tisamenes, who invaded Achaea in the 11th century BC, after they had been driven out by the Dorians who had settled in the Achaean centres of the eastern Peloponnese. As is indicated by the finds of archaeological excavations, Achaea has been inhabited since very early times, since approximately 6000 BC. Most of the prehistoric constructions belong to the Mycenean period, among them the cyclopean walls that surround the acropolis of the "Teichos" on cape Araxos, and that of Aegira in Aegialeia, and the settlement at "Portes", which used to function as a control post and provisioning centre. The finds of recent excavations also show that the role the region played and the position it occupied in the Mycenean world was quite considerable.
When the Achaeans settled in Achaea, they founded important cities, while the Ionian Aegialeans, after their defeat at Helice, their cultural centre, by the invading Achaeans, were forced to seek refuge first in Athens and later in Asia Minor, where they founded the cities of Miletus, Ephesus, and other Ionian colonies.
The Achaeans settled in twelve cities in Achaea. In 280 BC was established the Achaean League, which, in the beginning, comprised four cities. The principal aim and purpose of the establishment of the League was to rid the Achaean cities of the rulers appointed by the Macedonians and of the Macedonian guard.
Within a period of eight years, the Achaean League embraced all the flourishing cities of Achaea, which numbered about ten. The seat of the League was Aeghion. Up until 255 BC the supreme command was held by two generals (strategoi), while from 255 on it was entrusted to one *strategos* aided by other notables.
From 245 BC on, the strategos at the head of the League was the Sicyonian, Aratos. Decisions were made by a council consisting of representatives of the various cities. The power of the League grew when cities outside Achaea were admitted as members.
In 192 BC Sparta was annexed to the Achaean Confederacy.
The efforts of the Spartans to break away from the League, and the intervention of the Romans in the quarrels between the Greek cities, led the League to take up arms against the Romans. In 146 BC the

View of the site on which stands the monastery of Aghia Lavra

MINOAN LINES
MINOAN LINES

Roman general Mummius defeated the armies of the League, a Roman victory which put an end to the autonomy of the Greek cities.

Achaea embraced Christianity at an earlier date than the rest of Greece. The apostle Andrew taught and suffered martyrdom in Patras in 68 AD. Patras flourished greatly during Byzantine times, when it was an important commercial and manufacturing centre. In 1205 Achaea was taken by the Franks, in whose possession it remained until 1430, when it passed into the hands of Constantine Palaeologus. In 1460 it was captured by the Turks and in 1687 was conquered by the Venetians, whose rule lasted until 1715. The inhabitants of the region had already, since 1600, begun to build and to establish settlements in the highlands, to avoid the Turkish yoke.

On the 25th of March 1821, the Archbishop of Old Patras, Germanos, raised the banner of freedom in St. George's square in Patras, but the city was only liberated in 1828 by the forces of the French general Maison.

PATRAS

Capital of the prefecture of Achaea is the attractive town of Patras, built along the coasts washed by the waters of the Patraic gulf. The city was said to have been founded by the Achaean Spartan, Patreus, who abandoned his native city in order not to cooperate with the Dorian invaders. According to Pausanias, the city of Patras was formed by the amalgamation of three small rural settlements - Arhoe, Antheia and Messati - which probably took place around 550 BC.

The surrounding area had already been inhabited since Mycenean times, as is evidenced by the archaeological finds at the sites of Boudeni, Agrapithia, Bala, Achaia-Clauss and Kallithea.

From Mycenean times up to the 7th and 6th centuries BC the inhabitants of Patras and the surrounding area were mainly farmers. In 146 BC the armies of Mummius destroyed and sacked the city of Corinth, but Patras was spared. Thus, while Corinth lay in ruins, Patras began to develop, thanks to the privilege of relative autonomy it enjoyed. In Roman times its position opposite the coasts of Italy was particularly appreciated. The city was favoured in the 2nd century AD by the Roman emperors and especially by Hadrian. Fine mansions and public buildings - a gymnasium, odeon, bath - adorned Roman Patras, which began to spread out eastwards, westwards and southwards, towards the sea.

In Pausanias' day it gave the impression of a cosmopolitan city, as its residents represented a mixture of cultures and races.

The medieval fortifications of Patras were built in the 6th century AD. A considerable

Left: View of Patras (aerial photograph)

Above: Patras, the Odeon.

Below: A scene from the carnival of Patras.

Patras: The castle and the city (aerial photograph). ›

Above: Lithograph of Patras.

Below: The church of St. Andrew.

amount of ancient building material was used in the construction of the castle.
In the 7th century AD the economy of the city began to acquire new vigour thanks to the development of new activities such as carpet-weaving, silkworm farming, the processing of silk and the manufacture of silk and linen fabrics. The 9th century was a period of economic prosperity. During the period of Latin rule, the Franks refortified the city. Following its liberation from the Turks in 1828, Patras began to develop rapidly, as a consequence of which it is today the third largest city in Greece and the first in size and importance in the Peloponnese.

Above the modern city rises the medieval castle with its fortified enclosure, and its moat which used to be filled with water. The fortress was impregnable in medieval times. The view from up here is magnificent: below, the town spreads out all the way to the sea, while in the distance rises the imposing mass of the mountains of Roumeli.
At the foot of the citadel spreads the old town, which still retains quite a number of attractive neo-classical houses.
The city is divided into what is known as the Lower and the Upper towns. Ascending streets lead from one to the other. The town plan was designed in 1829 by a Greek officer serving in the French army, Stamatis Voulgaris, who was also a friend of the first governor of Greece, John Capodistrias. The Lower Town, the "marine" town, is distinguished by its well-laid-out streets and wide squares.
In its centre, the two and three-storied arcaded houses, revealing the influence of the West, lend the city its particular character. George I square, with its playing fountain, its winged lions and the neo-classical building designed by Ernest Ziller which today houses the Municipal Theatre, is one of the particularly attractive corners of the town. Further to the south lies 25th March Square, where we may see the restored Roman Odeon, dating from 160 AD, which is older but smaller than that of Herodes Atticus in Athens. Close by are the church of the Pantanassa, with its impressive belfry, and the Byzantine church of the Pantocrator.
The grandest church in Patras is that dedicated to the city's patron saint, St. Andrew. Adjacent to the new domed church we find the older basilica of St. Andrew. A marble plaque set in the wall informs us that the church was built in 1835. However, its construction was completed at a later date. Next to the basilica is a small kiosk, through which one descends to the

The Achaia-Clauss area, with the winery overlooking the fertile plain, and the sea in the distance.

aghiasma, the fountain of holy water on the spot on which St. Andrew is said to have suffered his martyrdom.
Here, in Pausanias' time was the divining fountain of Demeter and a shrine dedicated to the goddess.
One of the most attractive squares of the town is the one known as "Psila Alonia" - "the high threshing floor". It is the "balcony" of Patras and is adorned with tall palm trees, a sundial and a bust of Greece's national poet, Costis Palamas. Here excavations have brought to light the foundations of a building complex of the Roman period. Every year, at Carnival time, the town abandons itself to revelry and merry-making, attracting thousands of visitors who come to take part in the fun. The spectacular procession of floats, accompanied by hundreds of dancing masqueraders, parades through the centre of town on the last Sunday of Carnival, marking the end and climax of the festivities, which will linger for a long time in the memory of those who participated in them. Two and a half kilometres south-east of Patras, we shall visit the Byzantine monastery of the *Gerokomeion*, while north of the city, on a verdant hill which offers a fine view of the surrounding country, we shall find the Achaia-Clauss winery housed in an impressive, castle-like old building.
Nine kilometres beyond the Achaia-Clauss estate, we shall come upon the 14th -century monastery of Oblou, set within a forest of plane trees. At a short distance from the settlements of Boudeni, Kallithea and Clauss, to the north-east and north of Patras, have been brought to light Mycenean cemeteries dating from around 1450/1400 BC to 1050 BC.

The Museums of Patras

ARCHAEOLOGICAL MUSEUM
It contains finds dating from all the periods, uncovered in the excavations carried out in the surrounding area. (Vassilissis Olgas Square, Aratou and Maisonos streets, no.41)

FOLK MUSEUM
It is housed in a room of the Municipal Centre of Literature and Art (Logou ke Technis) on George I Square, and displays works of Greek artists.

ETHNOLOGICAL MUSEUM
Also housed in the above building, it includes among its exhibits military uniforms, guns, swords, captured weapons etc.

MUSEUM OF POPULAR ART
Housed in a neo-classical building, its collection includes regional costumes, embroideries, jewellery, household utensils, various implements etc.

PRESS AND PRINTING MUSEUM
This Museum also is housed in rooms of the Centre of Literature and Art. Among its exhibits are various documents related to the 1821 revolution and to later years, engravings, old maps, rare editions, newspapers of the Peloponnese dating to before 1900 etc. There is also a library in which one may find series of newspapers, old periodicals etc.

Above: Kato Achayiá

Below left: The sandy beach of Kalogria.

Above right: Antirrhion.

Below right: Rhion.

THE ACHAEAN COAST

ITINERARY 1

We follow the road which stretches out to the west of Patras, the old highway running through the fertile plain connecting Patras with Pyrgos.

Our route runs along the western shore of the Gulf of Patras. On our right stretches the sea, with its endless beaches and golden strands and a string of pretty villages hiding among rich verdure. The village of Kato Achayia, with its wide beach, is built on the site of ancient Dyme. Dyme was the second largest city of western Achaea, after Patras, and it played an important role in Hellenistic and Roman times. In 210 BC it was plundered by the Roman Poplius Sulpicius.

When Pausanias visited the city he found

a sanctuary dedicated to the Great Mother and to Attis, gods of Lydio-Phrygian origin, whose cult was brought to Dyme by the Romans who settled there during the reign of Augustus. Attis was a priest of the Great Mother, who died at an early age. The worship of the two divinities included the celebration of mysteries.

Further west we encounter the village of Lakkopetra, after which we come to Araxos. South of cape Araxos and at a short distance from the lagoon with the fish hatcheries, we find the so-called "castle of Kalogria" referred to by Polybius as the Wall (Teichos) of the Dymeans. The cyclopean wall built in the Mycenean period was restored in medieval times.

South of Araxos stretches the golden beach of Kalogria bordered by the green pine forest of Strophilia.

ITINERARY 2

To the north and east of Patras extends the coastal zone which reaches all the way to Corinthia. Characteristic of this area is the lush vegetation, the picturesque coves and the dozens of villages, lapped by the waves of the Corinthian gulf, which emerge, one after the other, as we drive along.

Our first stop, Rhion, is an important crossroads of sea and land communications, since it links the Peloponnese to continental Greece. Here is the entrance to the gulf of Corinth. Crowning the headland of Rhion is

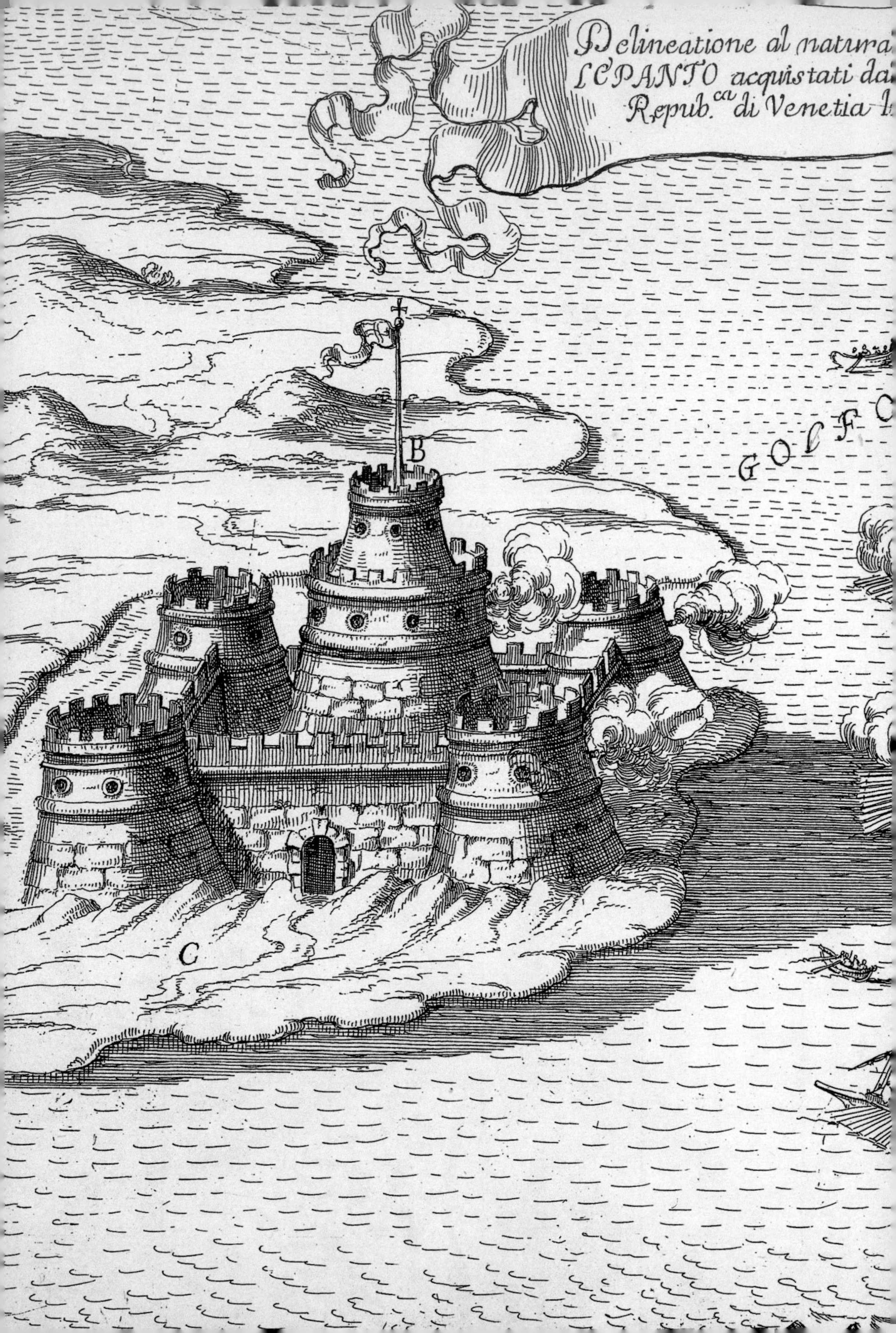
Delineatione al natura
LEPANTO acquistati da
Repub.ca di Venetia
B
C
GOLFO

elli famosi Dardanelli di
mi della Potentissima
Luglio. 1687
LEPANTO
DI
A
E
D

← **Coloured lithograph of Rhion and Antirrhion. (Giacomo de Rossi, *Teatro de la guerra contro il Turco*, Roma 1687).**

Above: Aighion.

Below: Platanos

the mighty fortress of the Morea, while, across the waters at Antirrhion rises the castle of Roumeli, guarding the shores of continental Greece. Both fortresses were built by the Turkish sultan Bayazit II, in 1499, to control the entrance to the gulf of Corinth. They were restored by the Venetians in 1713.

The Rhion fortress is triangular in shape. The landward side was protected by a wide moat which communicated with the sea and which filled with sea water. Sturdy towers strengthened the defences of the castle on the sea and land sides. According to Strabo, at Rhion there was a shrine of Poseidon. After Rhion we come to the charming fishing village of Psathopyrgos, one of the most attractive villages of the area. We move on to Lambiri, with its lovely beach, to verdant Longos, basking by its pebbly shore, and finally arrive at Aighion, the second largest town of the province.

Already in antiquity Aighion was the second most important city of Achaea after the disappearance of Helike, and the political centre of the Achaean League.

The city was continuously inhabited since prehistoric times, as excavations prove. When Pausanias visited the city in the second century BC, Aighion still retained some of its former glory. During the periods of Frankish and Turkish rule, at which time it was known as Vostitsa, it was one of the important centres of the Peloponnese.

Aighion was one of the first towns of the Peloponnese to be liberated from the Turkish yoke in 1821. The city is built on three levels, as it was also in antiquity, starting from the seashore and climbing upwards. The town is thus divided into Upper and Lower Aighion. The attractive square of Psila Alonia in the upper town offers a wide view over the open bay of Aighion. The lower town charms us with its

small harbour, its twelve-spouted fountain, known as "fountain of the mole", and its shady square with the three plane trees, among which stands out the centuries-old tree with the huge bole, known as the "plane tree of Pausanias".

Of the churches of Aighion, of interest are the cathedral of Phaneromeni, designed by Ernest Ziller, and the church of Panaghia Trypiti or Zoodochos Pighi, wedged in a steep cliff in a luxuriantly green setting.

East of Aighion, at a place not yet exactly determined - somewhere between the villages of Rizomylos and Rhodia - lay the ancient city of Helike. In the winter of 373 BC, a violent earthquake, the epicentre of which was in the western part of the gulf of Corinth, shook the area, with devastating results for the neighbouring coasts of the Peloponnese and continental Greece.

Helike, an important political and religious centre of the Achaeans, sank into the sea. In ancient times one could still make out the submerged ruins of the city when the sea was calm, as is testified by three reliable witnesses - Pausanias, Pliny and Ovid.

Continuing our journey along a coastal strip dotted with seaside villages, we come to Diakofto, lying in a luxuriantly green setting. This is the starting point for the tiny cog railway which leads up to Mega Spelaion and Kalavryta.

After Diakofto, other attractive seaside villages follow. We pass, in turn, Trapeza, Platanos and, just before we come to the borders of Corinthia, Akrata, and Aeghira.

Above: The beach of Trapeza, also known as "Punta".

Below: View of Akrata.

Left: Psathopyrgos.

THE ACHAEAN HIGHLANDS

ITINERARY 1

It is in the highlands of Achaea that we find the most impressive beauty spots. Among the mighty masses of the three mountain ranges than run through the region - the Panachaikon, the Erymanthus, and the Aroania or Chelmos - lie small peaceful valleys, flower-decked fields and plateaux, rise fir-clad peaks, covered with snow the whole year long, flow gentle streams and murmuring brooks, open up awesome ravines.

Up the verdant slopes climb charming villages, their two- or three-storied houses bearing the obvious stamp of the skilled master-builders who produced them, artisans from Langadia, from Epirus, or from the community of Nonacus, Kalavryta - the renowned Varvarites - who used to go from village to village building houses.

It was not difficult to guess their origin, which was revealed by the characteristic features of their work. Those of the Langadian and Epirots were fairly similar. Those of the Varvarites differed, as they

Above and below: The beautiful gorge of the Buraicos. One of the enchanting corners of highland Achaea.

usually used more wood than the others. The houses are made of stone and are usually covered with slate roofs. One of the sides often has a projecting section formed by the fireplace. The *kato'i*, the lower floor, is used as a storeroom and a shelter for the livestock. The residential quarters occupied the *ano'i* , the upper floor.

On a level space, in a prominent position, stands the church. This space constitutes the social centre of the village Here is to be found also the traditional fountain. The houses communicate with one another through stepped streets and are grouped in neighbourhoods. A village may have two, three, or more neighbourhoods.

In the mountain villages of Kalavryta, built in the 18th or the beginning of the 19th century, still survive today towers and towered houses with battlements and machicolations above the main entrance.

Many of the villages in the Achaean highlands are famed for the abundance of their waters and the luxuriance of their vegetation. Quite a few of these (Alpochori, Vessini), have been characterised as traditional. Worth mentioning here are the names of certain of these mountain settlements.

South of Patras, on the slopes of Mt. Erymanthus, lies Kalentzi, by a thick forest of firs, and also verdant Alpochori. Further

The village of Kerpine.

towards the south-east, on the Panachaikon and Erymanthus, lie Halandritsa, with its ruined Frankish castle, Katarractis, Kalanistra, Kalamos, Michas - on a walnut-covered slope - and Ano and Kato Vlasia. Further east, around Kalavryta, we find Flamboura, from where a dirt road leads to the monastery of Makelaria, built, as the inscription informs us, in 532 AD by Justinian's general, Belissarius.

Further south lies Kryoneri, with its attractive traditional fountain and abundant waters, verdant Kertezi, famed for its wine and its savoury bean soup, Ano and Kato Kleitoria. Also the village of Arsania, built at an altitude of 930 metres, Pankrati, with its "grapevine of Pausanias", Daphne, Paos,and any number of other picturesque villages. North of Kalavryta, among its setting of fir trees, we find Fteri gazing out over the Corinthian gulf, Zachlorou in the mountain valley of the Buraicos, and, further south, the important village of Kerpine. where one can see houses built by the famous master-masons of the Peloponnese, the Varvarites.

To the south lies Lousou, and the fortress-house of Petmezas, equipped with a defensive tower, a circular bastion and crenellated battlements. Outside the village, by the small chapel of the Panaghia, have come to light the remains of the sanctuary of Artemis Hemera and of the ancient city of Lousae.

The temple of the goddess consisted of a central building, with a front and back porch and a cella, and of rectangular porticoes running along the north and south sides. It was probably built in the second half of the 4th century BC.

South of Lousae lies the village of Kastria

Left page: Views of the cave of Limnes at Kastria.

Above: A dense forest of fir trees surrounds the Tsivlos lake in the vicinity of the village of Zarouchla. Another idyllic spot in the highlands of Achaea.

and the beautiful cave of Limnes, said to be the cave where the daughters of Proetus found refuge. In the cave are thirteen small lakes with clear, transparent waters, each situated on a different level. The stalactites and stalagmites mirrored in the calm waters and the iridescent colours make this a magic, fairy-tale place. The temperature inside the cave is 15º C. When the cave was explored, not far from its entrance were found fossilised bones of hippopotami, 300,000 years old, of deer, 100,000 years old, and also human bones of a more recent date.

To the east lies the village of Zarouchla, dominated by the Photelas tower, Peristera and Solos. Here starts the path for the arduous ascent of the Chelmos, leading to the Neraidorachi ("Nymphs' Peak") and from there to the "Waters of the Styx". Today the inhabitants of the region call these

CHELMOS

On the high slopes of Mt. Chelmos, at an altitude of 1650 to 2100 metres, at the place called Vathia Lakka, there is a ski centre disposing of three drawn and one elevated ski-lift and two runs for each lift. A comfortable tarred road from Kalavryta (14 kms) winding through a fir-covered area leads to the centre. A little higher up, at 2100 metres, at the site of "Diaselo Avgou" stands the B. Leontopoulos refuge. There is another mountain refuge on the slopes of the Panachaikon range, at Psarthi (1420 m altitude), known as the S. Gerokostopuolos refuge. It is reached by way of Patras.

Above: The beach at Diakofto.

The old locomotive of the railway.

Right: The cog railway climbs up the steep track in the Buraicos gorge.

waters "Mavroneri", meaning "Black Water", because, seen from above, the waters flowing at the bottom of the ravine look black. Trickling out of the entrails of a precipitous cliff, the waters drip down over the rocks into the gorge, eventually joining the river Krathis.

ITINERARY 2

South of Diakofto, between the peaks of the Chelmos, at an altitude of 657 metres, lies the picturesque village of Kalavryta, built on the site of the ancient city of Kynaitha. Just beyond the village, at an altitude of 1100 metres, on top of a towering peak, stood the castle built by the barons de Tournais, which is known today as "Kastro tis Orias" - "Castle of the Fair Lady". It is said that it was from this castle that the beautiful daughter of the baron of

Above: The railway station at Zachlorou.

Below: The picturesque station at Mega Spelaion.

Above: View of Kalavryta.

Right: The monument to the heroes of the War of Independence at Aghia Lavra.

Halandritsa, Catherine Palaeologus, plunged to her death, in order not to fall into the hands of the Turks who had taken the castle. During the years of Frankish rule, Kalavryta was the seat of one of the twelve baronies of the Morea. In 1330, the town passed into the hands of the Byzantines, who sold it to the Knights of St. John of Rhodes. In 1463 it was taken by the Turks. The cog railway which leads to Kalavryta starts at Diakofto and runs along the deep ravine of the Bouraicos river, which streams down from the Chelmos mountains.

The untamed beauty of the gorge is breathtaking. To the right and left of the narrow railway track which winds up the steep sides of the ravine, a profusion of verdure spreads out in striking contrast to the bare, precipitous walls of rock.

The train stops first at the place called Treklia, after which it continues its course to Zachlorou. East of Zachlorou, at an altitude of 900 metres, is built the monastery of Mega Spelaion. Clinging to the face of a vertical cliff, the eight stories of the modern edifice were built in 1943, following the destruction of the older monastery.

The first monastery was built in the 4th century by two brothers, the monks Symeon and Theodore. In the *katholikon* of the present monastery is kept the icon of the Holy Virgin holding the Child on her right arm, executed in relief, using wax and mastic, the work - as tradition would have it - of the Apostle Luke. In the museum of the monastery are displayed sacred relics and mementoes, carved wooden crosses, manuscripts, illuminated Gospels, etc. there is a guest-house attached to the monastery. Southwest of Kalavryta, at a distance of approximately 6 kilometres, stands the monastery of Aghia Lavra, on a site surveying the valley of the Bouraicos river. It was founded in 961 by Athanasius Athonitis on the site known as Paliomonastiro, not far from the present monastery. Of the first monastery, which was burnt down by the Turks in 1585, all that remains is a two-aisled church, while the new monastery was moved, in 1689, further south, to the spot on which it stands today. In the courtyard of the new monastery was raised in 1821 the banner of the War of Independence, which is kept, along with the very old gospel donated to the monastery by Catherine the Great, the gold crosses and other precious objects, in the sacristy of the monastery. In the church can be seen a carved wooden iconostasis, wall paintings darkened by the smoke of the fires which devastated it at various times, and the icon of Aghia Lavra. Opposite the monastery, on a hill, stands a memorial to the heroes of the War of Independence. Our visit to the monastery of Aghia Lavra brings to an end our tour of the Peloponnese, a region rich in history, lore and tradition.

Above: The monastery of Mega Spelaion.

Below: The monastery of Aghia Lavra.

TRAVEL INFORMATION HOW TO GET TO THE PELOPONNESE

By bus/car

There are frequent bus services to the capitals of the prefectures and the main towns of the Peloponnese, which start from the KTEL bus station in Athens, 100 Kifissou street. The main bus lines are:

1. Corinth, Loutraki, Kiato, Derveni (information: tel. no.01/512.92.32)

2. Argos, Nauplion, Asclepieion (Lygourio), Kranidi (information: tel. no. 01/ 513.45.88)

3. Tripolis, Megalopolis, Leonidion (information: tel. no. 01/513.45.75)

4. Sparta, Gytheion (information: tel.no.-01/ 512.42.93)

5. Kalamata (via Tripolis), Messene, Corone, Pylos, Filiatra, Gargaliani, Kyparissia (information: tel.no.-01/513.42.93)

6. Pyrgos, Andravida, Gastouni, Amalias, Olympia, Zacharo (information: tel.no.01/ 513.41.10)

7. Patras, Aighion, Kalavryta (information: tel.no.01/513.73.10)

Thessalonike is also linked to Corinth by KTEL bus, but the services are less frequent. Information: KTEL, Corinth, tel.no.-0741/25642. Patras is linked by KTEL buses to Thessalonike and to Messolonghi-Aetolikon-Agrinion. Information: KTEL, Patras, tel.061/623868.

KTEL buses also run between all the main towns and larger villages of the prefectures. For further information contact the local KTEL offices.

By train

The main towns of the Peloponnese are connected to Athens by rail. Information from the OSE (Greek Railways) offices in Athens, tel.01/522.24.91 or from the local OSE offices.

By boat/car ferry

1. There is a boat/ferry-boat service between Piraeus and Palaia Epidavros, Hermione, Nauplion, and Porto Heli. Palaia Epidavros, Hermione, Porto Heli are also linked to the islands of the Argosaronic Gulf, while Nauplion is also linked by boat to the Cyclades. Information from the Piraeus Port Authority, tel.no.01/412.45.33.

2. There is a ferry-boat service between Kalamata and the islands of Kythera and Crete (Castelli in Chania). Information from the Kalamata Port Authority, tel.no.0721/22218.

3. Patras is the main port for connections to the islands of the Ionian Sea, Igoumenitsa and Italy. This is where boats to the islands of Cephalonia, Ithaca and Corfu, to Igoumenitsa, and to Brindisi, Bari and Ancona in Italy, start from. Information: Patras Port Authority, tel. no.061/34.10.02.

4. Boats to the island of Zakynthos leave from Kyllene. Information: Kyllene Port Authority, tel.no.0623/92211.

5. Ferry-boats run regularly from Rhion to Antirrhion (the crossing takes 15 minutes). Information: tel.no.061/991203. Also from Aighion to Aghios Nikolaos in Phokis (a 45' crossing). Information: Aighion Port Authority, tel.0691/28888.

ARTISTIC EVENTS

Besides the local fêtes which take place at various times of the year in many parts of the Peloponnese, a variety of artistic events are also organised, mainly during the summer months, of which the most important is the Epidaurus Festival, during which performances of ancient drama and comedy are staged at the ancient theatre.

In the small ancient theatre of Palaia Epidavros there is also a festival which mainly comprises concerts and musical events. Nauplion presents a yearly event, entitled "Musical August", with the participation of well-known artists.

Cultural events are also organised in the summer by the Municipalities of Monemvasia and Kalamata, while, at the end of August, a wine festival takes place at Nemea.

By Hydrofoil

From the harbour of Zea in Piraeus hydrofoils run to the eastern Peloponnese (Palaia Epidavros, Hermione, Porto Heli, Tolo, Astros, Leonidion, Kyparissi, Monemvasia, Kythera. Services are more frequent in the summer; services are suspended during the winter months.

By plane

Athens is linked by air only to Kalamata. The airport is at a distance of 8 kms from the town. Information: Olympic Airways, Athens. Tel.no.01/966.66.66 and Kalamata: tel.no.0721/22376.

Road network

The road network of the Peloponnese is good, There are tarred roads leading to almost every part of the prefectures.

In the towns and tourist areas there are taxis equipped with taximeters, as well as car and bike rental agencies. In these areas there are also travel agencies which organise excursions to surrounding areas of interest and to archaeological sites.

Ski centres and mountain refuges

Ski centres

Arcadia: Mt. Maenalon, at the Ostrakina plateau, 1600 m altitude, 5 runs, 3 ski lifts and a chalet offering meals and accommodation.

Access from Tripolis (30 kms). Information: Tripolis Mountaineering club, tel. 071/233342, ski centre tel. 0796/22227.

Achaea: Mt. Aroania (Chelmos), at Vathia Lakka, at an altitude of 1650 m to 2100 m. Two runs to each lift, 3 chair lifts and one cable lift. There is a ski rental shop and a chalet offering meals. Access from Athens (214 kms) from Patras (100 kms) and from Kalavryta (14 kms).

Information: Kalavryta ski centre, tel. 0692/22661, 22174.

Mountain refuges

Corinthia: There are two refuges on Mt. Kyllene (Zereia). One is situated at an altitude of 1520 m and the other at 1680 m. Access from Ano Trikkala. Information from the Mountaineering Club of Corinth, tel. 074/22970.

Arcadia: At an altitude of 1600 m on the Ostrakina plateau on Mt. Maenalon. Through here passes the European E4 Trail. Access to the refuge from Tripolis. Information from the refuge (tel. no.0796/22227) or from the Mountaineering Club of Tripolis (071/232243).

Laconia: There are two refuges, one on Mt. Parnon and the other on Mt. Taygetus.

That of Mt. Parnon is situated at the site of Arnomoussa, at an altitude of 1400 m. Access from Argos or Tripolis or Sparta. Information from the Sparta Mountaineering Club, tel. 0731/22574.

That of the Taygetus is situated at Varvara-Dereki, at an altitude of 1600 m. Information from the Mountaineering Club of Sparta. Access from Sparta.

Achaea: There are two refuges, one on the Panachaikon and the other on Mt. Chelmos (Aroania).

That of the Panachaikon is at the site of Psarthi, at an altitude of 1420 m. Access from Patras. Information from the Moun-

Food and Entertainment

The Peloponnese has something to offer to satisty most tastes and interests. Of course, there is a greater choice in the towns than in the less populated areas or those off the beaten track, but, no matter where one may go, there will always be a taverna, ouzerie or coffee-shop which will be ready to welcome the traveller for a simple meal or a cup of coffee. In the towns and the tourist resorts there is a larger choice. The visitor can choose between restaurants of every kind, ouzeries, tavernas, pizza parlours, coffee shops, pastry shops etc. There will be entertainment in the evenings in the form of bars, discos, pubs etc.

taineering Association of Patras, tel. 061/273912. That of the Chelmos mountain is at the site of Diaselo Avgou, at an altitude of 2100 m. Access from Kalavryta. Information from the Mountaineering Association of Kalavryta, 0692/226611.

MINERAL SPRINGS AND SPAS

In the Peloponnese there are mineral springs at Loutraki, Methana, Kyllene and Kaiaphas.

Loutraki (Corinthia)

There are three specially organised thermal establishments and centres for mineral water therapy. For information contact the Municipality of Loutraki, tel. 0744/22423.

Methana

There are three hydrotherapy centres with 136 individual baths. Information from the Municipality of Methana, tel. 0298/92324.

Kyllene (Elis)

There is a hydrotherapy centre with 37 individual baths, inhalation rooms and Turkish baths and 63 inhalation therapy machines. Information from the Community Centre, tel. 0623/95221 and from the Baths, tel. 0623/96270.

Kaiaphas (Elis)

There is a hydrotherapy centre with 26 baths and 2 bathing pools inside the cave. Information from the Municipality of Zacharo, tel. 0625/31277 and at the Baths tel. 0625/31709.

SPORTS

Besides the water sports which can be enjoyed on the beaches, the Peloponnese is also a place for mountain trekking or climbing, skiing and walking. The European E4 Long Distance Trail ends in the Peloponnese. In the mountains of the region - the Panachaikon, Zereia or Kyllene mountains, the Aroania or Chelmos range, Mts. Maenalon, Parnon and Taygetus - there are mountain refuges, while on the Maenalon and the Aroania there are ski centres.

LOCAL EVENTS FETES

In the villages and towns of the Peloponnese many local fetes and traditional festivities take place throughout the year. We shall only mention here those that occur in the region during the Carnival period and around Greek Orthodox Easter. The most important Carnival event, not only of the Peloponnese but of all of Greece is the Patras Carnival. The climax of the festivities occurs during the last week of the Carnival period, with various events and two great processions, the one on the evening of the last Saturday and the other in the early afternoon of the last Sunday of Carnival. Other events of the Patras Carnival are a treasure hunt, the farewell to the King of the Carnival on the evening of the last Sunday of Carnival, with dancing, fireworks etc. late into the night. Other Carnival festivities with their own local characteristics also take place in Messene on Shrove Sunday. In the various neighbourhoods fires are lit, around which locals and visitors feast and make merry, to the accompaniment of music. In Methone, the popular ceremony known as "Tou Koutrouli o Gamos" ("Koutrouli's Wedding") takes place. It is a custom which has its roots in the 14th century. After the "Wedding" everyone can join in the festivities, which include food and wine. Easter in the Peloponnese has its own particular character. In Kalamata there is a competition, which has its roots in the 1821 struggle of the Greeks for independence. The participants, clad in traditional costumes and armed with paper tubes filled with gunpowder, engage in a mock battle. The event takes place in the Messeniakos football stadium. At Leonidion, on the eve of Easter Sunday, the midnight sky is filled with lighted balloons, while outside the church is enacted the "burning of Judas". On Easter Sunday, in the square of the small town, a grand fete is held. In Tripolis, on Easter Sunday there is similar merry-making, and the community offers lamb on the spit, various snacks and local wine, while folk dance groups dance traditional dances to the accompaniment of music played by folk musicians.

BIBLIOGRAPHY

Chatzidakis M., *Mystras. The Medieval City and the Castle*, Athens 1989.
Christou Ch. *Αρχαία Σπάρτη*, Sparta 1960.
EKDOTIKI ATHINON (eds), *Greek Mythology*
EKDOTIKI ATHINON (eds), *Ιστορία του ελληνικού έθνους*.
Gritsopoulos T., *Μυστράς*, Athens 1966.
Kaltsa N., *Αρχαία Μεσσήνη*, Athens 1989.
Karpodini-Dimitriadi E., *Κάστρα της Πελοποννήσου*, Athens 1993.
Kokkini S. *Τα μουσεία της Ελλάδος*, Athens 1976.
Lambrinoudaki B. *Αργολίδα*,
MELISSA (eds), *Architecture of the Peloponnese*.
Motsios G. *Το ελληνικό μοιρολόγι*, Athens 1995.
Mylonas G., *Μυκήναι*, Athens 1994.
Papahadji N., *Μυκήνες-Επίδαυρος-Τίρυνθα-Ναύπλιο*, Athens 1978.
Papahadji N., Παυσανίου *Ελλάδος Περιήγησις*, Athens 1994.
Petrocheilou A., *The Greek Caves*, Athens 1985
Vassiliades D. *Οδοιπορία στις μορφές και το ύφος του ελληνικού χώρου*, Athens 1979.

CATEG.	NAME	TEL.	BEDS
	CORINTHIA		
	ALMYRI (0741)		
C	APHRODITE (FF)	33602	18
C	TO PANORAMA TOU NIKOU (FF)	33432	64
	ANO TRIKALA (0743)		
C	ASTERIA	91207	25
	ANCIENT CORINTH (0741)		
A	XENIA	31208	3
	ASSOS (0741)		
C	VILLA CONSTANZIA (FF)	86666	27
	VRACHATI (0741)		
B	ALKYON (FF)	52010	66
	GALATAKI (0741)		
B	OREA ELENI	33470	42
	ISTHMIA (0741)		
A	KING SARON	37273	305
	ISTHMUS (0741)		
B	ISTHMIA (M)	23454	140
	KASTANIA (0747)		
B	XENIA	61283	34
	KIATO (0742)		
B	TRITON	23421	59
C	GALINI	22207	45
C	PAPPAS	22358	76
C	PEFKIAS	28650	22
	KOKKONI (0742)		
B	KARAVAS VILLAGE	32091	88
C	ANGELA	32486	260
C	KOKKONI BEACH	33108	64
	KORFOS (0741)		
B	KORFOS	95217	20
	CORINTH (0741)		
C	ACROPOLIS	21104	49
C	EPHYRA	22434	85
C	CONSTANTATOS	22120	48
C	CORINTHOS	26701	64
C	BELLE	22068	31
	LAFKA (0747)		
C	LAFKA	31220	15
	LECHAION (0741)		
B	SYMI	21474	177
C	CORINTHIAN BEACH	25666	108
C	LECHAION BEACH (FF)	71625	46
	LOUTRA ELENIS (0741)		
B	POLITIS	33401	50
C	KAKANAKOS	33211	30
C	MYRTO GARDEN	33616	41
C	SEA VIEW	33551	42
	LOUTRAKI (0744)		
A	AKTI LOUTRAKI	22338	69
A	ACHILLEION	22271	110
A	THEOXENEIA	22257	50
A	KARELEION	22347	76
A	PALACE	26695	83
A	PAOLO	28742	140
A	PARK	22270	115

CATEG.	NAME	TEL.	BEDS
A	PEFKAKI	22426	71
B	AIGLI	22344	48
B	BARBARA	64338	165
B	VASSILIKON	22366	55
B	GRAND HOTEL	22348	58
B	EXELSCIOR	22254	60
B	HELIOCHARI	62427	16
B	KONTIS	22481	70
B	MARINOS	22575	97
B	BAKOS	65130	80
B	BEAU RIVAGE	22323	49
B	PALMYRA	22325	66
B	PAPPAS	28103	153
C	AEOLOS APARTMENTS (FF)	28526	41
C	ACROPOLE	22265	42
C	ALEXANDROS	21350	34
C	ALCYONIS	28173	49
C	ANDREOU	22280	24
C	ARION	22628	52
C	GALANOPOULOS	64801	28
C	GALAXY	28282	72
C	DRITSAS	28028	37
C	ELPIS	28263	122
C	ILION	23177	44
C	ISTHMIA	42510	50
C	COSMOPOLITE	22336	69
C	LOUTRAKI	21466	40
C	MARION	22346	93
C	MARGOT	63542	53
C	MON REPOS	22123	56
C	BELLE BY	26747	32
C	BRETA	22349	34
C	MITZYTHRA	26260	83
C	OIKONOMION	22326	48
C	OLYMPIA	21377	108
C	PETIT PALAIS	22267	69
C	PLAZA	22260	50
C	POSEIDONION	23273	72
C	SENGAS	22623	44
C	PHILOXENIA	91294	26
C	HOLIDAYS ANGELOPOULOS	21662	96
	LYKOPORIA (0743)		
C	ALCYON	51221	26
	MELISSI (0743)		
B	LIDO (FF)	61570	34
C	XYLOKASTRON BEACH	61190	154
C	SIKYON BEACH	28432	186
	BOUTSI LOUTRAKIOU (0744)		
A	CLUB POSEIDON	26411	758
	NERANTZA (0742)		
B	GOLDEN SUN (FF)	–	16
C	NERANTZA	32329	48
	XYLOKASTRO (0743)		
A	ARION	22230	120
B	APOLLON	22239	60
B	RALLIS	22219	132

CATEG.	NAME	TEL.	BEDS
B	FADIRA	22648	92
C	VILLA CREOLI	25360	14
C	LEDA (FF)	28116	65
C	MIRAMARE	22375	56
C	PERIANDROS	22272	39
	PALAIO KALAMAKI (0741)		
A	KALAMAKI BEACH	37653	153
	STOMIO (0743)		
C	GEORGIADES (FF)	51737	26
	SYKIA (0743)		
C	PARADEISOS	28121	54
	TRIKALA (0743)		
C	TA TRIKALA	91260	41
	ARGOLID		
	ARGOS (0751)		
C	MYCENAE	68754	42
C	TELESILLA	68317	60
	ANCIENT EPIDAURUS (0753)		
A	ELENI	41364	15
C	XENIA II	22003	48
	VIVARI (0752)		
C	ARETI	92391	19
C	VANESSA (FF)	92124	14
C	MARINA	92248	38
	DREPANO (0752)		
B	DANTIS BEACH	92294	121
C	PLAKA	92020	277
	HERMIONE (0754)		
B	COSTA PERLA	31112	362
B	LENA-MARIE	31450	228
	CANDIA		
B	CANDIA HOUSE	–	22
	COSTA (0754)		
B	CAP D'OR	51360	284
B	LIDO	57395	72
	KRANIDI (0754)		
C	HERMIONIDA	21750	52
	LYGOURIO (0753)		
C	ABATON (M)	22059	32
	MYCENAE (0751)		
B	LA PETITE PLANETE	66240	56
C	AGAMEMNON	76222	16
	NAUPLION (0752)		
LUX.	XENIA PALACE	28981	102
LUX.	XENIA PALACE BUNGALOWS	28981	108
A	AMPHITRYON	27366	80
A	XENIA	28981	98
B	AGAMEMNON	28021	74
B	ASPASIA	61183	21
C	ATHENA	27685	26
C	AMALIA	27068	16
C	VICTORIA	27420	71
C	BYRON (Tr.H)	22351	26
C	GALINI	27346	72
C	DIOSCUROI	28550	93
C	ELENA	23217	147

CATEG.	NAME	TEL.	BEDS
C	NAUPLIA	28167	104
C	HOTEL DES ROSES ANNEXE	27223	50
C	PARK (Tr.H)	27428	135
C	REX	28094	94
C	HOTEL DES ROSES	27223	24
	NEA KIOS (0751)		
C	IGNATIA	51479	52
	NEA TIRYNS (0752)		
A	AMALIA	24401	319
	PALAIA EPIDAVROS (0753)		
B	MARIALENA (FF)	41090	24
C	AEGAEON	41381	16
C	AKTIS	41407	16
C	APOLLON	41295	72
C	VERDELIS INN	41332	54
C	HELLAS	41226	36
C	MIKE	41213	25
C	MARONIKA	41391	35
C	PAOLA BEACH	41397	52
C	PLAZA	41395	17
C	POSEIDON	41211	18
C	RENA	41311	13
C	SARONIS	41514	72
C	CHRISTINA	41451	34
	PLEPI (0754)		
A	HYDRA BEACH HELIOS CLUBП	41080	516
A	PORTO HYDRA	41112	522
	PORTO HELI (0754)		
A	COSMOS	51327	279
A	PORTO HELI	51400	404
A	HINITSA BEACH	57401	385
B	ALCYON	51161	171
B	APOLLON BEACH	51431	303
B	VERVERONTA	51342	463
B	YIOULI	51217	310
B	GALAXY	–	325
B	LA CITE	51265	308
C	PORTO (harbour)	51410	20
C	ROZOS	51416	42
C	TOURIST VILLAGE OF AGIOS AEMILIANOS (FF)	51518	200
	SALADI (0754)		
B	SALADI BEACH	71391	776
	TOLO (0752)		
A	ASTERIA (FF)	58175	37
B	DOLPHIN	59220	42
B	SOLON	59204	50
B	SOFIA	59567	88
C	AKTAEON	59084	39
C	ALCYONIS (FF)	59074	10
C	APOLLON	59015	88
C	ARIS	59510	58
C	ARTEMIS	59458	39
C	ASINE BEACH	59347	16
C	ELENAS	59158	34
C	EPIDAURIA	59219	70
C	HESPERIA	59339	82
C	ZEUS	59089	31

CATEG.	NAME	TEL.	BEDS
C	ELECTRA	59105	34
C	HELIOS	59503	62
C	THETIS	59203	30
C	KNOSSOS	59174	31
C	CORONIS	59292	36
C	KYANI AKTI	59012	26
C	MINOA	59207	83
C	PAVLOS	59028	24
C	POSEIDONION	59345	69
C	RITSAS HOTEL	59418	58
C	ROMVI	59331	33
C	SOCRATES (FF)	59403	12
C	SPARTACUS	59521	18
C	TOLO	59248	72
C	TOLO II	59248	33
C	FLISVOS	59137	66
C	PHRYNE	59188	36
C	CHRISTINA	59001	37

ARCADIA

CATEG.	NAME	TEL.	BEDS
	VYTINA (0795)		
A	XENIA (M)	22218	40
B	VILLA VALOS	22210	92
C	AEGLI	22316	23
C	MAENALON	22217	37
	DIMITSANA (0795)		
	KAZAKOS HOSTEL	31000	15
C	DIMITSANA	31518	52
	DYRRACHION (0791)		
C	PALLADION	71221	34
	ISSARI (0791)		
C	ISSAREIKO SPITI	81200	20
	LANGADIA (0795)		
C	KENTRIKON	43221	36
C	LANGADIA (M)	43202	55
	LEONDARI (0791)		
C	LEONDARI GUEST HOUSE, ARCADIA	61107	41
	LEONIDION (0757)		
C	KAMARIA (FF)	22757	40
	MAGOULIANA (0795)		
A	COSMOPOULOS	82350	29
C	KAMBEAS	22666	42
	MEGALOPOLIS (0791)		
C	APOLLON	24828	24
C	LETO	22302	27
	PARALIA TYROU (0757)		
C	APOLLON	41393	23
C	GOLDEN BEACH	41072	38
C	KAMVYSIS	41424	40
C	BLUE SEA	41369	41
	PARALIO ASTROS (0755)		
C	APHRODITE (FF)	51596	11
C	KANELLOPOULOS	–	38
C	CRYSTAL (FF)	51313	62
C	PARADEISOS (FF)	51186	71

CATEG.	NAME	TEL.	BEDS
	STEMNITSA (0795)		
C	TRIKOLONION	81297	38
	TRIPOLIS (071)		
B	ARCADIA	225551	85
C	ALEX	223465	59
C	ANAKTORIKON	222545	58
C	ARTEMIS	225221	126
C	GALAXY	225195	150
C	MAENALON	222450	58

LACONIA

CATEG.	NAME	TEL.	BEDS
	ANAVRYTI (0731)		
C	ANAVRYTI	91288	16
	AREOPOLIS (0733)		
A	LONTAS (Tr.H.)	51360	9
A	KAPETANAKOS TOWER (Tr.H.)	51233	16
B	LIMENI VILLAGE	51111	75
C	KOURIS	51340	21
C	MANI	51190	35
	VATHEIA (0733)		
Tr.H	GIANNAKAKOS TOWER	55244	6
Tr.H	EXARCHAKOS TOWER	55244	14
Tr.H	KERAMIDAS TOWER	55244	9
Tr.H	MITSAKOS TOWER	55244	8
Tr.H	PAPADONGONAS TOWER	55244	9
Tr.H	TSELEPIS TOWER	55244	2
	VAMVAKOU		
C	VAMVAKOU	–	17
	GEROLIMENAS (0733)		
B	ARCHONTIKO (Tr.FF)	54285	26
B	TSITSIRIS TOWER (Tr.H)	54297	46
	GEFYRA, MONEMVASIA (0732)		
B	PHILOXENIA	61716	37
	GLYKOVRYSSI (0735)		
C	AMALIA	91224	37
	GYTHEION (0733)		
A	LACONIS (B)	22666	148
B	GYTHEION (Tr.H)	23452	16
B	CAVO GROSSO (B)	23488	54
B	BELLE HELENE	93001	180
C	ZEUS (FF)	22212	47
C	LARISSEION	22021	150
C	MILTON	22091	30
C	PANTHEON	22284	99
	DYROS (0733)		
C	DYROS	52306	25
	ELAIA MOLAON (0732)		
C	GORGIA (FF)	57333	21

CATEG.	NAME	TEL.	BEDS
ELAPHONISSOS (ISLAND) (0734)			
C	ASTERI TIS ELAPHONISSOU	61271	21
C	ELAPHONISSOS	61268	21
MONEMVASIA (0732)			
A	KELLIA GUEST HOUSE (Tr.H)	61520	40
A	ANO MALVASIA (Tr.H)	61323	34
A	BYZANTINO (Tr.H)	61254	28
A	MALVASIA II (Tr.FF)	61323	16
B	VENETIA (FF)	61734	10
B	VILLA TROUGAKOS (FF)	61177	22
B	THEOPHANO (Tr.FF)	61212	9
B	MALVASIA (Tr.H)	61323	16
B	PABLITO HOUSE (Tr.FF)	61254	7
B	PANOS (FF)	61480	18
C	CASTRO (Tr.H)	61413	23
C	LOULOUDI TIS MONEMVASIAS (FF)	61395	40
C	MINOA	61209	46
C	MONEMVASIA	61381	18
MYSTRAS (0731)			
B	BYZANTION	93309	38
NEAPOLIS (0734)			
B	LIMIRA MARE	22208	206
C	AIVALI	22287	50
C	ARSENAKOS	22991	29
OITYLO (0733)			
A	OITYLO	51300	36
SPARTA (0731)			
A	LEDA	23601	75
B	MENELAION	22161	88
C	APOLLON	22491	88
C	DIOSCUROI	28484	60
C	LACONIA	28951	62
C	MANIATIS	22665	150
C	SPARTA INN	21021	281

MESSENIA

CATEG.	NAME	TEL.	BEDS
AGIOS ANDREAS (0725)			
C	AIPIA	31368	37
C	AKROYIALI	31266	27
C	ANGELOS	31368	34
C	KASIMIOTIS (FF)	31333	50
C	LONGAS BEACH	31583	28
C	FRANGISKO	–	58
AGIOS AVGOUSTINOS (0722)			
B	CLUB AQUARIUS SAN AGOSTINO BEACH	22151	633
C	SIAS BUNGALOWS (B)	22027	85
AKROYIALI			
C	APOLLON	–	81
ALAGONIA (0721)			
C	TAYGETUS	76236	27
ACHLADOCHORI (0722)			
LUX.	ANATOLI TOU HELIOU	32122	162
LUX	SUNRISE VILLAGE	32122	162
C	ICARUS 31511	32	
VERGA (0721)			
B	MESSENIAN BAY	41001	138
C	PHOTINI	93494	48
VOUNARIA (0725)			
C	CASTELLI	41560	61
GARGALIANI (0763)			
B	IONIAN VIEW	22494	12
YIALOVA (0723)			
C	VILLA ZOE	22025	55
C	PYLOS (FF)	–	19
KALAMATA (0721)			
A	ELITE	25015	94
A	ELITE VILLAGE	–	172
A	PHARAE PALACE	94421	139
B	PHILOXENIA	23166	373
C	VALASSIS	23849	128
C	BYZANTIO	86824	86
C	GALAXIAS	86002	56
C	NEDON	26811	20
C	PANORAMA	41202	37
C	FLISVOS	82282	75
C	HAIKOS	82886	112
KALO NERO (0761)			
B	OASIS (FF)	72561	80
KARDAMYLI (0721)			
B	KALAMITSI	73131	48
C	ANNISKA (FF)	73000	60
C	HESPERIDES (FF)	73173	50
C	THEANO (FF)	73222	18
C	KARDAMYLIL BEACH	73180	46
C	PATRIARCHEAS	73366	32
CORONE (0725)			
C	MARINOS (B)	22522	34
C	AUBERGE DE LA PLAGE	22401	83
KYPRARISSIA (0761)			
B	AGIOS NEKTARIOS BEACH	24464	36
B	KYPARISSIA BEACH	24492	50
B	TSOLARIDES	22145	53
B	HOTEL KANELLAKIS	–	36
C	APOLLON	24411	52
C	BASILIKON	22655	45
C	IONION	22511	57
MARATHOPOLIS (0763)			
C	ARTINA	61400	54
METHONE (0723)			
B	AMALIA (B)	31193	65
B	ANNA	31585	15
B	MOTHON (FF)	31611	15
B	ODYSSEUS	31600	17
C	ALEX	31219	38
C	VILLA PENELOPE (FF)	–	18
C	YIOTA	31290	27
C	METHONE BEACH	31544	23
MESSENE (0722)			
C	DROSSIA	23248	14
C	CLEOPATRA INN	23138	52
C	LYSANDROS	22921	40
C	MESSENE	23002	37
MIKRA MANTINEIA (0721)			
C	TAYGETUS BEACH	42000	50
NOMITSIS (0721)			
B	O PYRGOS (Tr.H)	74414	9
PETALIDI			
B	SUNRISE SARELAS (FF)		18
PETROCHORI (0723)			
B	NAVARONE	41571	109
PYLOS (0723)			
B	MIRAMARE	22751	30
C	ARVANITIS	22641	42
C	GALAXY	22780	62
C	KARALIS	22960	67
C	KARALIS BEACH	23021	24
C	NELEUS	22518	24
STOUPA (0721)			
B	REMVI (FF)	77720	46
C	ECHMEA	77717	23
C	CLEOPATRA (FF)	77538	26
C	LEUKTRON	54322	61
C	MAISTRELI	54595	11
C	STOUPA	77308	36
PHILIATRA (0761)			
C	LIMENARI	32935	65
PHOENIKOUS (0723)			
C	PORTO PHOENICIA	71358	52
C	JENNY BEACH (FF)	–	12
C	PHOENIKOUNTA	71208	58
HAROKOPIO			
C	KARAMITSOU LIAROU (B)	–	16
CHRANI			
C	VILLA MARIA (FF)	–	23

ELIS

CATEG.	NAME	TEL.	BEDS
AMALIAS (0622)			
C	HELLENIS	28975	27
C	CORIBOS	27555	21
C	OLYMPIC INN	28632	77
ANDRITSAINA (0626)			
B	THEOXENIA	22219	46
ARKOUDI (0623)			
C	ARKOUDI	96480	77
C	LINDSAY	96483	83
C	BRATIS	96350	77
C	ROBINA (FF)	–	19
C	SOULIS (FF)	96379	19

CATEG.	NAME	TEL.	BEDS
	VARTHOLOMIO (0623)		
C	ALPHA	41707	57
C	ARTEMIS	41405	20
C	FENGAROGNEMATA	41222	30
	VRANAS (0623)		
C	TAXIARCHIS	41440	48
	GASTOUNI (0623)		
C	ODYSSEUS	32726	18
	GLYFA (0623)		
C	KYPRIOTIS	96372	36
	ZACHARO(0625)		
C	NESTOR	31206	46
C	REX	31221	66
	KAIAPHAS (0625)		
C	GERANION	31710	77
C	KAIAPHAS LAKE	32954	19
C	JENNY	32252	16
	KASTRO KYLLINIS (0623)		
A	ROBINSON CLUB KYLLINI BEACH	95205	624
C	PARADISE	95209	81
C	CHRYSSI AKTI	95224	20
	KATAKOLO (0621)		
B	ZEPHYROS	41170	18
C	IONIO	41494	19
	KOUROUTAS (0622)		
C	AKTI KOUROUTA	22902	44
C	FOUR SEASONS	27311	95
	KRESTAINA (0625)		
C	ATHENA	23150	40
	LOUTRA KYLLINIS (0623)		
A	XENIA	96270	160
C	IONION	92318	45
C	XENIA	96275	150
	LYGHIA (0623)		
B	HELIDONIA (FF)	96393	48
	OLYMPIA (0624)		
A	AMALIA	22190	272
A	ANTONIOS	22348	121
A	EUROPE	22650	77
B	ALTIS	23101	116
B	APOLLON	22522	183
B	NEDA	22563	75
B	NEON OLYMPIA	22506	59
B	XENIA	22510	72
B	XENIOS ZEUS (M)	22522	72
B	OLYMPIC VILLAGE HOTEL	22211	97
C	ARTEMIS	22255	28
C	ELIS	22547	106
C	HERCULES	22696	25
C	CRONION	22502	41
C	OENOMAUS	22056	44
C	OLYMPIAKI DADA	22668	42
C	PELOPS	22543	37
C	PHIDIAS	22667	17
	PYRGOS (0621)		
C	ELIDA	28046	64
C	IONIAN SEA	28828	107
C	LETRINA	25150	128
C	MARILEE	28133	51

CATEG.	NAME	TEL.	BEDS
C	OLYMPUS	23650	71
C	PANTHEON	29746	89
	SKAFIDIA (0621)		
A	OLYMPIA	94647	665

ACHAEA

CATEG.	NAME	TEL.	BEDS
	AIGHION (0691)		
B	GALINI	26150	59
C	TELIS	28200	64
	AKRATA (0696)		
A	AKRATA BEACH	31180	56
	DIAKOFTO (0691)		
C	CHRIS-PAUL	41715	46
	ELAIONAS (0691)		
C	AFRICA (FF)	41751	37
C	CHRISELEN (B)	41526	23
	ZAROUCHLA (0696)		
B	O PYRGOS TIS ZAROUCHLAS (Tr.H)	51252	12
	KALAVRYTA (0692)		
B	VILLA KALAVRYTA (FF)	22712	16
B	PHILOXENIA	22422	48
B	CHELMOS	22217	45
C	MARIA	22296	29
	KALENTZI (0694)		
C	XENIA KALENTZIOU	31240	43
	KALOGRIA (0693)		
B	KALOGRIA BEACH	31380	156
B	CHRISTINA BEACH	31469	84
	KAMINIA (061)		
C	POSEIDON	671602	60
	KATO ALISSOS (0693)		
C	TARANTELLA	71205	62
	KATO ACHAIA (0693)		
C	ACHAIA	22678	29
	KLEITORIA (0692)		
B	MONT CHELMOS	31221	38
	KOUKOULI (061)		
C	KOUKOS ATE	322987	63
	KRATHION (0696)		
B	KRATION (FF)	31964	46
C	SILVER BEACH	31663	65
	LAKKOPETRA (0693)		
A	LAKKOPETRA BEACH	51713	385
B	IONIAN BEACH (B)	51300	150
	LAMBIRI (0691)		
C	GALINI	31231	23
	LONGOS (0691)		
B	LONGOS BEACH	72197	267
C	SPAY BEACH	71724	72
	BOZAITIKA (061)		
B	ACHAIA BEACH	991801	165
B	THE TZAKI	653960	96
	NIKOLEIKA (0691)		
B	POSEIDON BEACH	81400	168
C	THEMISTO	81888	37

CATEG.	NAME	TEL.	BEDS
	NIKOPHOREIKA (0693)		
A	PAULINA	24040	168
C	ACHAIOS	22501	76
C	WHITE CASTLE	23390	89
	VUE (061)		
C	YIOTIS	522224	38
	PATRAS (061)		
A	ASTIR	277502	222
A	MOREAS	425494	180
B	GALAXY	278815	98
C	ADONIS	224213	107
C	ACROPOLE	279809	64
C	ATLANTA	220019	39
C	DELPHINI	421001	135
C	EL GRECO	272931	43
C	KOUKOS	324520	43
C	MARI	331302	48
C	MEDITERRANEE	279602	165
C	OLYMPIC	224103	75
C	RANIA	220114	54
	RHION (061)		
A	PORTO RIO	992102	504
B	APOLLON (FF)	990426	18
C	GEORGIOS	992627	26
C	RHION BEACH	991421	162
	RHODIA (0691)		
B	EDEN BEACH	81195	48
	RODINI (061)		
B	RODINI (FF)	931341	86
	SELIANITIKA (0691)		
B	A-B (FF)	71716	30
C	KANELI	72442	68
C	PANAGIOTIS	71840	18
C	PLACE	72200	48
	PHILIA (0692)		
C	GEORGAKION	31245	14
	FTERI (0691)		
C	FTERES	98233	17
	PSATHOPYRGOS (061)		
B	FLORIDA (M)	931279	156

Note:

1. There are also D- and E-class hotels, rooms to rent and camping sites. For information on these, contact the local police. For reservations, contact the Chamber of Hotel Industry of Greece, Stadiou 24, Athens 105 64, TLX. 0214269 XEPE GR., Fax: 01-3225449 and 01-3236962. FF= furnished flats, M = motel, B = bungalows, Tr.FF - traditional furnished flats, Tr.H = traditional hotel, LUX = luxury class.

TEXTS: REGINA MOUSTERAKI

ART EDITORS: TH. ANAGNOSTOPOULOS, TH. PRESVYTES

MONTAGE: PERGAMOS

ENGLISH TRANSLATION: DAPHNE KAPSAMBELIS

PHOTOGRAPHS: C. ADAM, G. GIANNELOS, G. KOUROUPIS,

C. MITRELLIS, V. VOUTSAS, ARCHAEOLOGICAL PROCEEDS FUND

PRINTING AND BOOKBINDING: PERGAMOS